**OLD TESTAMENT 2022**

# Come, Follow Me—
# For Individuals and Families

Living, Learning, and Teaching the Gospel of Jesus Christ

Published by
The Church of Jesus Christ of Latter-day Saints
Salt Lake City, Utah

# Contents

**Introductory Materials**

Conversion Is Our Goal . . . . . . . . . . . . . . . . . . . . . . . . . . . . . . . . . . . . . . . . . . . . . . . . . . . . . . . . . . . . . . . . . . . . . vii

Using *Come, Follow Me—For Individuals and Families* . . . . . . . . . . . . . . . . . . . . . . . . . . . . . . . . . . . . . . . viii

Ideas to Improve Your Personal Scripture Study . . . . . . . . . . . . . . . . . . . . . . . . . . . . . . . . . . . . . . . . . . . . . . x

Ideas to Improve Your Family Scripture Study. . . . . . . . . . . . . . . . . . . . . . . . . . . . . . . . . . . . . . . . . . . . . . . . xii

Additional Resources. . . . . . . . . . . . . . . . . . . . . . . . . . . . . . . . . . . . . . . . . . . . . . . . . . . . . . . . . . . . . . . . . . . . . . xv

Teaching Young Children . . . . . . . . . . . . . . . . . . . . . . . . . . . . . . . . . . . . . . . . . . . . . . . . . . . . . . . . . . . . . . . . . xvii

Including Sacred Music in Your Gospel Learning . . . . . . . . . . . . . . . . . . . . . . . . . . . . . . . . . . . . . . . . . . . . . xix

Old Testament Overview. . . . . . . . . . . . . . . . . . . . . . . . . . . . . . . . . . . . . . . . . . . . . . . . . . . . . . . . . . . . . . . . . . . xx

Thoughts to Keep in Mind: Reading the Old Testament . . . . . . . . . . . . . . . . . . . . . . . . . . . . . . . . . . . . . . . . . 1

**December 27–January 2:** Moses 1; Abraham 3. . . . . . . . . . . . . . . . . . . . . . . . . . . . . . . . . . . . . . . . . . . . . . . . . 3

**January 3–9:** Genesis 1–2; Moses 2–3; Abraham 4–5 . . . . . . . . . . . . . . . . . . . . . . . . . . . . . . . . . . . . . . . . . . 7

**January 10–16:** Genesis 3–4; Moses 4–5 . . . . . . . . . . . . . . . . . . . . . . . . . . . . . . . . . . . . . . . . . . . . . . . . . . . . 11

**January 17–23:** Genesis 5; Moses 6 . . . . . . . . . . . . . . . . . . . . . . . . . . . . . . . . . . . . . . . . . . . . . . . . . . . . . . . . . 15

**January 24–30:** Moses 7. . . . . . . . . . . . . . . . . . . . . . . . . . . . . . . . . . . . . . . . . . . . . . . . . . . . . . . . . . . . . . . . . . . 19

**January 31–February 6:** Genesis 6–11; Moses 8 . . . . . . . . . . . . . . . . . . . . . . . . . . . . . . . . . . . . . . . . . . . . . . 23

Thoughts to Keep in Mind: The Covenant. . . . . . . . . . . . . . . . . . . . . . . . . . . . . . . . . . . . . . . . . . . . . . . . . . . . . 27

**February 7–13:** Genesis 12–17; Abraham 1–2. . . . . . . . . . . . . . . . . . . . . . . . . . . . . . . . . . . . . . . . . . . . . . . . 29

**February 14–20:** Genesis 18–23 . . . . . . . . . . . . . . . . . . . . . . . . . . . . . . . . . . . . . . . . . . . . . . . . . . . . . . . . . . . 33

**February 21–27:** Genesis 24–27 . . . . . . . . . . . . . . . . . . . . . . . . . . . . . . . . . . . . . . . . . . . . . . . . . . . . . . . . . . . 37

Thoughts to Keep in Mind: The House of Israel . . . . . . . . . . . . . . . . . . . . . . . . . . . . . . . . . . . . . . . . . . . . . . . 41

**February 28–March 6:** Genesis 28–33 . . . . . . . . . . . . . . . . . . . . . . . . . . . . . . . . . . . . . . . . . . . . . . . . . . . . . . 43

**March 7–13:** Genesis 37–41 . . . . . . . . . . . . . . . . . . . . . . . . . . . . . . . . . . . . . . . . . . . . . . . . . . . . . . . . . . . . . . 47

**March 14–20:** Genesis 42–50 . . . . . . . . . . . . . . . . . . . . . . . . . . . . . . . . . . . . . . . . . . . . . . . . . . . . . . . . . . . . . 51

**March 21–27:** Exodus 1–6 . . . . . . . . . . . . . . . . . . . . . . . . . . . . . . . . . . . . . . . . . . . . . . . . . . . . . . . . . . . . . . . . 55

**March 28–April 3:** Exodus 7–13 . . . . . . . . . . . . . . . . . . . . . . . . . . . . . . . . . . . . . . . . . . . . . . . . . . . . . . . . . . . 59

**April 4–10:** Exodus 14–17. . . . . . . . . . . . . . . . . . . . . . . . . . . . . . . . . . . . . . . . . . . . . . . . . . . . . . . . . . . . . . . . 63

**April 11–17:** Easter . . . . . . . . . . . . . . . . . . . . . . . . . . . . . . . . . . . . . . . . . . . . . . . . . . . . . . . . . . . . . . . . . . . . . . 67

**April 18–24:** Exodus 18–20. . . . . . . . . . . . . . . . . . . . . . . . . . . . . . . . . . . . . . . . . . . . . . . . . . . . . . . . . . . . . . . 71

**April 25–May 1:** Exodus 24; 31–34. . . . . . . . . . . . . . . . . . . . . . . . . . . . . . . . . . . . . . . . . . . . . . . . . . . . . . . . . 75

Thoughts to Keep in Mind: The Tabernacle and Sacrifice . . . . . . . . . . . . . . . . . . . . . . . . . . . . . . . . . . . . . . 79

**May 2–8:** Exodus 35–40; Leviticus 1; 16; 19 . . . . . . . . . . . . . . . . . . . . . . . . . . . . . . . . . . . . . . . . . . . . . . . . 82

**May 9–15:** Numbers 11–14; 20–24 . . . . . . . . . . . . . . . . . . . . . . . . . . . . . . . . . . . . . . . . . . . . . . . . . . . . . . . . 86

**May 16–22:** Deuteronomy 6–8; 15; 18; 29–30; 34 . . . . . . . . . . . . . . . . . . . . . . . . . . . . . . . . . . . . . . . . . . . 90

Thoughts to Keep in Mind: The Historical Books in the Old Testament . . . . . . . . . . . . . . . . . . . . . . . . . . . 94

**May 23–29:** Joshua 1–8; 23–24 . . . . . . . . . . . . . . . . . . . . . . . . . . . . . . . . . . . . . . . . . . . . . . . . . . . 97

**May 30–June 5:** Judges 2–4; 6–8; 13–16 . . . . . . . . . . . . . . . . . . . . . . . . . . . . . . . . . . . . . . . 101

**June 6–12:** Ruth; 1 Samuel 1–3. . . . . . . . . . . . . . . . . . . . . . . . . . . . . . . . . . . . . . . . . . . . . . . . . . 105

**June 13–19:** 1 Samuel 8–10; 13; 15–18 . . . . . . . . . . . . . . . . . . . . . . . . . . . . . . . . . . . . . . . . 109

**June 20–26:** 2 Samuel 5–7; 11–12; 1 Kings 3; 8; 11 . . . . . . . . . . . . . . . . . . . . . . . . . . . . 113

**June 27–July 3:** 1 Kings 17–19 . . . . . . . . . . . . . . . . . . . . . . . . . . . . . . . . . . . . . . . . . . . . . . . . . 117

**July 4–10:** 2 Kings 2–7. . . . . . . . . . . . . . . . . . . . . . . . . . . . . . . . . . . . . . . . . . . . . . . . . . . . . . . . . . 121

Thoughts to Keep in Mind: "Jesus Will Say to All Israel, 'Come Home'" . . . . . . . . . . . . . . . . . . . 125

**July 11–17:** 2 Kings 17–25 . . . . . . . . . . . . . . . . . . . . . . . . . . . . . . . . . . . . . . . . . . . . . . . . . . . . . 128

**July 18–24:** Ezra 1; 3–7; Nehemiah 2; 4–6; 8 . . . . . . . . . . . . . . . . . . . . . . . . . . . . . . . . . . 132

**July 25–31:** Esther . . . . . . . . . . . . . . . . . . . . . . . . . . . . . . . . . . . . . . . . . . . . . . . . . . . . . . . . . . . . . 136

Thoughts to Keep in Mind: Reading Poetry in the Old Testament . . . . . . . . . . . . . . . . . . . . . . . . 140

**August 1–7:** Job 1–3; 12–14; 19; 21–24; 38–40; 42 . . . . . . . . . . . . . . . . . . . . . . . . . . . . 142

**August 8–14:** Psalms 1–2; 8; 19–33; 40; 46. . . . . . . . . . . . . . . . . . . . . . . . . . . . . . . . . . . . . 146

**August 15–21:** Psalms 49–51; 61–66; 69–72; 77–78; 85–86 . . . . . . . . . . . . . . . . . . . . 150

**August 22–28:** Psalms 102–103; 110; 116–119; 127–128; 135–139; 146–150 . . . . . . 154

**August 29–September 4:** Proverbs 1–4; 15–16; 22; 31; Ecclesiastes 1–3; 11–12 . . . . . . 158

Thoughts to Keep in Mind: Prophets and Prophecy. . . . . . . . . . . . . . . . . . . . . . . . . . . . . . . . . . . 162

**September 5–11:** Isaiah 1–12 . . . . . . . . . . . . . . . . . . . . . . . . . . . . . . . . . . . . . . . . . . . . . . . . . . 164

**September 12–18:** Isaiah 13–14; 24–30; 35 . . . . . . . . . . . . . . . . . . . . . . . . . . . . . . . . . . . . 168

**September 19–25:** Isaiah 40–49 . . . . . . . . . . . . . . . . . . . . . . . . . . . . . . . . . . . . . . . . . . . . . . . 172

**September 26–October 2:** Isaiah 50–57 . . . . . . . . . . . . . . . . . . . . . . . . . . . . . . . . . . . . . . . . 176

**October 3–9:** Isaiah 58–66 . . . . . . . . . . . . . . . . . . . . . . . . . . . . . . . . . . . . . . . . . . . . . . . . . . . . 180

**October 10–16:** Jeremiah 1–3; 7; 16–18; 20 . . . . . . . . . . . . . . . . . . . . . . . . . . . . . . . . . . . 184

**October 17–23:** Jeremiah 30–33; 36; Lamentations 1; 3. . . . . . . . . . . . . . . . . . . . . . . . . . 188

**October 24–30:** Ezekiel 1–3; 33–34; 36–37; 47 . . . . . . . . . . . . . . . . . . . . . . . . . . . . . . . . 192

**October 31–November 6:** Daniel 1–6 . . . . . . . . . . . . . . . . . . . . . . . . . . . . . . . . . . . . . . . . . . 196

**November 7–13:** Hosea 1–6; 10–14; Joel . . . . . . . . . . . . . . . . . . . . . . . . . . . . . . . . . . . . . . 200

**November 14–20:** Amos; Obadiah . . . . . . . . . . . . . . . . . . . . . . . . . . . . . . . . . . . . . . . . . . . . . 204

**November 21–27:** Jonah; Micah. . . . . . . . . . . . . . . . . . . . . . . . . . . . . . . . . . . . . . . . . . . . . . . 208

**November 28–December 4:** Nahum; Habakkuk; Zephaniah . . . . . . . . . . . . . . . . . . . . . . . . 212

**December 5–11:** Haggai; Zechariah 1–3; 7–14 . . . . . . . . . . . . . . . . . . . . . . . . . . . . . . . . . 216

**December 12–18:** Malachi. . . . . . . . . . . . . . . . . . . . . . . . . . . . . . . . . . . . . . . . . . . . . . . . . . . . . 220

**December 19–25:** Christmas . . . . . . . . . . . . . . . . . . . . . . . . . . . . . . . . . . . . . . . . . . . . . . . . . . . 224

# Conversion Is Our Goal

The aim of all gospel learning and teaching is to deepen our conversion to Heavenly Father and Jesus Christ and help us become more like Them. For this reason, when we study the gospel, we're not just looking for new information; we want to become a "new creature" (2 Corinthians 5:17). This means relying on Heavenly Father and Jesus Christ to help us change our hearts, our views, our actions, and our very natures.

But the kind of gospel learning that strengthens our faith and leads to the miracle of conversion doesn't happen all at once. It extends beyond a classroom into our hearts and homes. It requires consistent, daily efforts to understand and live the gospel. Gospel learning that leads to true conversion requires the influence of the Holy Ghost.

The Holy Ghost guides us to the truth and bears witness of that truth (see John 16:13). He enlightens our minds, quickens our understandings, and touches our hearts with revelation from God, the source of all truth. The Holy Ghost purifies our hearts. He inspires in us a desire to live by truth, and He whispers to us ways to do this. Truly, "the Holy Ghost . . . shall teach [us] all things" (John 14:26).

For these reasons, in our efforts to live, learn, and teach the gospel, we should first and foremost seek the companionship of the Spirit. This goal should govern our choices and guide our thoughts and actions. We should seek after whatever invites the influence of the Spirit and reject whatever drives that influence away—for we know that if we can be worthy of the presence of the Holy Ghost, we can also be worthy to live in the presence of Heavenly Father and His Son, Jesus Christ.

# Using *Come, Follow Me—For Individuals and Families*

## Who Is This Resource For?

This resource is for every individual and family in the Church. It is designed to help you learn the gospel—whether on your own or with your family. If you haven't studied the gospel regularly in the past, this resource can help you get started. If you already have a good habit of gospel study, this resource can help you have more meaningful experiences.

## How Should I Use This Resource?

Use this resource in any way that is helpful to you. You may find it helpful as a guide or aid for personal and family scripture study. You could also use it for home evening. The outlines highlight important principles found in the Old Testament, suggest study ideas and activities for individuals and families, and provide places to record your impressions.

*Come, Follow Me—For Individuals and Families* is not meant to replace or compete with other good things you are doing. Follow the Spirit's guidance to determine how to approach your own study of the word of God.

## How Does This Resource Relate to What Happens at Church?

The outlines in this resource are organized according to a weekly reading schedule. The *Come, Follow Me* resources for Primary, for Sunday School, and for Aaronic Priesthood quorums and Young Women classes follow the same schedule. To support your efforts to learn and live the gospel at home, your teachers at church will give you opportunities to share your experiences, thoughts, and questions about the scripture passages that you have been studying at home.

Because Sunday School is taught only twice a month, Sunday School teachers may choose to skip or combine outlines to keep up with the weekly schedule. This may also be necessary (for both Sunday School and Primary) on weeks when regular Church meetings are not held because of stake conference or other reasons. During these weeks you are invited to continue to study the Old Testament at home.

## Do I Need to Follow the Schedule?

The schedule will help you read selections from the Old Testament and the Pearl of Great Price by the end of the year. In addition, following the same schedule as others can lead to meaningful experiences at home, at church, and elsewhere. But don't feel bound by the schedule or compelled to read every verse; the schedule is simply a guide to help you pace yourself. The important thing is that you are learning the gospel individually and as a family.

### Note about the Old Testament Reading Schedule

The suggested *Come, Follow Me* reading schedule for 2022 does not include every chapter in the Old Testament. Because the Old Testament is longer than other volumes of scripture, some chapters and books have been omitted to make the reading schedule more manageable for you and your family.

Chapters and books were selected to avoid redundancy and to highlight passages that testify of Jesus Christ, are rich in doctrine, and are especially relevant to our day. For example, the suggested reading schedule does not include 1 and 2 Chronicles because much of the content of those books duplicates material found in 1 and 2 Kings. The schedule also doesn't include the Song of Solomon, because the Prophet Joseph Smith taught that it is not inspired scripture (see Guide to the Scriptures, "Song of Solomon," scriptures.ChurchofJesusChrist.org). However, remember that this is just a *suggested* study schedule. Your personal and family scripture study should be guided by personal revelation.

# Ideas to Improve Your Personal Scripture Study

Here are some simple ways to enhance your study of the word of God in the scriptures.

## Look for Truths about Jesus Christ

The scriptures teach us that all things testify of Christ (see 2 Nephi 11:4; Moses 6:63), so consider noting or marking verses that teach about the Savior and how to follow Him.

## Look for Inspiring Words and Phrases

You may find that certain words and phrases in the scriptures impress you, as if they were written specifically for you. They may feel personally relevant and inspire and motivate you. Consider marking them in your scriptures or writing them in a study journal.

## Look for Gospel Truths

Sometimes gospel truths (often called doctrine or principles) are stated directly, and sometimes they are implied through an example or story. Ask yourself, "What eternal truths are taught in these verses?"

## Listen to the Spirit

Pay attention to your thoughts and feelings, even if they are unrelated to what you are reading. Those impressions may be the very things that your Heavenly Father wants you to learn.

## Liken the Scriptures to Your Life

Consider how the stories and teachings you are reading apply to your life. For example, you could ask yourself, "What experiences have I had that are similar to what I am reading?" or "How can I follow the example of this person in the scriptures?"

## Ask Questions as You Study

As you study the scriptures, questions may come to mind. These questions might relate to what you are reading or to your life in general. Ponder these questions and look for answers as you continue studying the scriptures.

## Use Scripture Study Helps

To gain additional insights into the verses you read, use the footnotes, the Topical Guide, the Bible Dictionary, the Guide to the Scriptures (scriptures.ChurchofJesusChrist.org), and other study helps.

## Consider the Context of the Scriptures

You can find meaningful insights about a scripture if you consider its context—the circumstances or setting of the scripture. For example, knowing the background and beliefs of the people a prophet spoke to can help you understand the intent of his words.

## Record Your Thoughts and Feelings

There are various ways to record the impressions that come as you study. For example, you could mark a meaningful word or phrase and record your thoughts as a note in your scriptures. You could also keep a journal of the insights, feelings, and impressions you receive.

## Study the Words of Latter-day Prophets and Apostles

Read what latter-day prophets and apostles have taught about the principles you find in the scriptures (for example, see conference.ChurchofJesusChrist.org and Church magazines).

## Share Insights

Discussing insights from your personal study is not only a good way to teach others, but it also helps strengthen your understanding of what you have read.

## Live by What You Learn

Scripture study should not only inspire us but also lead us to change the way we live. Listen to what the Spirit prompts you to do as you read, and then commit to act on those promptings.

Elder David A. Bednar said: "We should not expect the Church as an organization to teach or tell us everything we need to know and do to become devoted disciples and endure valiantly to the end [see Doctrine and Covenants 121:29]. Rather, our personal responsibility is to learn what we should learn, to live as we know we should live, and to become who the Master would have us become. And our homes are the ultimate setting for learning, living, and becoming" ("Prepared to Obtain Every Needful Thing," *Ensign* or *Liahona,* May 2019, 102).

# Ideas to Improve Your Family Scripture Study

Regular family scripture study is a powerful way to help your family learn the gospel. How much and how long you read as a family is not as important as being consistent in your efforts. As you make scripture study an important part of your family life, you will help your family members come closer to Heavenly Father and Jesus Christ and build their testimonies on the foundation of God's word.

Consider the following questions:

- How can you encourage family members to study the scriptures on their own?

- What can you do to encourage family members to share what they are learning?

- How can you emphasize the principles you are learning in the Old Testament in everyday teaching moments?

Remember that the home is the ideal place for gospel learning. You can learn and teach the gospel at home in ways that are not possible in a Church class. Be creative as you think of ways to help your family learn from the scriptures. Consider some of the following ideas to enhance your family scripture study.

## Use Music

Sing songs that reinforce the principles taught in the scriptures. A suggested hymn or children's song is listed in each weekly outline. You might ask family members questions about words or phrases in the lyrics. In addition to singing, your family can perform actions that go with the songs or listen to the songs as background music while they are doing other activities. For more ideas, see "Including Sacred Music in Your Gospel Learning" in this resource.

## Share Meaningful Scriptures

Give family members time to share scripture passages that they have found meaningful during their personal study.

## Use Your Own Words

Invite family members to summarize in their own words what they learn from the scriptures you study.

## Apply the Scriptures to Your Life

After reading a scripture passage, ask family members to share ways the passage applies to their lives.

## Ask a Question

Invite family members to ask a gospel question, and then spend time looking for verses that can help answer the question.

## Display a Scripture

Select a verse you find meaningful, and display it where family members will see it often. Invite other family members to take turns selecting a scripture to display.

## Make a Scripture List

As a family, choose several verses that you would like to discuss during the coming week.

## Memorize Scriptures

Select a scripture passage that is meaningful to your family, and invite family members to memorize it by repeating it daily or playing a memorization game.

## Share Object Lessons

Find objects that relate to the gospel principles in the scripture passages you are reading as a family. Invite family members to talk about how each object relates to the teachings in the scriptures.

## Pick a Topic

Let family members take turns choosing a topic that the family will study together. Use the Topical Guide, the Bible Dictionary, or the Guide to the Scriptures (scriptures.ChurchofJesusChrist.org) to find scripture passages about the topic.

## Draw a Picture

Read a few verses as a family, and then allow time for family members to draw something that relates to what you read. Spend time discussing one another's drawings.

## Act Out a Story

After reading a story, invite family members to act it out. Afterward, talk about how the story relates to the things that you are experiencing individually and as a family.

President Russell M. Nelson said: "I promise that as you diligently work to remodel your home into a center of gospel learning, over time *your* Sabbath days will truly be a delight. *Your* children will be excited to learn and to live the Savior's teachings, and the influence of the adversary in *your* life and in *your* home will decrease. Changes in your family will be dramatic and sustaining" ("Becoming Exemplary Latter-day Saints," *Ensign* or *Liahona,* Nov. 2018, 113).

# Additional Resources

Most of these resources can be found in the Gospel Library app and at ChurchofJesusChrist.org.

## Hymns and Children's Songbook

Sacred music invites the Spirit and teaches doctrine in a memorable way. In addition to using the print versions of *Hymns* and *Children's Songbook,* you can find audio and video recordings of many hymns and children's songs at music.ChurchofJesusChrist.org and in the Sacred Music and Gospel Media apps.

## Seminary and Institute Manuals

Seminary and institute manuals provide historical background and doctrinal commentary for principles and accounts found in the scriptures.

## Church Magazines

The *Friend, For the Strength of Youth,* and the *Liahona* magazines provide stories and activities that can supplement the principles you are teaching from *Come, Follow Me—For Individuals and Families.*

## Gospel Topics

In Gospel Topics (topics.ChurchofJesusChrist.org) you can find basic information about a variety of gospel subjects, along with links to helpful resources, such as related general conference addresses, articles, scriptures, and videos. You can also find Gospel Topics Essays, which offer in-depth information about doctrinal and historical issues.

## Old Testament Stories

*Old Testament Stories* can help children learn the doctrine and stories found in the Old Testament. You can also find videos of these stories in the Gospel Library app and at MediaLibrary. ChurchofJesusChrist.org.

## Scripture Stories Coloring Book— Old Testament

This resource contains fun coloring activity pages designed to enhance children's learning from the Old Testament.

## Videos and Art

Artwork, videos, and other media can help your family understand doctrine and visualize stories related to the scriptures. Visit Gospel Media at MediaLibrary.ChurchofJesusChrist.org to browse the Church's collection of media resources. Gospel Media is also available as a mobile app. Many images that you can use are found in the *Gospel Art Book*.

## Teaching in the Savior's Way

*Teaching in the Savior's Way* can help you learn about and apply principles of Christlike teaching.

# Teaching Young Children

If you have young children in your family, here are some activities that can help them learn:

- *Sing.* Hymns and songs from *Children's Songbook* teach doctrine powerfully. Use the topics index at the back of the *Children's Songbook* to find songs that relate to the gospel principles you are teaching. Help your children relate the messages of the songs to their lives. (See also "Including Sacred Music in Your Gospel Learning" in this resource.)

- *Listen to or act out a story.* Young children love stories—from the scriptures, from your life, from your family history, or from Church magazines. Look for ways to involve them in storytelling. They can hold pictures or objects, draw pictures of what they are hearing, act out the story, or even help tell the story. Help your children recognize the gospel truths in the stories you share.

- *Read a scripture.* Young children may not be able to read very much, but you can still engage them in learning from the scriptures. You may need

to focus on a single verse, key phrase, or word. The children may even be able to memorize short phrases from the scriptures if they repeat them a few times. As they hear the word of God, they will feel the Spirit.

- *Look at a picture or watch a video.* When you show your children a picture or video related to a gospel principle or scripture story, ask them questions that help them learn from what they are seeing. For example, you could ask, "What is happening in this picture or video? How does it make you feel?" The Gospel Media app, MediaLibrary.ChurchofJesusChrist.org, and children.ChurchofJesusChrist.org are good places to look for pictures and videos.

- *Create.* Children can build, draw, or color something related to the story or principle they are learning.

- *Participate in object lessons.* A simple object lesson can help your children understand a gospel principle that is difficult to comprehend. When using object lessons, find ways to let your children participate. They will learn more from an interactive experience than from just watching a demonstration.

- *Role-play.* When children role-play a situation they are likely to encounter in real life, they are better able to understand how a gospel principle applies to their lives.

- *Repeat activities.* Young children may need to hear concepts multiple times to understand them. Don't be afraid to repeat stories or activities often. For example, you might share a scripture story several times in different ways—reading from the scriptures, summarizing in your own words, showing a video, letting your children help you tell the story, inviting them to act out the story, and so on.

# Including Sacred Music in Your Gospel Learning

Singing Primary songs and hymns can bless you and your family in many ways. These ideas can help you use sacred music as you strive to learn and live the gospel.

- *Learn doctrinal principles.* Look for truths taught in the songs you sing or listen to. This may lead to gospel discussions about these truths throughout the day. Sing or listen to Primary songs or hymns that teach about Jesus Christ and His gospel. Pay attention to ways the Holy Ghost testifies of the Savior and His teachings.

- *Recognize music's power.* Singing or listening to Primary songs and hymns can be a blessing in times of need. For instance, singing a song could calm a child at bedtime, create joy as your family works together, uplift a neighbor who is sick, or comfort someone who feels anxious.

- *Share experiences.* Share personal and family experiences that relate to the messages of the songs. You can also share related scripture stories.

- *Involve your family.* Your family will learn more from songs if they are actively participating.

To involve family members, you could invite an older child to help teach a song to younger siblings or invite children to teach the family a song they learned in Primary. You could also let family members take turns leading a song.

- *Be creative.* Use a variety of ways to learn sacred music as a family. For instance, you could use gestures that go with words and phrases in a song. Or you could take turns acting out parts of a song while other family members try to guess the song. Your family might enjoy singing songs at different speeds or volumes. The Gospel Library app and the Gospel for Kids app have audio recordings and videos that can help you learn the songs. You could also make playlists of sacred music to listen to.

For more ideas, see the sections "Using Music to Teach Doctrine" and "Helping Children Learn and Remember Primary Songs and Hymns," found in "Instructions for Singing Time and the Children's Sacrament Music Presentation" in *Come, Follow Me— For Primary*.

# Old Testament Overview

## THE PATRIARCHS

Adam and Eve

Enoch

Noah

Melchizedek

Abraham and Sarah

Isaac and Rebekah

Jacob and Leah, Rachel, Bilhah, Zilpah

Joseph and Asenath

## EXODUS

Moses and Zipporah

Joshua

## JUDGES

Deborah
Gideon
Samson

Ruth

Hannah
Samuel

## UNITED MONARCHY

Saul
David
Solomon

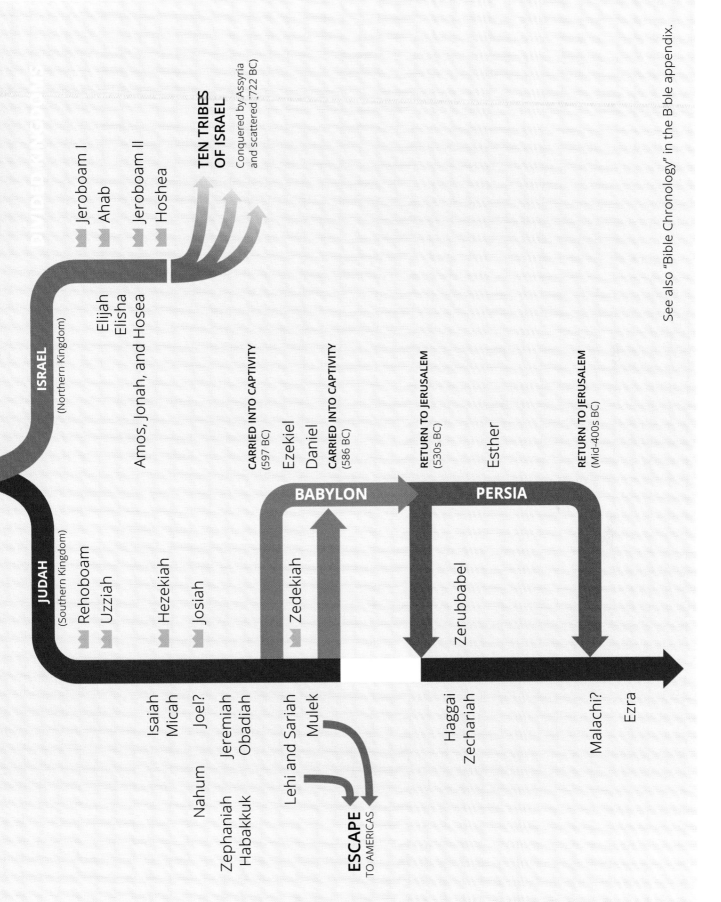

DIVIDED KINGDOMS

ISRAEL
(Northern Kingdom)

Jeroboam I
Ahab
Jeroboam II
Hoshea

Elijah
Elisha

Amos, Jonah, and Hosea

**TEN TRIBES
OF ISRAEL**

Conquered by Assyria
and scattered (722 BC)

JUDAH
(Southern Kingdom)

Rehoboam
Uzziah

Hezekiah

Josiah

Isaiah
Micah    Joel?

Nahum

Zephaniah   Jeremiah
Habakkuk    Obadiah

Lehi and Sariah
Mulek

**ESCAPE**
TO AMERICAS

**CARRIED INTO CAPTIVITY**
(597 BC)

Ezekiel
Daniel

**CARRIED INTO CAPTIVITY**
(586 BC)

Zedekiah

**BABYLON**

**RETURN TO JERUSALEM**
(530s BC)

Esther

**PERSIA**

Zerubbabel

Haggai
Zechariah

**RETURN TO JERUSALEM**
(Mid-400s BC)

Malachi?

Ezra

See also "Bible Chronology" in the Bible appendix.

# Reading the Old Testament

## Find Personal Meaning

When you consider your opportunity to study the Old Testament this year, how do you feel? Eager? Uncertain? Afraid? All of those emotions are understandable. The Old Testament is one of the oldest collections of writings in the world, and that can make it both exciting and intimidating. These writings come from an ancient culture that can seem foreign and sometimes strange or even uncomfortable. And yet in these writings we see people having experiences that seem familiar, and we recognize gospel themes that witness of the divinity of Jesus Christ and His gospel.

Yes, people like Abraham, Sarah, Hannah, and Daniel lived lives that, in some ways, were very different from ours. But they also experienced family joy and family discord, moments of faith and moments of uncertainty, and successes and failures—like all of us do. More importantly, they exercised faith, repented, made covenants, had spiritual experiences, and never gave up in their efforts to obey God.

If you wonder whether you and your family can find personal meaning in the Old Testament this year, keep in mind that Lehi and Sariah's family did. Nephi shared stories about Moses and teachings from Isaiah when his brothers needed encouragement or correction or perspective. When Nephi said, "My soul delighteth in the scriptures" (2 Nephi 4:15), he was talking about scriptures that are now part of the Old Testament.

## Seek the Savior

If you wonder whether you and your family can come closer to Jesus Christ through studying the Old Testament, keep in mind that the Savior Himself invites us to do so. When He told the leaders of the Jews, "The scriptures . . . testify of me" (John 5:39), He was talking about the writings we call the Old Testament. To find the Savior in what you read, you may need to ponder patiently and seek spiritual guidance. Sometimes the references to Him seem very direct, as in Isaiah's declaration "Unto us a child is born, unto us a son is given: . . . and his name shall be called . . . The Prince of Peace" (Isaiah 9:6). In other places, the Savior is represented more subtly, through symbols and similarities—for example, through the descriptions of animal sacrifices (see Leviticus 1:3–4) or the account of Joseph forgiving his brothers and saving them from famine.

If you seek greater faith in the Savior as you study the Old Testament, you will find it. Perhaps this could be the aim of your study this year. Pray that the Spirit will guide you to find and focus on passages, stories, and prophecies that will bring you closer to Jesus Christ.

*Old Testament Prophet,* Judith A. Mehr

## Divinely Preserved

Don't expect the Old Testament to present a thorough and precise history of humankind. That's not what the original authors and compilers were trying to create. Their larger concern was to teach something about God—about His plan for His children, about what it means to be His covenant people, and about how to find redemption when we don't live up to our covenants. Sometimes they did it by relating historical events as they understood them—including stories from the lives of great prophets. Genesis is an example of this, as are books like Joshua, Judges, and 1 and 2 Kings. But other Old Testament writers did not aim to be historical at all. Instead, they taught through works of art like poetry and literature. The Psalms and the Proverbs fit in this category. And then there are the precious words of prophets, from Isaiah to Malachi, who spoke the word of God to ancient Israel—and, through the miracle of the Bible, still speak to us today.

Did all of these prophets, poets, and compilers know that their words would be read by people all over the world thousands of years later? We don't know. But we marvel that this is exactly what has happened. Nations rose and fell, cities were conquered, kings lived and died; but the Old Testament outlasted them all, from generation to generation, from scribe to scribe, from translation to translation. Of course some things were lost or modified, and yet somehow so much was miraculously preserved.[1]

These are just a few things to keep in mind as you read the Old Testament this year. Maybe God preserved these ancient writings because He knows you and what you are going through. Maybe He has prepared a spiritual message for you in these words, something that will draw you closer to Him and build your faith in His plan and His Beloved Son. Perhaps He will lead you to a passage or an insight that will bless someone you know—a message you can share with a friend, a family member, or a fellow Saint. There are so many possibilities. Isn't that exciting to think about?

### Books in the Old Testament

In most Christian versions of the Old Testament, the books are organized differently from how they were arranged when they were first compiled into one collection. So while the Hebrew Bible groups the books into three categories—the law, prophets, and writings—most Christian Bibles arrange the books into four categories: law (Genesis–Deuteronomy), history (Joshua–Esther), poetic books (Job–Song of Solomon), and prophets (Isaiah–Malachi).

Why are these categories important? Because knowing what *kind* of book you are studying can help you understand *how* to study it.

Here's something to keep in mind as you begin reading "the law," or the first five books of the Old Testament. These books, which are attributed to Moses, probably passed through the hands of numerous scribes and compilers over time. Still, the books of Moses are the inspired word of God, even though they are—like any work of God transmitted through mortals—subject to human imperfections (see Moses 1:41; Articles of Faith 1:8). The words of Moroni, referring to the sacred Book of Mormon record that he helped compile, are helpful here: "If there are faults they are the mistakes of men; wherefore, condemn not the things of God" (title page of the Book of Mormon). In other words, a book of scripture need not be free from human error in order to be the word of God.

**Note**

1. President M. Russell Ballard said: "It is not by chance or coincidence that we have the Bible today. Righteous individuals were prompted by the Spirit to record both the sacred things they saw and the inspired words they heard and spoke. Other devoted people were prompted to protect and preserve these records" ("The Miracle of the Holy Bible," *Ensign* or *Liahona,* May 2007, 80).

# Moses 1; Abraham 3

"THIS IS MY WORK AND MY GLORY"

As you read what God said to Moses and to Abraham, ponder what He might also be saying to you.

RECORD YOUR IMPRESSIONS

The Bible begins with the words "in the beginning God created the heaven and the earth" (Genesis 1:1). But what was there *before* this "beginning"? And *why* did God create all of this? Through the Prophet Joseph Smith, the Lord has shed light on these questions.

For example, He gave us the record of a vision in which Abraham saw our existence as spirits "before the world was" (see Abraham 3:22–28). The Lord also gave us an inspired translation or revision of the first six chapters of Genesis, called the book of Moses—which doesn't begin with "in the beginning." Instead, it begins with an experience Moses had that provides some context for the well-known Creation story. Together, these latter-day scriptures are a good place to start our study of the Old Testament because they address some fundamental questions that can frame our reading: Who is God? Who are we? What is God's work, and what is our place in it? The opening chapters of Genesis could be seen as the Lord's response to Moses's request: "Be merciful unto thy servant, O God, and tell me concerning this earth, and the inhabitants thereof, and also the heavens" (Moses 1:36).

# Ideas for Personal Scripture Study

### MOSES 1

## As a child of God, I have a divine destiny.

President Dieter F. Uchtdorf taught, "Much of the confusion we experience in this life comes from simply not understanding who we are" ("The Reflection in the Water" [Church Educational System fireside for young adults, Nov. 1, 2009], ChurchofJesusChrist .org). Heavenly Father knows this, and so does Satan. God's first message to Moses included the truths "thou art my son" and "thou art in the similitude of mine Only Begotten" (Moses 1:4, 6). In contrast, Satan addressed Moses as just a "son of man" (Moses 1:12). How would your life and decisions be different if you thought of yourself like Satan wants you to, as a "son [or daughter] of man"? How does knowing and remembering that you are a child of God bless your life?

What verses or phrases in Moses 1 give you a sense of your divine worth?

*Christ and the Creation,* by Robert T. Barrett

### MOSES 1:12–26

## I can resist Satan's influence.

As Moses 1 clearly shows, powerful spiritual experiences do not exempt us from temptation. In fact, one of Satan's tactics is to tempt us to doubt those experiences or what we learned from them. As you read about Moses's response to Satan in verses 12–26, what do you learn that can help you stay true to the testimony you have received? What helps you resist Satan's other temptations? (see, for example, verses 15 and 18).

Based on what you learn, you could make a plan for resisting temptation. For example, you could complete the statement "When I am tempted to _____, I will _____."

See also Matthew 4:1–11; Helaman 5:12; Gary E. Stevenson, "Deceive Me Not," *Ensign* or *Liahona,* Nov. 2019, 93–96; "I Am a Son of God" (video), ChurchofJesusChrist.org.

### MOSES 1:27–39; ABRAHAM 3

## God's work and glory is to help me gain eternal life.

After beholding a vision of God's creations, Moses made a request of the Lord: "Tell me . . . why these things are so" (Moses 1:30). What impresses you about the Lord's response in Moses 1:31–39?

Abraham also had a visionary experience, recorded in Abraham 3. What do you find in verses 22–26 that could help answer Moses's request?

Consider listing other truths that Moses and Abraham learned in their visions: truths about God, about themselves, and about the purposes of God's creations. How do these truths affect the way you view yourself and the world around you?

See also Dieter F. Uchtdorf, "You Matter to Him," *Ensign* or *Liahona,* Nov. 2011, 19–22; Gospel Topics, "Premortality," topics.ChurchofJesusChrist.org.

### ABRAHAM 3:22–23

## Were others besides Abraham "chosen before [they were] born"?

"In the premortal spirit world, God appointed certain spirits to fulfill specific missions during their mortal lives. This is called foreordination. . . . The doctrine of foreordination applies to all members of the Church, not just to the Savior and His prophets" (Gospel Topics, "Foreordination," topics .ChurchofJesusChrist.org).

## How did we get the books of Moses and Abraham?

The book of Moses is the first part of Joseph Smith's inspired translation of the Bible. The book of Abraham was revealed to Joseph Smith during his work with Egyptian papyri. These books, found today in the Pearl of Great Price, provide much information about Moses, Abraham, and other prophets that is not found in the Old Testament. To learn more about how we got these books, see "Joseph Smith Translation of the Bible" (Church History Topics, ChurchofJesusChrist.org/study/history/topics) and "Translation and Historicity of the Book of Abraham" (Gospel Topics, topics .ChurchofJesusChrist.org).

## Ideas for Family Scripture Study and Home Evening

**Moses 1:2–6; Abraham 3:11–12.** You could invite family members to look for phrases in the song "I Am a Child of God" (*Children's Songbook,* 2–3) that relate to the truths taught in these scriptures.

**Moses 1:4, 30–39.** Would your family enjoy looking at some of "the workmanship of [God's] hands"? (verse 4). Maybe you could read these verses in a park or under the stars at night. You could then talk about why God created the world and about how we participate in His "work and [His] glory" (verse 39).

**Moses 1:18.** What advice can we share to help each other "judge between" God and Satan? (See also Moroni 7:12–18; Doctrine and Covenants 50:23–24.)

**Abraham 3:24–26.** You could give family members a fun but challenging task that allows them to prove they can follow instructions, such as folding a paper airplane or following a recipe. How is this activity similar to the purpose of our mortal life as described in these verses?

For more ideas for teaching children, see this week's outline in *Come, Follow Me—For Primary.*

Suggested song: "I Am a Child of God," *Children's Songbook,* 2–3.

### Improving Personal Study

**Look for gospel truths.** In the scriptures, sometimes gospel truths are stated directly; sometimes they are implied through an example or story. Ask yourself, "What eternal truth is taught in these verses?"

*Moses Overcomes Satan,* by Joseph Brickey

# Genesis 1–2; Moses 2–3; Abraham 4–5

"IN THE BEGINNING GOD CREATED THE HEAVEN AND THE EARTH"

Even if you have read about the Creation before, there is always more to learn from the scriptures. Pray for guidance from the Holy Ghost to help you find new understanding.

RECORD YOUR IMPRESSIONS _____

_____

_____

Because the world around us is so beautiful and majestic, it is hard to imagine the earth when it was "without form, and void," "empty and desolate" (Genesis 1:2; Abraham 4:2). One thing the Creation story teaches us is that God can make something magnificent out of something unorganized. That's helpful to remember when life seems chaotic. Heavenly Father and Jesus Christ are Creators, and Their creative work with us is not finished. They can make light shine in dark moments in our lives. They can form solid ground in the midst of life's stormy seas. They can command the elements, and if we obey Their word like the elements did, They can transform us into the beautiful creations we were meant to be. That's part of what it means to be created in God's image, after His likeness (see Genesis 1:26). We have the potential to become like Him: exalted, glorified, celestial beings.

For an overview of the book of Genesis, see "Genesis" in the Bible Dictionary.

## Ideas for Personal Scripture Study

**GENESIS 1:1–25; MOSES 2:1–25; ABRAHAM 4:1–25**

### Under the direction of Heavenly Father, Jesus Christ created the earth.

Elder D. Todd Christofferson said, "Whatever the details of the creation process, we know that it was not accidental but that it was directed by God the Father and implemented by Jesus Christ" ("Why Marriage, Why Family," *Ensign* or *Liahona,* May 2015, 51). While there's a lot we don't know about exactly how the world was created, ponder what you learn about the Creation from what God has revealed in Genesis 1:1–25; Moses 2:1–25; and Abraham 4:1–25. What do you notice in these accounts that is similar? What do you notice that is different? What thoughts do you have about Heavenly Father and Jesus Christ as you read about the Creation?

See also Doctrine and Covenants 101:32–34.

*Creation,* by Joan Hibbert Durtschi

**GENESIS 1:27–28; 2:18–25; MOSES 3:18, 21–25; ABRAHAM 5:14–19**

### Marriage between a man and a woman is ordained of God.

"Adam and Eve were joined together in marriage for time and for all eternity by the power of [the] everlasting priesthood" (Russell M. Nelson, "Lessons from Eve," *Ensign,* Nov. 1987, 87). Why is this truth important to know? Ponder this as you read Genesis 1:27–28; 2:18–25; Moses 3:18, 21–25; and Abraham 5:14–19. If you would like to learn more about marriage within God's plan, read and ponder the resources listed below. What do these resources prompt you to do to improve your marriage or to prepare for marriage in the future?

See also Matthew 19:4–6; 1 Corinthians 11:11; Linda K. Burton, "We'll Ascend Together," *Ensign* or *Liahona,* May 2015, 29–32; "The Family: A Proclamation to the World," ChurchofJesusChrist.org.

**GENESIS 2:2–3; MOSES 3:2–3; ABRAHAM 5:2–3**

### God blessed and sanctified the Sabbath day.

God made the Sabbath day holy, and He asks us to keep it holy. Elder David A. Bednar taught, "The Sabbath is God's time, a *sacred time* specifically set apart for worshipping Him and for receiving and remembering His great and precious promises" ("Exceeding Great and Precious Promises," *Ensign* or *Liahona,* Nov. 2017, 92). How could you use this statement and Genesis 2:2–3; Moses 3:2–3; or Abraham 5:2–3 to explain to someone why you choose to honor the Sabbath day? How has the Lord blessed you for keeping His day holy?

See also Isaiah 58:13–14; Doctrine and Covenants 59:9–13; "The Sabbath Is a Delight" (video), ChurchofJesusChrist.org.

## Ideas for Family Scripture Study and Home Evening

**Genesis 1:1–25; Moses 2:1–25; Abraham 4:1–25.** How can you make learning about the Creation fun for your family? You could take your family on a search outside for the kinds of things that were made during each period of the Creation story, such as stars, trees, or animals. You might also show pictures of things created in each period and invite family members to put the pictures in order after reading one of the accounts of the Creation together. What do these creations teach us about Heavenly Father and Jesus Christ?

**Genesis 1; Moses 2; Abraham 4.** One way to approach the Creation story is to invite your family to find how many times in Genesis 1 or Moses 2 God calls the things that he made "good." What does this suggest about how we should treat God's creations—including ourselves? What do we learn from the way these events are worded in Abraham 4?

**Genesis 1:26–27; Moses 2:26–27; Abraham 4:26–27.** Why is it important to know that we were created in God's image? How does it affect the way we feel about ourselves, others, and God?

If you have small children, you might want to read together Moses 2:27 and play a simple game: Show a picture that depicts Heavenly Father and Jesus Christ, such as picture 90 in the *Gospel Art Book* (2009), and ask family members to take turns pointing to a part of Heavenly Father's or Jesus's body. Then the other family members could point to that same part on their bodies.

**Genesis 1:28; Moses 2:28; Abraham 4:28.** "God's commandment for His children to multiply and replenish the earth remains in force" ("The Family: A Proclamation to the World," ChurchofJesusChrist .org). Family members could role-play how to explain our beliefs about this commandment to those who do not know this truth or who believe differently.

**Genesis 1:28; Moses 2:28; Abraham 4:28.** What does it mean to "have dominion . . . over every living thing that moveth upon the earth"? (see also Doctrine and Covenants 59:16–21). How can our family fulfill our responsibility to care for the earth?

For more ideas for teaching children, see this week's outline in *Come, Follow Me—For Primary.*

Suggested song: "My Heavenly Father Loves Me," *Children's Songbook,* 228–29.

## Improving Our Teaching

**Apply the scriptures to our lives.** After reading a passage of scripture, invite family members to apply it to their lives. For instance, how does Moses 3:1–3 apply to our observance of the Sabbath each week? (See *Teaching in the Savior's Way,* 21.)

*The Creation,* by Annie Henrie Nader

*Adam and Eve*, by Douglas M. Fryer

# Genesis 3–4; Moses 4–5

THE FALL OF ADAM AND EVE

As you study Genesis 3–4 and Moses 4–5, consider what the Lord is trying to teach you. Record these truths and your spiritual impressions, and reflect on them throughout the week.

RECORD YOUR IMPRESSIONS _____

At first, the story of the Fall of Adam and Eve might seem like a tragedy. Adam and Eve were cast out of the beautiful Garden of Eden. They were thrown into a world where pain, sorrow, and death are ever present (see Genesis 3:16–19). And they were separated from their Heavenly Father. But because of the truths restored through the Prophet Joseph Smith in the book of Moses, we know that the story of Adam and Eve is actually one of hope—and an essential part of God's plan for His children.

The Garden of Eden was beautiful. But Adam and Eve needed something more than beautiful surroundings. They needed—and we all need—an opportunity to grow. Leaving the Garden of Eden was the necessary first step toward returning to God and eventually becoming like Him. That meant facing opposition, making mistakes, learning to repent, and trusting the Savior, whose Atonement makes possible progression and "the joy of our redemption" (Moses 5:11). So when you read about the Fall of Adam and Eve, focus not on the seeming tragedy but on the possibilities—not on the paradise Adam and Eve lost but on the glory their choice allows us to receive.

# Ideas for Personal Scripture Study

**GENESIS 3:1–7; MOSES 4; 5:4–12**

## The Fall was a necessary part of God's plan to redeem His children.

Adam and Eve's Fall brought physical and spiritual death into the world. It also brought adversity, sorrow, and sin. These all seem like reasons to regret the Fall. But the Fall was part of Heavenly Father's plan to redeem and exalt His children through "the sacrifice of the Only Begotten of the Father" (Moses 5:7). As you study Genesis 3:1–7; Moses 4; 5:4–12, what truths do you find that help you understand the Fall and how Christ's Atonement overcomes it? Questions like these might help:

- How did the Fall affect Adam and Eve? How does it affect me?

- Why did Adam and Eve offer sacrifices? What did those sacrifices symbolize? What can I learn from the angel's words in these verses?

- Why were Adam and Eve "glad" after their Fall? What do I learn from this account about God's plan to redeem me through Jesus Christ?

Because of the Book of Mormon and other latter-day revelations, we have a unique perspective on the Fall. For example, consider what the prophet Lehi taught his family about Adam and Eve in 2 Nephi 2:15–27. How do Lehi's teachings clarify what happened in the Garden of Eden and help us understand why it was important?

See also 1 Corinthians 15:20–22; Mosiah 3:19; Alma 12:21–37; Doctrine and Covenants 29:39–43; Articles of Faith 1:3; Dallin H. Oaks, "The Great Plan," *Ensign* or *Liahona,* May 2020, 93–96; Dallin H. Oaks, "Opposition in All Things," *Ensign* or *Liahona,* May 2016, 114–17; Jeffrey R. Holland,

"Where Justice, Love, and Mercy Meet," *Ensign* or *Liahona,* May 2015, 104–6.

*Leaving Eden,* by Annie Henrie Nader

**GENESIS 3:16; MOSES 4:22**

## What does it mean that Adam was to "rule over" Eve?

This passage of scripture has sometimes been misunderstood to mean that a husband is justified in treating his wife unkindly. In our day, the Lord's prophets have taught that while a husband should preside in the home in righteousness, he should see his wife as an equal partner (see "The Family: A Proclamation to the World" [ChurchofJesusChrist.org]). Elder Dale G. Renlund and Sister Ruth Lybbert Renlund explained that a righteous husband "will seek to minister; he will acknowledge error and seek forgiveness; he will be quick to offer praise; he will be considerate of family members' preferences; he will feel the great weight of responsibility to provide 'the necessities of life and protection' for his family; he will treat his wife with the utmost respect and deference. . . . He will bless his family" (*The Melchizedek Priesthood: Understanding the Doctrine, Living the Principles* [2018], 23).

**MOSES 5:4–9, 16–26**

## God will accept my sacrifices if I offer them with a willing and obedient heart.

Adam and Eve learned that animal sacrifices were symbolic of Christ's atoning sacrifice, and they made this "known unto their sons and their daughters" (Moses 5:12). As you study Moses 5:4–9, 16–26, consider the different attitudes of two of their sons, Cain and Abel, toward these sacrifices. Why did the Lord accept Abel's sacrifice but not Cain's?

What kinds of sacrifices does the Lord ask of you? Is there anything in Moses 5:4–9, 16–26 that changes the way you think about those sacrifices?

See also Psalm 4:5; 2 Corinthians 9:7; Omni 1:26; 3 Nephi 9:19–20; Moroni 7:6–11; Doctrine and Covenants 97:8; Jeffrey R. Holland, "Behold the Lamb of God," *Ensign* or *Liahona,* May 2019, 44–46.

## Ideas for Family Scripture Study and Home Evening

**Genesis 3; Moses 4.** What can you do to help your family better understand the Fall of Adam and Eve? You could copy the pictures from "Adam and Eve" (in *Old Testament Stories*) and cut them out. Then you could work together to put the pictures in order as you discuss the experiences of Adam and Eve. Why was the Fall necessary in Heavenly Father's plan of salvation? Watching the video "The Fall" (ChurchofJesusChrist.org) could help answer this question.

**Moses 4:1–4.** What do we learn about God, Jesus Christ, and Satan from these verses? Why is agency so important to God's plan that Satan would want to destroy it?

**Moses 5:5–9.** What did God command Adam and Eve to do to help them think about the Savior? What has God given us to help us think about the Savior?

**Moses 5:16–34.** What does it mean to be our "brother's keeper"? How can we better care for each other as a family?

For more ideas for teaching children, see this week's outline in *Come, Follow Me—For Primary.*

Suggested song: "Choose the Right Way," *Children's Songbook,* 160–61.

### Improving Personal Study

**Use scripture study helps.** As you study the scriptures, use the footnotes, Topical Guide, Bible Dictionary, Guide to the Scriptures, and other study helps to gain additional insights.

*Similitude,* by Walter Rane

# Genesis 5; Moses 6

"TEACH THESE THINGS FREELY UNTO YOUR CHILDREN"

As you read and ponder Genesis 5 and Moses 6, record the spiritual impressions you receive. What messages do you find that are valuable to you and your family?

RECORD YOUR IMPRESSIONS

Most of Genesis 5 is a list of the generations between Adam and Eve and Noah. We read a lot of names, but we don't learn much about them. Then we read about Enoch, six generations from Adam, who is described with this intriguing but unexplained line: "And Enoch walked with God: and he was not; for God took him" (Genesis 5:24). Surely there's a story behind that. But without further explanation, the list of generations resumes.

Thankfully, Moses 6 reveals the details of Enoch's story—and it's quite a story. We learn of Enoch's humility, his insecurities, the potential God saw in him, and the great work he performed

as God's prophet. We also get a clearer picture of the family of Adam and Eve as it progressed through the generations. We read of Satan's "great dominion" but also of parents who taught children "the ways of God" and of "preachers of righteousness" who "spake and prophesied" (Moses 6:15, 21, 23). Especially precious is what we learn about the doctrine these parents and preachers taught: faith, repentance, baptism, and receiving the Holy Ghost (see Moses 6:50–52). That doctrine, like the priesthood that accompanies it, "was in the beginning [and] shall be in the end of the world also" (Moses 6:7).

## Ideas for Personal Scripture Study

**MOSES 6:26–36**

### A prophet is a seer.

As you study Moses 6:26–36, what do you learn about eyes, darkness, and seeing? In Enoch's time, who could not "see afar off"? Why were these people unable to see truth? What was Enoch able to see? What has built your faith that modern-day prophets are seers? (see verse 36; Guide to the Scriptures, "Seer," scriptures.ChurchofJesusChrist.org).

**MOSES 6:26–47**

### God calls us to do His work despite our inadequacies.

It's not unusual to feel overwhelmed with what the Lord has called us to do. Even Enoch felt that way when the Lord called him to be a prophet. As you read Moses 6:26–36, look for why Enoch felt overwhelmed and what the Lord said to give him courage. In verses 37–47, look for ways the Lord supported Enoch and empowered him to do His work (see also Moses 7:13). You might compare Enoch's experience with that of other prophets who felt inadequate, such as Moses (see Exodus 4:10–16), Jeremiah (see Jeremiah 1:4–10), Nephi (see 2 Nephi 33:1–4), and Moroni (see Ether 12:23–29). What do you feel God wants you to learn from these scriptures about the work He has given you to do?

See also Jacob 4:6–8.

**MOSES 6:48–68**

### The doctrine of Christ is central to God's plan of salvation.

Because we have the book of Moses, we know that God has been teaching His children how to find forgiveness and redemption ever since the beginning. In the scriptures, these teachings are sometimes called the doctrine of Christ (see 2 Nephi 31:13–21). As you study Moses 6:48–68, search for what we must know and do to be redeemed. You may find it helpful to write your own summary of what Enoch taught. Why is it important to know that these truths have been taught since the days of Adam and Eve? What do you feel prompted to do as a result of studying these teachings?

**MOSES 6:51–62**

### "Teach these things freely unto your children."

Adam and Eve were taught the precious truths of the gospel of Jesus Christ. But the Lord's words in Moses 6:27–28 make clear that in the generations before Enoch, many people weren't living those truths anymore. The Lord wanted Enoch to restore the truths that had been lost—along with the commandment originally given to Adam: "Teach these things freely unto your children" (Moses 6:58). As you read Moses 6:51–62, what do you learn about Jesus Christ? What do you find that would be especially valuable to the rising generation? What can you do to help pass these truths on to future generations?

Parents should teach their children the gospel.

# Ideas for Family Scripture Study and Home Evening

**Genesis 5; Moses 6:5–25, 46.** Reading about the "book of remembrance" that Adam and Eve's family kept may inspire your family to make your own book of remembrance. Discuss as a family what you would like to include. Maybe you have photos, stories, or documents from your family history. You might choose to include things that are happening in your family now. What will future generations find valuable? You could also discuss how the phrases "by the spirit of inspiration" (Moses 6:5) and "the pattern given by the finger of God" (Moses 6:46) could guide your efforts. Consider saving information from your book of remembrance on FamilySearch.org.

**Moses 6:53–62.** How would we answer Adam's question found in Moses 6:53? What answers do we find in verses 57–62?

**Moses 6:59.** What does it mean to be "born again into the kingdom of heaven"? What can we do to continue to be born again throughout our lives? For help, see Alma 5:7–14, 26; Guide to the Scriptures, "Born Again, Born of God," scriptures.ChurchofJesusChrist.org; David A.

Bednar, "Always Retain a Remission of Your Sins" (*Ensign* or *Liahona,* May 2016, 59–62).

**Moses 6:61.** What do we learn about the Holy Ghost from this verse?

**Moses 6:63.** What are some of the things that "bear record of [Christ]"? (see also 2 Nephi 11:4). Consider inviting family members to share something that they see "in the heavens above" or "on the earth" that helps them learn about Jesus Christ. For example, how do trees, rocks, or the sun remind us of the Savior? What do the titles "living water" and "bread of life" teach us about Him? (John 4:10–14; 6:35).

For more ideas for teaching children, see this week's outline in *Come, Follow Me—For Primary.*

Suggested song: "I'll Go Where You Want Me to Go," *Hymns,* no. 270.

## Improving Personal Study

**Look for symbols.** In the scriptures, objects or events can often represent or symbolize spiritual truths. These symbols can enrich your understanding of doctrine. For instance, what do you learn from the symbols of eyes and clay in Moses 6:35?

*Adam and Eve Teaching Their Children,* by Del Parson

*Love One Another, by Emma Donaldson Taylor*

# Moses 7

"THE LORD CALLED HIS PEOPLE ZION"

As you read and ponder Moses 7, record your spiritual impressions. By doing this, you show that you value guidance from the Lord and that you want to receive more of His guidance.

RECORD YOUR IMPRESSIONS

Throughout history, people have tried to achieve what Enoch and his people accomplished: building an ideal society where there is no poverty or violence. As God's people, we share this desire. We call it building Zion, and it includes—in addition to caring for the poor and promoting peace—making covenants, dwelling together in righteousness, and becoming one with each other and with Jesus Christ, "the King of Zion" (Moses 7:53). Because the work of establishing Zion continues in our day,

it's helpful to ask, How did Enoch and his people do it? How did they become "of one heart and one mind" (Moses 7:18) despite the wickedness around them? Among the many details Moses 7 gives us about Zion, a particularly valuable one for Latter-day Saints might be this: Zion is not just a city—it is a condition of the heart and spirit. Zion, as the Lord has taught, is "the pure in heart" (Doctrine and Covenants 97:21). So perhaps the best way to build Zion is to start in our own hearts and homes.

# Ideas for Personal Scripture Study

### MOSES 7:16–21, 27, 53, 62–69

## Enoch's efforts are a pattern for building Zion in our own lives.

Because Moses 7 is a record of how God's followers successfully built Zion, it can instruct and inspire us today as we strive to do the same. Consider using a table like this one to record what you learn about Zion from Moses 7:16–21, 27, 53, 62–69.

| Verse | What do you learn about Zion? | What does this suggest about your efforts to build Zion? |
|---|---|---|
| 7:18 | The people of Zion were "of one heart and one mind." | We need to be united as families and as a Church. |
| 7:21 | "In process of time, [Zion] was taken up into heaven." | Building Zion is a gradual process. |
| | | |
| | | |

### MOSES 7:18–19, 53

## God's people should strive to be "of one heart and one mind."

Moses 7:18–19 lists important characteristics of the people whom the Lord called Zion. Why do you think these characteristics are necessary to build Zion? How is Zion, as described in this chapter, different from other united groups or organizations in the world? As you ponder this question, you might think about these words of Jesus Christ in verse 53: "I am Messiah, the King of Zion." What does it mean to have Jesus Christ as our King? How does He help us develop the characteristics of Zion?

See also Philippians 2:1–5; 4 Nephi 1:15–18; Doctrine and Covenants 97:21; 105:5.

We should strive to be "of one heart and one mind" (Moses 7:18).

### MOSES 7:21, 23–24, 27, 69

## What happened to the city of Enoch?

The phrases "taken up" (Moses 7:21, 23), "lifted up" (Moses 7:24), "caught up" (Moses 7:27), and "fled" (Moses 7:69) refer to Zion and the people of Enoch being translated and taken to heaven. People who are translated "are changed so that they do not experience pain or death" as mortals (Guide to the Scriptures, "Translated Beings," "Zion," scriptures.ChurchofJesusChrist.org; see also 3 Nephi 28:4–9, 15–18, 39–40).

### MOSES 7:28–69

## God weeps for His children.

Some people see God as a distant being who isn't emotionally affected by what happens to us. But Enoch saw a vision in which God wept for His children. As you read Moses 7:28–40, look for the reasons God wept. In the remainder of Enoch's vision, described in Moses 7:41–69, what evidence do you find that God is "merciful and kind forever"? (Moses 7:30; see verses 43, 47, and 62 for examples).

MOSES 7:62

## In the last days God will gather His elect.

Verse 62 describes events of the last days. Consider what phrases like these might mean: "righteousness will I send down out of heaven," "truth will I send forth out of the earth," "righteousness and truth will I cause to sweep the earth as with a flood." What do these phrases teach you about God's work in the latter days?

# Ideas for Family Scripture Study and Home Evening

**Moses 7:18–19.** To help family members visualize what it means to be "of one heart," maybe you could make a paper heart and cut it into puzzle pieces, enough for each family member to have one piece. Family members could write their name on their piece and then work with each other to put the heart together. While completing the puzzle you might talk about things you love about each family member.

**Moses 7:28–31, 35.** What do we learn about God from these verses?

**Moses 7:32.** Why did God give us agency? What might we say to someone who feels that God's commandments limit our agency? Reading 2 Nephi 2:25–27 might add to this discussion.

**Moses 7:59–67.** As your family reads Moses 7:59–67, try marking or noting things the Lord tells Enoch about the last days—for example, that God will "gather out [His] elect" (verse 62) and that there will be "great tribulations among the wicked" (verse 66). How can we have faith and hope despite the wickedness in the last days? As part of this discussion, consider reading these words from Elder Ronald A. Rasband: "Take heart, brothers and sisters. Yes, we live in perilous times, but as we stay on the covenant path, we need not fear. I bless you that as you do so, you will not be troubled by the times in which we live or the troubles that come your way. I bless you to choose to stand in holy places and be not moved. I bless you to believe in the promises of Jesus Christ, that He lives and that He is watching over us, caring for us and standing by us" ("Be Not Troubled," *Ensign* or *Liahona,* Nov. 2018, 21).

For more ideas for teaching children, see this week's outline in *Come, Follow Me—For Primary.*

Suggested song: "Love at Home," *Hymns,* no. 294.

## Improving Our Teaching

**Be observant.** As you pay attention to what is happening in your children's lives, you will find excellent teaching opportunities. Your children's comments and questions throughout the day can also signal possible teaching moments. (See *Teaching in the Savior's Way,* 16.)

*City of Zion Translated,* by Del Parson

# Genesis 6–11; Moses 8

"NOAH FOUND GRACE IN THE EYES OF THE LORD"

Stories in the scriptures can often teach us multiple spiritual lessons. As you read about the Great Flood and the Tower of Babel, seek inspiration about how these accounts apply to you.

RECORD YOUR IMPRESSIONS

Generations of Bible readers have been inspired by the story of Noah and the Flood. But we who live in the latter days have special reason to pay attention to it. When Jesus Christ taught how we should watch for His Second Coming, He said, "As it was in the days of Noah, so it shall be also at the coming of the Son of Man" (Joseph Smith—Matthew 1:41). In addition, phrases that describe Noah's day, like "corrupt" and "filled with violence," could just as easily be describing our time (Genesis 6:12–13; Moses 8:28). The story of the Tower of Babel also feels applicable to our day, with its description of pride followed by confusion and division among God's children.

These ancient accounts are valuable not just because they show us that wickedness repeats itself throughout history. More important, they teach us what to do about it. Noah "found grace in the eyes of the Lord" (Moses 8:27) despite the wickedness around him. And the families of Jared and his brother turned to the Lord and were led away from the wickedness in Babel (see Ether 1:33–43). If we wonder how to keep ourselves and our families safe during our own time of corruption and violence, the familiar stories in these chapters have much to teach us.

# Ideas for Personal Scripture Study

### GENESIS 6; MOSES 8

## There is spiritual safety in following the Lord's prophet.

Thanks to the restored gospel, we know a lot more about Noah than what is found in the Old Testament. Joseph Smith's inspired translation of Genesis 6, found in Moses 8, reveals that Noah was one of God's great prophets. He was ordained and sent forth to preach the gospel of Jesus Christ, he walked and talked with God, and he was chosen to reestablish God's children on the earth after the Flood (see also *Teachings of Presidents of the Church: Joseph Smith* [2007], 104, 201). What do you learn about prophets from Noah's experiences?

As you read about Noah's day, you might notice similarities to our day. For example:

- Moses 8:18, 20–21, 23–24 (rejection of God's servants)

- Moses 8:21 (complacency and worldliness)

- Moses 8:22 (evil imaginations and thoughts)

- Moses 8:28 (corruption and violence)

What are prophets teaching today about the gospel of Jesus Christ that could keep you safe in today's world? As you read about Noah's experiences, what inspires you to follow the Lord's prophets today?

See also Mosiah 13:33; Doctrine and Covenants 21:4–7.

### GENESIS 9:8–17

## Tokens or symbols help us remember our covenants with the Lord.

Gospel covenants can be represented by a sign, symbol, or "token" (Genesis 9:12). For example, think about how the bread and water of the sacrament or the waters of baptism bring to mind sacred truths related to your covenants. According to Genesis 9:8–17, what can a rainbow bring to your mind? What does Joseph Smith Translation, Genesis 9:21–25 (in the Bible appendix) add to your understanding? Why does the Lord want you to remember Him and the covenants you have made?

See also Gerrit W. Gong, "Always Remember Him," *Ensign* or *Liahona,* May 2016, 108–11.

### GENESIS 11:1–9

## The only way to reach heaven is by following Jesus Christ.

Ancient Babel, or Babylon, has long been used as a symbol for wickedness and worldliness (see Revelation 18:1–10; Doctrine and Covenants 133:14). As you study Genesis 11:1–9, ponder the insights provided by the prophet Mormon, who wrote that it was Satan "who put it into the hearts of the people to build a tower sufficiently high that they might get to heaven" (Helaman 6:28; see also verses 26–27). What warnings does the story of the Tower of Babel have for you?

See also Psalm 127:1.

Illustration of the Tower of Babel, by David Green

# Ideas for Family Scripture Study and Home Evening

**Genesis 6–8.** How might you use the story of Noah's ark to teach your family how following the prophet can keep us spiritually safe? (see "Noah and His Family," in *Old Testament Stories*). Maybe your family could work together to build a simple toy boat out of paper or blocks. As you read Genesis 6–7, you could compare the safety provided by the boat to the safety we find in following the prophet. You may want to discuss recent counsel from the prophet and write his words of counsel on your boat.

What else has God given us that might be compared to the ark that saved Noah's family? These resources suggest some answers, though there are many others: 2 Nephi 9:7–13; Doctrine and Covenants 115:5–6; and President Russell M. Nelson's message "Becoming Exemplary Latter-day Saints" (*Ensign* or *Liahona,* Nov. 2018, 113–14).

**Moses 8:17.** What does it mean for the Lord's Spirit to "strive" with us? (see 1 Nephi 7:14; Doctrine and Covenants 1:33). When have we experienced the Spirit striving with us?

**Genesis 9:8–17.** Young children might enjoy drawing or coloring a rainbow while you talk about what it represents (see also Joseph Smith Translation, Genesis 9:21–25 [in the Bible appendix]). You might also discuss things that help us remember our covenants, such as the sacrament, which helps us remember our baptismal covenant to follow Jesus Christ (see Doctrine and Covenants 20:75–79).

**Genesis 11:1–9.** It might be helpful to read Ether 1:33–43 as your family studies Genesis 11 and learns about the Tower of Babel. What do we learn from the families of Jared and his brother that can help our family find spiritual safety despite the wickedness in the world? What additional lessons do we learn from Noah and his family as they faced a similar challenge? (see Moses 8:13, 16–30).

For more ideas for teaching children, see this week's outline in *Come, Follow Me—For Primary.*

Suggested song: "Follow the Prophet," *Children's Songbook,* 110–11 (verse 3).

## Improving Personal Study

**Share your insights.** When you share what you learn from the scriptures, you not only bless others but also deepen your own understanding. What do you feel inspired to share from the scriptures with your family, friends, or ward members?

Depiction of Noah's ark, by Adam Klint Day

# The Covenant

Throughout the Old Testament, you will frequently read the word *covenant*. Today we usually think of covenants as sacred promises with God, but in the ancient world, covenants were also an important part of people's interactions with each other. For their safety and survival, people needed to be able to trust each other, and covenants were a way to secure that trust.

So when God spoke to Noah, Abraham, or Moses about covenants, He was inviting them to enter into a relationship of trust with Him. One of the best-known examples of a covenant in the Old Testament is the one God made with Abraham and Sarah—and then renewed with their descendants Isaac and Jacob (also called Israel). We often call this the Abrahamic covenant, although in the Old Testament it was known simply as "the covenant." You will see that the Old Testament is fundamentally the story of people who saw themselves as the inheritors of this covenant—the covenant people.

The Abrahamic covenant continues to be important today, especially to Latter-day Saints. Why? Because we are also the covenant people, whether or not we are direct descendants of Abraham, Isaac, and Jacob (see Galatians 3:27–29). For this reason, it is important to understand what the Abrahamic covenant is and how it applies to us today.

## What Is the Abrahamic Covenant?

Abraham wanted "to be a greater follower of righteousness" (Abraham 1:2), so God invited him into a covenant relationship. Abraham wasn't the first to have this desire, and he wasn't the first to

receive a covenant. He sought for "the blessings of the fathers" (Abraham 1:2)—blessings that were offered by covenant to Adam and Eve and thereafter to those who sought these blessings diligently.

God's covenant with Abraham promised wonderful blessings: an inheritance of land, a large posterity, access to priesthood ordinances, and a name that would be honored for generations to come. But the focus of this covenant was not just on the blessings Abraham and his family would *receive* but also on the blessing they would *be* to the rest of God's children. "Thou shalt be a blessing," God declared, "and in thee shall all families of the earth be blessed" (Genesis 12:2–3).

Did this covenant give Abraham, Sarah, and their descendants a privileged status among God's children? Only in the sense that it is a privilege to bless others. The family of Abraham were to "bear this ministry and Priesthood unto all nations," sharing "the blessings of the Gospel, which are the blessings of salvation, even of life eternal" (Abraham 2:9, 11).

This covenant was the blessing Abraham was longing for. After receiving it, Abraham said in his heart, "Thy servant has sought thee earnestly; now I have found thee" (Abraham 2:12).

That was thousands of years ago, but this covenant has been restored in our day (see 1 Nephi 22:8–12). And it is currently being fulfilled in the lives of God's people. In fact, the fulfillment of the covenant is building momentum in the latter days as God's work progresses, blessing families throughout the world. And anyone who, like Abraham, wants to be a greater follower of righteousness, anyone who seeks the Lord earnestly, can be a part of it.

## What Does the Abrahamic Covenant Mean to Me?

You are a child of the covenant. You made a covenant with God when you were baptized. You renew that covenant every time you partake of the sacrament. And you make sacred covenants in the temple. Together, these covenants make you a participant in the Abrahamic covenant, the fulness of which is found in temple ordinances. As President Russell M. Nelson taught, "Ultimately, in the holy temple, we may become joint heirs to the blessings of an eternal family, as once promised to Abraham, Isaac, Jacob, and their posterity."[1]

Through these covenants and ordinances, we become God's people (see Exodus 6:7; Deuteronomy 7:6; 26:18; Ezekiel 11:20). We become different from the world around us. Our covenants make it possible for us to be true, committed disciples of Jesus Christ. "Our covenants," President Nelson explained, "bind us to Him and give us godly power."[2] And when God blesses His people with His power, it is with the invitation and expectation that they will bless others—that they will "be a blessing" to "all the families of the earth" (Abraham 2:9, 11).

This is the precious understanding granted to us because of the Restoration of the Abrahamic covenant through the Prophet Joseph Smith. So when you read about covenants in the Old Testament, don't think just about God's relationship with Abraham, Isaac, and Jacob. Think also about His relationship with you. When you read about the promise of numberless posterity (see Genesis 28:14), don't think just about the millions who today call Abraham their father. Think also about God's promise to you of eternal families and eternal increase (see Doctrine and Covenants 131:1–4; 132:20–24). When you read about the promise of a land of inheritance, don't think just about the land promised to Abraham. Think also about the celestial destiny of the earth itself—an inheritance promised to the "meek" who "wait upon the Lord" (Matthew 5:5; Psalm 37:9, 11; see also Doctrine and Covenants 88:17–20). And when you read about the promise that God's covenant people will bless "all the families of the earth" (Abraham 2:11), don't think just about the ministry of Abraham or the prophets who descended from him. Think also about what you can do—as a covenant follower of Jesus Christ—to be a blessing to the families around you.

**Notes**

1. Russell M. Nelson, "Covenants," *Ensign* or *Liahona,* Nov. 2011, 88.

2. Russell M. Nelson, "Drawing the Power of Jesus Christ into Our Lives," *Ensign* or *Liahona,* May 2017, 41. President Linda K. Burton said: "Making and keeping covenants means choosing to bind ourselves to our Father in Heaven and Jesus Christ. It is committing to follow the Savior" ("The Power, Joy, and Love of Covenant Keeping," *Ensign* or *Liahona,* Nov. 2013, 111).

FEBRUARY 7–13

# Genesis 12–17; Abraham 1–2

"TO BE A GREATER FOLLOWER OF RIGHTEOUSNESS"

As you read about Abram and Sarai (later called Abraham and Sarah) and their family, ponder how their examples inspire you. Record impressions about what you can do "to be a greater follower of righteousness" (Abraham 1:2).

RECORD YOUR IMPRESSIONS

Because of the covenant God made with him, Abraham has been called "the father of the faithful" (Doctrine and Covenants 138:41) and "the Friend of God" (James 2:23). Millions today honor him as their direct ancestor, and others have been adopted into his family through conversion to the gospel of Jesus Christ. Yet Abraham himself came from a troubled family—his father, who had abandoned the true worship of God, tried to have Abraham sacrificed to false gods. In spite of this, Abraham's desire was "to be a greater follower of righteousness" (Abraham 1:2), and the account of his life shows that God honored his desire. Abraham's life stands as a testimony that no matter what a person's family history has been, the future can be filled with hope.

# Ideas for Personal Scripture Study

### ABRAHAM 1:1–19

## God will bless me for my faith and righteous desires.

Like many of us, Abraham lived in a wicked environment, yet he desired to be righteous. President Dallin H. Oaks taught the importance of having righteous desires: "As important as it is to lose every desire for sin, eternal life requires more. To achieve our eternal destiny, we will desire and work for the qualities required to become an eternal being. . . . If this seems too difficult—and surely it is not easy for any of us—then we should begin with a desire for such qualities and call upon our loving Heavenly Father for help with our feelings [see Moroni 7:48]" ("Desire," *Ensign* or *Liahona,* May 2011, 44–45). As you read Abraham 1:1–19, consider how these verses demonstrate what President Oaks taught. Questions like these might help:

- What did Abraham desire and seek after? What did he do to demonstrate his faith?

- What are your desires? Is there something you feel you should do to purify your desires?

- What challenges did Abraham face because of his righteous desires? How did God help him?

- What message do these verses have for those whose family members do not desire righteousness?

See also Matthew 7:7; "Deliverance of Abraham" (video), ChurchofJesusChrist.org; "Educate Your Desires, Elder Andersen Counsels" (ChurchofJesusChrist.org).

### ABRAHAM 2:10–11

## Who is included in the Abrahamic covenant?

When the Lord made His covenant with Abraham, He promised that this covenant would continue in Abraham's posterity, or "seed," and that "as many as receive this Gospel shall be . . . accounted thy seed" (Abraham 2:10–11). This means that the promises of the Abrahamic covenant apply to members of the Church today, whether they are literal descendants of Abraham or adopted into his family through baptism and conversion to the gospel of Jesus Christ (see Galatians 3:26–29; Doctrine and Covenants 132:30–32). To be counted as Abraham's seed, an individual must obey the laws and ordinances of the gospel.

### GENESIS 12:1–3; 13:15–16; 15:1–6; 17:1–8, 15–22; ABRAHAM 2:8–11

## The Abrahamic covenant blesses me and my family.

Because all members of the Church are included in the Abrahamic covenant, you might want to spend some time pondering why this covenant is meaningful in your life. Record your thoughts about the following questions:

How can the promises found in Abraham 2:8–11 bless me and my family? (see also Genesis 12:1–3; 13:15–16). _____

_____

What do I learn about the Abrahamic covenant from Genesis 15:1–6; 17:1–8, 15–22? _____

_____

What do I feel inspired to do to help fulfill the promise that "all the families of the earth shall be blessed"? (Abraham 2:11). _____

_____

You might consider that some of the earthly blessings promised to Abraham and Sarah, such as inheriting a promised land and being parents of a great posterity, have eternal parallels. These include an inheritance in the celestial kingdom (see Doctrine and Covenants 132:29) and eternal marriage with eternal posterity (see Doctrine and Covenants 131:1–4; 132:20–24, 28–32). It is "in the temple," President Russell M. Nelson taught, that "we receive our ultimate blessings, as the seed of Abraham, Isaac, and Jacob" ("The Gathering of Scattered Israel," *Ensign* or *Liahona,* Nov. 2006, 80).

See also Joseph Smith Translation, Genesis 15:9–12; 17:3–12 (in the Bible appendix); Bible Dictionary, "Abraham, covenant of"; "Thoughts to Keep in Mind: The Covenant," in this resource.

# Ideas for Family Scripture Study and Home Evening

**Genesis 13:5–12.** What did Abraham do to create peace in his family? Perhaps your family members could practice being a peacemaker like Abraham by role-playing how to resolve conflicts that are likely to arise in your family.

**Genesis 13:16; 15:2–6; 17:15–19.** How can you help your family understand the Lord's promise in these verses—that even though Abraham and Sarah did not yet have children, their posterity would be as numerous as the dust of the earth, stars in the sky, or sand on the seashore? (see also Genesis 22:17). Perhaps you could show family members a container of sand, look at the stars, or use the picture that accompanies this outline. How can we trust God's promises even when they seem impossible?

**Genesis 14:18–20.** What do we learn about Melchizedek from Joseph Smith Translation, Genesis 14:25–40? (in the Bible appendix; see also Alma 13:13–19). How can we "[establish] righteousness" as Melchizedek did? (verse 36). What else about Melchizedek's ministry inspires us?

*Melchizedek Blesses Abram,* by Walter Rane

**Genesis 16.** Reading about Hagar could be an opportunity to discuss how the Lord helps us when we feel wronged. You might point out that "Ishmael" means "God hears." When have we felt that the Lord heard and helped us when we felt wronged? (see Genesis 16:11).

For more ideas for teaching children, see this week's outline in *Come, Follow Me—For Primary.*

Suggested song: "I Want to Live the Gospel," *Children's Songbook,* 148.

## Improving Our Teaching

**Be available and accessible.** Some of the best teaching moments start as a question or concern in the heart of a family member. Let your family members know through your words and actions that you are eager to hear them. (See *Teaching in the Savior's Way,* 16.)

God promised that Abraham's and Sarah's posterity would number "as the stars of the heaven" (Genesis 22:17). *Pondering God's Promise,* by Courtney Matz.

*Sarah and Isaac, by Scott Snow*

# Genesis 18–23

"IS ANY THING TOO HARD FOR THE LORD?"

Read and ponder Genesis 18–23, and record your impressions. You can use the ideas in this outline to help you study these chapters, and you may also be inspired to search for other messages in the scriptures that the Lord has specifically for you.

RECORD YOUR IMPRESSIONS_____

_____

_____

Abraham's life, filled with events both heartbreaking and heartwarming, is evidence of a truth Abraham learned in a vision—that we are on earth to be proven, "to see if [we] will do all things whatsoever the Lord [our] God shall command" (Abraham 3:25). Would Abraham himself prove faithful? Would he continue to have faith in God's promise of a large posterity, even when he and Sarah were still childless in their old age? And once Isaac was born, would Abraham's faith endure the unthinkable—a command to sacrifice the very son through whom God had promised to fulfill that covenant? Abraham did prove faithful. Abraham trusted God, and God trusted Abraham. In Genesis 18–23, we find stories from the lives of Abraham and others that can prompt us to think about our own ability to believe God's promises, to flee wickedness and never look back, and to trust God regardless of the sacrifice.

# Ideas for Personal Scripture Study

### GENESIS 18:9–14; 21:1–7

## The Lord fulfills His promises in His own time.

The Lord has made glorious promises to the faithful, but sometimes the circumstances of our lives can cause us to wonder how those promises can possibly be fulfilled. Abraham and Sarah may have felt that way at times. What do you learn from their experiences? It may be helpful to begin your study by reviewing what the Lord had promised Abraham in Genesis 17:4, 15–22. How did Abraham and Sarah react? (see also Joseph Smith Translation, Genesis 17:23 [in Genesis 17:17, footnote *b*]; Genesis 18:9–12). How did the Lord respond to help them have greater faith in His promises? (see Genesis 18:14).

What do you find in these verses that builds your faith? What other experiences—in your life or someone else's—have strengthened your faith that the Lord will fulfill His promises to you in His own time and way?

See also Doctrine and Covenants 88:68.

### GENESIS 19:12–29

## The Lord commands us to flee wickedness.

What lessons do you learn about fleeing wickedness as you read about Lot and his family? For example, what impresses you about what the angels said and did to help Lot and his family escape destruction? (see Genesis 19:12–17). How does the Lord help you and your family flee or find protection from evil influences in the world?

For more about the sins of Sodom and Gomorrah, see Ezekiel 16:49–50 and Jude 1:7–8.

See also Joseph Smith Translation, Genesis 19:9–15 (in the Bible appendix).

*Fleeing Sodom and Gomorrah,* by Julius Schnorr von Carolsfeld

### GENESIS 19:26

## What did Lot's wife do wrong?

Elder Jeffrey R. Holland taught:

"Apparently, what was wrong with Lot's wife was that she wasn't just *looking* back; in her heart she wanted to *go* back. It would appear that even before she was past the city limits, she was already missing what Sodom and Gomorrah had offered her. . . . She did not have faith. She doubted the Lord's ability to give her something better than she already had. . . .

"To all [people] of every generation, I call out, 'Remember Lot's wife' [Luke 17:32]. Faith is for the future. Faith builds on the past but never longs to stay there. Faith trusts that God has great things in store for each of us and that Christ truly is the 'high priest of good things to come' (Hebrews 9:11)" ("The Best Is Yet to Be," *Ensign,* Jan. 2010, 24, 27).

### GENESIS 22:1–19

## Abraham's willingness to sacrifice Isaac is a similitude of God and His Son.

We don't know all the reasons God commanded Abraham to offer Isaac as a sacrifice; we do know it was a test of his faith in God (see Genesis 22:12–19). As you read Genesis 22:1–19, what do you learn from Abraham's experience?

Abraham's willingness to sacrifice his son was "a similitude of God and his Only Begotten Son" (Jacob 4:5). As you ponder the similarities between

Abraham's test and God the Father's offering of His Son as a sacrifice for us, what do you feel for your Heavenly Father?

There are also similarities between Isaac and the Savior. Consider reading Genesis 22:1–19 again, looking for these similarities.

See also "Akedah (The Binding)" (video), ChurchofJesusChrist.org.

# Ideas for Family Scripture Study and Home Evening

**Genesis 18:14.** Are there stories from the scriptures, from your family history, or from your own life you could share that have taught you that nothing is too hard for the Lord?

**Genesis 18:16–33.** What do we learn about Abraham's character from these verses? How can we follow his example? (See also Alma 10:22–23.)

**Genesis 19:15–17.** These verses can help your family members prepare for times when they need to flee from wicked situations. What might some of these situations be? For example, you might have a discussion about inappropriate media or the temptation to gossip. How can we flee from such situations?

**Genesis 21:9–20.** What impresses your family about the way God treated Hagar and Ishmael after Sarah and Abraham cast them out?

**Genesis 22:1–14.** How can you help your family see the connection between the story of God commanding Abraham to sacrifice Isaac and the Savior's atoning sacrifice? You could show pictures of Abraham and Isaac and of the Crucifixion (see "Abraham and Isaac," in *Old Testament Stories*) while family members discuss similarities they see between these events. You could also sing a hymn or song about the Savior's sacrifice, such as "He Sent His Son" (*Children's Songbook,* 34–35), and look for phrases that describe the Savior's sacrifice.

What have we been asked to sacrifice as a family? How have these sacrifices brought us closer to God?

For more ideas for teaching children, see this week's outline in *Come, Follow Me—For Primary.*

Suggested song: "God Loved Us, So He Sent His Son," *Hymns,* no. 187.

## Improving Personal Study

**Listen to the Spirit.** As you study, pay attention to your thoughts and feelings, even if they seem unrelated to what you are reading. Those impressions may be the very things God wants you to know.

Illustration of Abraham and Isaac, by Jeff Ward

Illustration of Rebekah by Dilleen Marsh

FEBRUARY 21–27

# Genesis 24–27

THE COVENANT IS RENEWED

As you read Genesis 24–27, pay attention to spiritual insights you receive. Pray to know how the principles you find are relevant to your life.

RECORD YOUR IMPRESSIONS

God's covenant with Abraham included the promise that through Abraham and his posterity "shall all the families of the earth be blessed" (Abraham 2:11). That's not a promise that could be fulfilled in one generation: in many ways, the Bible is the story of God's ongoing fulfilment of His promise. And He began by renewing the covenant with the family of Isaac and Rebekah. Through their experiences, we learn something about being part of the covenant. Their examples teach us about kindness, patience, and trust in God's promised blessings. And we learn that it's well worth giving up any worldly "pottage" (Genesis 25:30) in order to secure God's blessings for ourselves and our children for generations to come.

## Ideas for Personal Scripture Study

### GENESIS 24

### Marriage is essential to God's eternal plan.

Today many people make marriage a low priority or even consider it a burden. Abraham had a different perspective—to him, the marriage of his son Isaac was of highest importance. Why do you think it was so important to him? As you read Genesis 24, think about the importance of marriage in God's plan of salvation. You might also read Elder D. Todd

Christofferson's message "Why Marriage, Why Family" (*Ensign* or *Liahona,* May 2015, 50–53) and consider why "a family built on the marriage of a man and woman supplies the best setting for God's plan to thrive" (page 52).

Questions like the following might help you consider other important principles in this chapter:

**Genesis 24:1–14.** What did Abraham and his servant do to include the Lord in their efforts to find a wife for Isaac?

**Genesis 24:15–28, 55–60.** What qualities do you find in Rebekah that you would like to emulate?

What other insights do you find?

See also Doctrine and Covenants 131:1–4; "The Family: A Proclamation to the World," ChurchofJesusChrist.org.

### GENESIS 25:29–34

### I can choose between immediate gratification and things of greater value.

In Abraham's culture, the oldest son in a family typically received a position of leadership and privilege, called the birthright. This son received a greater inheritance from his parents, along with greater responsibilities for caring for the rest of the family.

As you read Genesis 25:29–34, consider why Esau might have been willing to give up his birthright in exchange for a meal. What lessons do you find for yourself in this account? For example, is there any "pottage" that is distracting you from blessings that are of most value to you? What are you doing to focus on and appreciate these blessings?

See also Matthew 6:19–33; 2 Nephi 9:51; M. Russell Ballard, "What Matters Most Is What Lasts Longest," *Ensign* or *Liahona,* Nov. 2005, 41–44.

### GENESIS 26:1–5

### The Abrahamic covenant was renewed through Isaac.

The covenant God made with Abraham was intended to continue through many generations, so Abraham and Sarah's legacy of covenant keeping would need to be passed down to Isaac, Jacob, and other faithful women and men among their posterity. As you read Genesis 26:1–5, look for some of the blessings of the covenant that God mentioned. What do you learn about God from these verses?

### GENESIS 26:18–25, 32–33

### Jesus Christ is the well of living water.

You may notice that wells and springs and other water sources play important roles in many Old Testament stories. This isn't surprising, because most of these stories happened in very dry places. As you read in Genesis 26 about Isaac's wells, ponder what water may symbolize in the scriptures. What insights do you find about spiritual wells of "living water"? (see John 4:10–15). How are you digging spiritual wells in your life? How is the Savior like living water to you? Note that the Philistines had "stopped" the wells (see Genesis 26:18). Is there anything in your life that is stopping your wells of living water?

A well in ancient Beer-sheba, where Abraham and Isaac dug wells.

**GENESIS 27**

## Were Rebekah and Jacob wrong to deceive Isaac?

We don't know the reasons behind the approach Rebekah and Jacob used to obtain a blessing for Jacob. It is helpful to remember that the Old Testament as we now have it is incomplete (see Moses 1:23, 41). There may be information missing from the original records that would explain what might seem troubling to us. However, we do know that it was God's will for Jacob to receive the blessing from Isaac because Rebekah had a revelation that Jacob was to rule over Esau (see Genesis 25:23). After Isaac acknowledged that he had blessed Jacob instead of Esau, he affirmed that Jacob "shall be blessed" (Genesis 27:33)—suggesting that God's will had been accomplished.

## Ideas for Family Scripture Study and Home Evening

**Genesis 24:2–4, 32–48.** Abraham asked a trusted servant to find a wife for Isaac, and the servant covenanted with Abraham that he would. How did Abraham's servant show faithfulness in keeping his covenant? How can we follow his example?

**Genesis 24:15–28, 55–60.** Your family could look in these verses for attributes that made Rebekah a worthy eternal companion for Isaac. Encourage family members to pick one of these attributes that they feel they should develop.

**Genesis 25:19–34; 27.** To review the stories of how Esau's birthright and blessing came to Jacob instead, you could write the sentences from "Jacob and Esau" (in *Old Testament Stories*) on separate strips of paper. Family members could work together to put the sentences in the correct order.

As you discuss Esau selling his birthright, you might also talk about what matters most to your family, like your relationships with Heavenly Father and Jesus Christ. Perhaps family members could find objects or pictures that represent what they consider to be of eternal value. Let them explain why they chose those things.

**Genesis 26:3–5.** To help your family understand the Abrahamic covenant, you could invite them to find the promises described in these verses. Why is it important for us to know about these promises today? (see "Thoughts to Keep in Mind: The Covenant," in this resource).

**Genesis 26:18–25, 32–33.** Why are wells important? How is Jesus Christ like a well of water?

For more ideas for teaching children, see this week's outline in *Come, Follow Me—For Primary.*

Suggested song: "Choose the Right," *Hymns,* no. 239.

### Improving Personal Study

**Memorize a scripture.** Elder Richard G. Scott taught, "A memorized scripture becomes an enduring friend that is not weakened with the passage of time" ("The Power of Scripture," *Ensign* or *Liahona,* Nov. 2011, 6).

*Esau Sells His Birthright to Jacob,* by Glen S. Hopkinson

# The House of Israel

Somewhere in the wilderness east of Canaan, Jacob nervously awaited an encounter with his twin brother, Esau. The last time Jacob had seen Esau, about 20 years earlier, Esau was threatening to kill him. Jacob had spent all night wrestling in the wilderness, seeking a blessing from God. As a result of Jacob's faith, persistence, and determination, God had answered his prayers. That night Jacob's name was changed to Israel, a name that means "he perseveres with God" (Genesis 32:28, footnote *b;* see also Genesis 32:24–32).[1]

Near the Jabbok River, Jacob received the name Israel.

This is the first time the name *Israel* appears in the Bible, and it's a name that perseveres throughout the book and throughout history. The name soon came to refer to more than just one man. Israel had 12 sons, and their descendants were collectively known as the "house of Israel," the "tribes of Israel," the "children of Israel," or the "Israelites."

Throughout history, the children of Israel attached great significance to their descent from one of the twelve tribes of Israel. Their lineage was an important part of their covenant identity. The Apostle Paul proclaimed that he was "of the tribe of Benjamin" (Romans 11:1). When Lehi sent his sons to Jerusalem to retrieve the plates of brass, one reason was that the plates contained "a genealogy

of his fathers" (1 Nephi 5:14; see also 1 Nephi 3:3). Lehi discovered that he was a descendant of Joseph, and his posterity's understanding of their connection to the house of Israel proved important to them in the years to come (see Alma 26:36; 3 Nephi 20:25).

In the Church today, you may hear about Israel in expressions like "the gathering of Israel." We sing about the "Redeemer of Israel," the "Hope of Israel," and "Ye Elders of Israel."[2] In these cases, we aren't talking or singing only about the ancient kingdom of Israel or the modern nation called Israel. Rather, we are referring to those who have been gathered from the nations of the world into the Church of Jesus Christ. We are referring to people who persevere with God, who earnestly seek His blessings, and who, through baptism, have become His covenant people.

Your patriarchal blessing declares your connection to one of the tribes of the house of Israel. That's more than an interesting piece of family history information. Being a part of the house of Israel means that you have a covenant relationship with Heavenly Father and Jesus Christ. It means that you, like Abraham, are meant to "be a blessing" to God's children (Genesis 12:2; Abraham 2:9–11). It means, in the words of Peter, that "ye are a chosen generation, a royal priesthood, an holy nation, a peculiar people; that ye should shew forth the praises of him who hath called you out of darkness into his marvellous light" (1 Peter 2:9). It means that *you* are one who "perseveres with God" as you honor your covenants with Him.

**Notes**

1. There are other possible meanings for the name Israel, including "God rules" or "God fights or perseveres."

2. *Hymns*, nos. 6, 259, and 319.

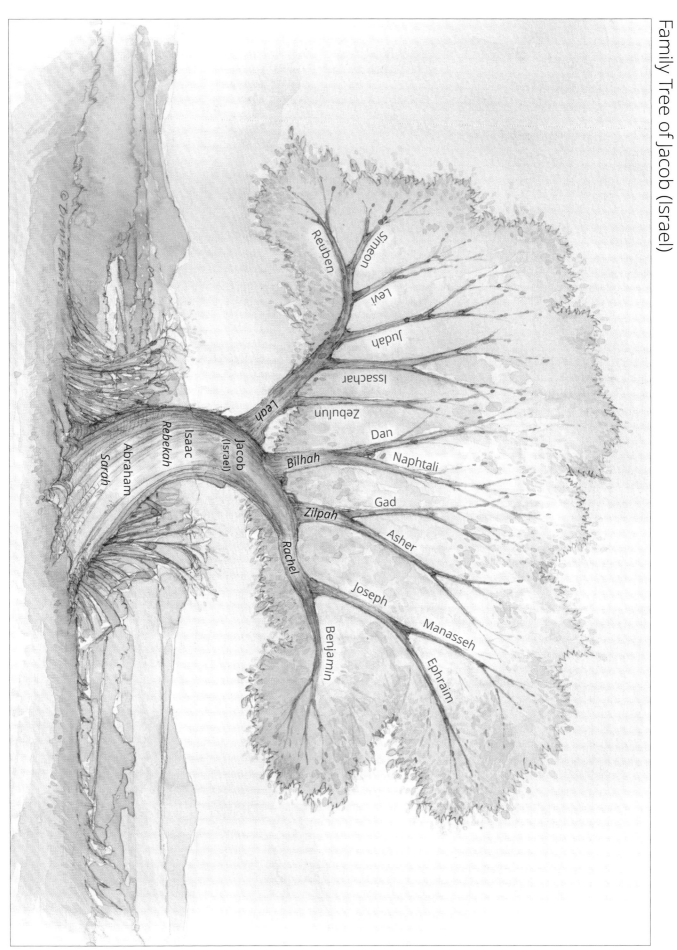

*Family Tree of Jacob (Israel)*, by Brent Evans

# Genesis 28–33

"SURELY THE LORD IS IN THIS PLACE"

As you read Genesis 28–33, ponder what you learn from the examples of Jacob and his family. Write down any impressions you receive.

RECORD YOUR IMPRESSIONS_____

_____

_____

Chapters 28 and 32 of Genesis tell of two spiritual experiences that the prophet Jacob had. Both happened in the wilderness but under very different circumstances. In the first experience, Jacob was traveling to his mother's homeland to find a wife and, along the way, spent the night on a pillow of stones. He may not have expected to find the Lord in such a desolate place, but God revealed Himself to Jacob in a life-changing dream, and Jacob declared, "Surely the Lord is in this place; and I knew it not" (Genesis 28:16). Years later, Jacob found himself in the wilderness again. This time, he was on his way back to Canaan, facing a potentially deadly reunion with his angry brother, Esau. But Jacob knew that when he needed a blessing, he could seek the Lord, even in the wilderness (see Genesis 32).

You may find yourself in your own wilderness seeking a blessing from God. Maybe your wilderness is a difficult family relationship, such as Jacob had. Maybe you feel distant from God or feel that you need a blessing. Sometimes the blessing comes unexpectedly; other times it is preceded by a wrestle. Whatever your need, you can discover that even in your wilderness, "the Lord is in this place."

# Ideas for Personal Scripture Study

### GENESIS 28; 29:1–18

## I am promised the blessings of Abraham in the temple.

On his way to Haran to find a wife, Jacob dreamed of a ladder stretching from the earth to heaven, with God standing above it. In the dream, God renewed with Jacob the same covenants He had made with Abraham and Isaac (see Genesis 28:10–17; see also Genesis 12:2–3; 26:1–4). President Marion G. Romney shared this thought about what the ladder could represent: "Jacob realized that the covenants he made with the Lord there were the rungs on the ladder that he himself would have to climb in order to obtain the promised blessings—blessings that would entitle him to enter heaven and associate with the Lord. . . . Temples are to us all what Bethel was to Jacob" ("Temples—The Gates to Heaven," *Ensign,* Mar. 1971, 16).

What other words and phrases in Genesis 28:10–22 suggest to you a connection between Jacob's experience and temple blessings? As you read these verses, think about the covenants you have made; what impressions come to you?

As you read Genesis 29:1–18, ponder how Jacob's marriage to Rachel was important to the covenant God renewed with Jacob in Bethel ("house of God"; see Genesis 28:10–19). Keep this experience in mind as you continue reading about Jacob's life in Genesis 29–33. How has the house of the Lord brought you closer to God?

See also Yoon Hwan Choi, "Don't Look Around, Look Up!" *Ensign* or *Liahona,* May 2017, 90–92.

### GENESIS 29:31–35; 30:1–24

## The Lord remembers me in my trials.

Even though Rachel and Leah lived in a time and culture different from ours, we can all understand some of the feelings they had. As you read Genesis 29:31–35 and 30:1–24, look for words and phrases describing God's mercy to Rachel and Leah. Ponder how God has "looked upon [your] affliction" and "remembered" you (Genesis 29:32; 30:22).

It is also important to remember that even though God hears us, in His wisdom He doesn't always give us exactly what we ask for. Consider studying Elder Brook P. Hales's message "Answers to Prayer" (*Ensign* or *Liahona,* May 2019, 11–14) to learn about different ways Heavenly Father answers us.

For more about the cultural background of this story, see *Old Testament Student Manual: Genesis–2 Samuel* (2003), 86–88.

### GENESIS 32–33

## The Savior can help us overcome discord in our families.

As Jacob returned to Canaan, he was "greatly afraid and distressed" about how Esau would receive him (Genesis 32:7). As you read in Genesis 32–33 about Jacob's encounter with Esau and his feelings leading up to it, you might ponder your own family relationships—perhaps one that needs healing. Maybe this story could inspire you to reach out to someone. Questions like these could help guide your reading:

- How did Jacob prepare to meet Esau?

- What stands out to you about Jacob's prayer found in Genesis 32:9–12?

- What do you learn about forgiveness from Esau's example?

- How can the Savior help us heal family relationships?

Illustration of Jacob and Esau embracing, by Robert T. Barrett

See also Luke 15:11–32; Jeffrey R. Holland, "The Ministry of Reconciliation," *Ensign* or *Liahona,* Nov. 2018, 77–79.

## Ideas for Family Scripture Study and Home Evening

**Genesis 28–33.** Use "Jacob and His Family" (in *Old Testament Stories*) to help children understand the events from these chapters. Maybe family members could pause at each picture and identify what is being taught, such as the importance of marriage, covenants, work, and forgiveness.

**Genesis 28:10–22.** You could use a ladder (or a picture of one) to talk about how our covenants are like a ladder. What covenants have we made, and how do they bring us closer to God? Family

members might enjoy drawing Jacob's dream, described in Genesis 28:10–22.

The hymn "Nearer, My God, to Thee" (*Hymns,* no. 100) was inspired by Jacob's dream. Your family could sing this song and discuss what each verse teaches.

**Genesis 32:24–32.** You might have family members who like to wrestle. Why is "wrestling" a good way to describe seeking blessings from the Lord? What do Enos 1:1–5; Alma 8:9–10 suggest about what it means to "wrestle . . . before God"?

**Genesis 33:1–12.** After many years of hard feelings, Jacob and Esau were reunited. If Jacob and Esau could talk to us today, what might they say to help us when there is contention in our family?

For more ideas for teaching children, see this week's outline in *Come, Follow Me—For Primary.*

Suggested song: "Dearest Children, God Is Near You," *Hymns,* no. 96.

### Improving Personal Study

**Look for Jesus Christ.** The Old Testament testifies of Jesus Christ through its stories and symbols. Consider noting or marking verses that point to the Savior and are especially meaningful to you.

*Jacob's Dream at Bethel,* by J. Ken Spencer

Illustration of Joseph of Egypt in prison, by Jeff Ward

MARCH 7–13

# Genesis 37–41

"THE LORD WAS WITH JOSEPH"

As you read Genesis 37–41, pray that the Holy Ghost will help you see how the scriptural passages relate to your life. Record any insights you receive.

RECORD YOUR IMPRESSIONS

Sometimes bad things happen to good people. Life teaches us that lesson clearly, and so does the life of Joseph, the son of Jacob. He was heir to the covenant God had made with his fathers, but he was hated by his brothers and sold into slavery. He refused to compromise his integrity when approached by Potiphar's wife and so was cast into prison. It seemed that the more faithful he was, the more hardship he faced. But all this adversity was not a sign of God's disapproval.

In fact, through it all, "the Lord was with him" (Genesis 39:3). Joseph's life was a manifestation of this important truth: God will not forsake us. "Following the Savior will not remove all of your trials," President Dieter F. Uchtdorf taught. "However, it will remove the barriers between you and the help your Heavenly Father wants to give you. God will be with you" ("A Yearning for Home," *Ensign* or *Liahona,* Nov. 2017, 22).

# Ideas for Personal Scripture Study

### GENESIS 37:1–28; 39; 41:9–45

## "The Lord was with Joseph" in his adversity.

Time and again, good fortune seemed to abandon Joseph, but the Lord never did. As you read Joseph's story, ponder questions like these: What did Joseph do to stay close to the Lord during his times of trial? How was the Lord "with him"? (Genesis 39:2–3, 21, 23).

You might also ask similar questions about your life. What evidence have you seen that the Lord has not forsaken you in your times of trial? Consider how you can share your experiences with family members and future generations (see 1 Nephi 5:14). What can you do now to prepare yourself to remain faithful when you face trials in the future?

See also John 14:18; Romans 8:28; Alma 36:3; Doctrine and Covenants 121:7–8; D. Todd Christofferson, "The Joy of the Saints," *Ensign* or *Liahona,* Nov. 2019, 15–18.

### GENESIS 37:5–11; 40; 41:1–38

## If I am faithful, the Lord will guide and inspire me.

Elder David A. Bednar taught, "Revelations are conveyed in a variety of ways, including, for example, dreams, visions, conversations with heavenly messengers, and inspiration" ("The Spirit of Revelation," *Ensign* or *Liahona,* May 2011, 88). The Lord used dreams to reveal truths to Joseph, Pharaoh's chief butler and baker, and Pharaoh. The Lord also revealed to Joseph how to interpret these dreams. What can you learn from Genesis 37:5–11; 40:5–8; 41:14–25, 37–38 about receiving and understanding revelation from the Lord? For instance, what can you learn from Joseph's example when revelation seems difficult to understand? (see Genesis 40:8; 41:16).

*Joseph Interpreting the Butler and Baker's Dreams,* by François Gérard

Ponder how the Lord is revealing His will to you. What are you doing to act on revelation the Lord has given you? How are you seeking additional guidance from Him?

See also Russell M. Nelson, "Revelation for the Church, Revelation for Our Lives," *Ensign* or *Liahona,* May 2018, 93–96; Michelle Craig, "Spiritual Capacity," *Ensign* or *Liahona,* Nov. 2019, 19–21.

### GENESIS 38; 39:7–20

## With the Lord's help, I can flee temptation.

When you are being tempted, Joseph's example can give you encouragement and strength. As you read about his experience in Genesis 39, notice things Joseph did to resist temptation. For example:

- He "refused" the advances of Potiphar's wife (verse 8).

- He recognized that sinning would offend God and others (verses 8–9).

- He "hearkened not" to the temptation, even though it continued "day by day" (verse 10).

- He "left his garment . . . and fled, and got him out" (verse 12).

With Joseph's example in mind, consider making a plan for avoiding and resisting temptation. For example, you could think of a temptation you face, write down situations to avoid, and make a plan to rely on Heavenly Father when the temptation arises (see 2 Nephi 4:18, 27–33).

Temptation: _____

Situations to avoid: _____

Plan to respond: _____

This account of Joseph's strength when faced with temptation is preceded by a very different account about his older brother Judah, found in Genesis 38. What do chapters 37, 38, and 39, taken together, teach you about chastity?

See also 1 Corinthians 10:13; 1 Nephi 15:23–24; 3 Nephi 18:17–18.

## Ideas for Family Scripture Study and Home Evening

**Genesis 37.** If you had been one of Joseph's brothers, what could you have done to keep jealousy from weakening your relationship with him? How would it help us to "speak peaceably" to each other? (verse 4).

**Genesis 39.** The videos "The Refiner's Fire" and "After the Storm" (ChurchofJesusChrist.org) relate the experiences of people who found strength by turning to the Lord during their trials. Maybe you could watch one of them and talk about what Joseph might say if he were to make a video about his experiences. You could sing together "I'm Trying to Be Like Jesus" (*Children's Songbook,* 78–79)

and look for advice your family could share with Joseph as he faced his trials.

**Genesis 39:7–12.** Reading these verses could provide an opportunity to discuss the law of chastity with your family. Here are some resources that could help with this discussion: Jacob 2:28; Alma 39:3–9; "Sexual Purity" (in *For the Strength of Youth* [2011], 35–37); "Sexual Intimacy Is Sacred and Beautiful" (in *Help for Parents* [2019], AddressingPornography.ChurchofJesusChrist.org).

**Genesis 41:15–57.** What do we learn from these verses about how the Lord blessed the people of Egypt through Joseph? What can we learn about preparing for future emergencies? Discuss what you can do to better prepared as a family. For ideas, see Gospel Topics, "Emergency Preparedness," topics.ChurchofJesusChrist.org.

For more ideas for teaching children, see this week's outline in *Come, Follow Me—For Primary.*

Suggested song: "Jesus Is Our Loving Friend," *Children's Songbook,* 58.

### Improving Personal Study

**Liken the scriptures to your life.** As you read, consider how the stories and teachings in the scriptures apply in your life. For example, how could Joseph's faithfulness in Egypt inspire you to stay faithful to the Lord in spite of adversity?

Illustration of Joseph's brothers taking away his coat, by Sam Lawlor

Illustration of Joseph of Egypt, by Robert T. Barrett

# Genesis 42–50

"GOD MEANT IT UNTO GOOD"

Reading the scriptures invites the Spirit. Listen for His promptings as you read, even if they don't seem directly related to what you're reading.

RECORD YOUR IMPRESSIONS

It had been about 22 years since Joseph was sold into Egypt by his brothers. He had suffered many trials, including being falsely accused and imprisoned. When he finally saw his brothers again, Joseph was the governor of all Egypt, second only to the pharaoh. He could easily have taken revenge on them, and considering what they had done to Joseph, that might seem understandable. And yet Joseph forgave his brothers. Not only that, but he helped them see divine purpose in his suffering. "God meant it unto good" (Genesis 50:20), he told them, because it put him in a position to save "all his father's household" (Genesis 47:12) from famine.

In many ways, Joseph's life parallels that of Jesus Christ. Even though our sins caused Him great suffering, the Savior offers forgiveness, delivering all of us from a fate far worse than famine. Whether we need to receive forgiveness or extend it—at some point we all need to do both—Joseph's example points us to the Savior, the true source of healing and reconciliation.

# Ideas for Personal Scripture Study

### GENESIS 45:1–8; 50:20

## "God sent me before you to preserve you."

As you have read about Joseph, have you noticed any similarities between his story and the atoning mission of Jesus Christ? You might ponder how Joseph's role in his family is similar to the Savior's role in God's family. What parallels do you see between Joseph's experiences and the mission of the Savior, who was sent "to save [us] by a great deliverance"? (Genesis 45:7).

### GENESIS 45; 50:15–21

## Forgiveness brings healing.

Reading about Joseph forgiving his brothers for the terrible things they did to him may prompt you to think about someone you are currently struggling to forgive. Or perhaps a difficult test of forgiveness is in your future. Either way, it might help to ponder why Joseph was able to forgive. What clues about Joseph's character and attitude do you find in Genesis 45; 50:15–21? How might his experiences have influenced him to be more forgiving? What does Joseph's example suggest about how you can become more forgiving with the Savior's help?

Notice also the blessings that came to Joseph's family because of his forgiveness. What blessings have you seen from forgiveness? Do you feel inspired to reach out to someone who has wronged you?

See also Genesis 33:1–4; Doctrine and Covenants 64:9–11; Larry J. Echo Hawk, "Even as Christ Forgives You, So Also Do Ye," *Ensign* or *Liahona*, May 2018, 15–16.

### GENESIS 49

## What does the symbolism in Jacob's blessings mean?

Jacob's blessings to his posterity contain vivid imagery, but some readers may also find them difficult to understand. Thankfully, the restored gospel gives us some additional understanding. When you read the blessing to Joseph in Genesis 49:22–26, read the following verses too, and see what insights they provide: 1 Nephi 15:12; 2 Nephi 3:4–5; Jacob 2:25; Doctrine and Covenants 50:44.

As you read about Judah's blessing in Genesis 49:8–12, remember that both King David and Jesus Christ are descendants of Judah. What words and phrases in these verses remind you of the Savior? When you study Judah's blessing, it may help to also read Revelation 5:5–6, 9; 1 Nephi 15:14–15; Doctrine and Covenants 45:59; 133:46–50.

If you'd like to learn more about Jacob's sons and the tribes of Israel who descended from them, there is an entry for each in the Guide to the Scriptures (scriptures.ChurchofJesusChrist.org).

### GENESIS 50:24–25; JOSEPH SMITH TRANSLATION, GENESIS 50:24–38 (IN THE BIBLE APPENDIX)

## "A seer shall the Lord my God raise up."

Through Joseph's dreams (see Genesis 37:5–11) and his interpretations of others' dreams (see Genesis 40–41), the Lord revealed things that would happen days or years in the future. But the Lord also revealed to Joseph what would happen in the coming centuries. Specifically, he learned about the prophetic missions of Moses and Joseph Smith. As you read Joseph's words in Genesis 50:24–25 and in Joseph Smith Translation, Genesis 50:24–38 (in the Bible appendix), ask yourself how knowing these things might have blessed Joseph and the children of Israel. Why do you think it was important for the Lord to restore this prophecy through Joseph Smith? (see also 2 Nephi 3).

How has Joseph Smith fulfilled the prophecies in Joseph Smith Translation, Genesis 50: 27–28, 30–33? (see Doctrine and Covenants 1:17–23; 20:7–12; 39:11; 135:3).

Illustration of Joseph of Egypt, by Paul Mann

## Ideas for Family Scripture Study and Home Evening

**Genesis 42–46.** Your family might enjoy acting out the story of Joseph reuniting with his brothers. ("Joseph and the Famine," in *Old Testament Stories* might help.) Have fun with it—use costumes and props if you'd like. Encourage family members to try to understand the emotions and perspectives of the characters. You might focus especially on the feelings of Joseph toward his brothers and on how they might have felt when he forgave them. This could lead to a discussion about how forgiveness can bless your family.

When Joseph met his brothers again after many years, how did they demonstrate that they had changed since he last saw them? What can we learn about repentance from their experiences?

**Genesis 45:3–11; 50:19–21.** Joseph recognized that although his experience in Egypt had been difficult, "God meant it unto good" (Genesis 50:20). Has your family experienced any trials that God turned into blessings?

A hymn about God's goodness during times of trial (such as "How Firm a Foundation" [*Hymns*, no. 85]) could enhance this discussion. What details from Joseph's experiences exemplify what the hymn teaches?

**Genesis 49:9–11, 24–25.** What do we find in these verses that teaches us about the roles and mission of Jesus Christ? (For help understanding phrases in these verses, see the material about Genesis 49 in "Ideas for Personal Scripture Study.")

For more ideas for teaching children, see this week's outline in *Come, Follow Me—For Primary.*

Suggested song: "How Firm a Foundation," *Hymns,* no. 85.

### Improving Our Teaching

**Use music.** Help family members find gospel truths in the lyrics of hymns and Primary songs. Look for ways to make sacred music a regular part of your gospel study.

*Jacob Blessing His Sons,* by Harry Anderson

Moses and the Burning Bush, by Harry Anderson

# Exodus 1–6

"I HAVE REMEMBERED MY COVENANT"

Begin your study with a prayer, and ask for help to find messages in Exodus 1–6 that are relevant to your life and to your service in God's kingdom.

RECORD YOUR IMPRESSIONS

The invitation to live in Egypt literally saved Jacob's family. But after hundreds of years, their descendants were enslaved and terrorized by a new pharaoh "who knew not Joseph" (Exodus 1:8). It would have been natural for the Israelites to wonder why God allowed this to happen to them, His covenant people. Did He remember the covenant He had made with them? Were they still His people? Could He see how much they were suffering?

There may be times when you've felt like asking similar questions. You might wonder, Does God know what I'm going through? Can He hear my pleas for help? The story in Exodus of Israel's deliverance from Egypt answers such questions clearly: God does not forget His people. He remembers His covenants with us and will fulfill them in His own time and way (see Doctrine and Covenants 88:68). "I will redeem you with a stretched out arm," He declares. "I am the Lord your God, which bringeth you out from under [your] burdens" (Exodus 6:6–7).

For an overview of the book of Exodus, see "Exodus, book of" in the Bible Dictionary.

# Ideas for Personal Scripture Study

### EXODUS 1–2

## Jesus Christ is my Deliverer.

One of the central themes in the book of Exodus is that God has power to free His people from oppression. The enslavement of the Israelites as described in Exodus 1 could be seen as a symbol of the captivity we all face because of sin and death (see 2 Nephi 2:26–27; 9:10; Alma 36:28). And Moses, the Israelites' deliverer, can be seen as a type, or representation, of Jesus Christ (see Deuteronomy 18:18–19; 1 Nephi 22:20–21). Read Exodus 1–2 with these comparisons in mind. You might notice, for example, that both Moses and Jesus were preserved from death as small children (see Exodus 1:22–2:10; Matthew 2:13–16) and that both spent time in the wilderness before beginning their ministry (see Exodus 2:15–22; Matthew 4:1–2). What other insights do you learn from Exodus about spiritual captivity? about the Savior's deliverance?

See also D. Todd Christofferson, "Redemption," *Ensign* or *Liahona,* May 2013, 109–12.

*Moses in the Bulrushes,* © Providence Collection/licensed from goodsalt.com

### EXODUS 3–4

## God gives power to those He calls to do His work.

Today we know Moses as a great prophet and leader. But Moses did not see himself that way when the Lord first called him. "Who am I," Moses wondered, "that I should go unto Pharaoh?" (Exodus 3:11). The Lord, however, knew who Moses really was—and who he could become. As you read Exodus 3–4, note how the Lord assured Moses and responded to his concerns. What do you find in these chapters that might inspire you when you feel inadequate? How does the Lord bless His servants with increased power to do His will? (see Moses 1:1–10, 24–39; 6:31–39, 47). When have you seen God do His work through you or others?

For more about the life and ministry of Moses, see "Moses" in the Bible Dictionary or Guide to the Scriptures.

### EXODUS 5–6

## The Lord's purposes will be fulfilled in His own time.

Although Moses courageously went before Pharaoh, just as God had commanded, and told him to release the Israelites, Pharaoh refused. In fact, he made the Israelites' lives harder. Moses and the Israelites may have wondered why things weren't working out even when Moses was doing what God asked him to do (see Exodus 5:22–23).

Have you ever felt you were doing God's will but didn't see the success you expected? Review Exodus 6:1–8, looking for what the Lord said to help Moses persevere. How has the Lord helped you persist in doing His will?

## EXODUS 6:3
### Who is Jehovah?

Jehovah is one of the names of Jesus Christ and refers to the premortal Savior. The Joseph Smith Translation clarifies that the prophets Abraham, Isaac, and Jacob knew the Lord by this name (see Exodus 6:3, footnote *c*). Usually, when the phrase "the Lord" appears in the Old Testament, it refers to Jehovah. In Exodus 3:13–15, the title "I AM" is also a reference to Jehovah (see also Doctrine and Covenants 38:1; 39:1).

# Ideas for Family Scripture Study and Home Evening

**Exodus 1–2.** Several women played critical roles in God's plan to raise up a deliverer for the Israelites. As a family, you could read about the midwives Shiphrah and Puah (Exodus 1:15–20); Moses's mother, Jochebed, and his sister, Miriam (Exodus 2:2–9; Numbers 26:59); Pharaoh's daughter (Exodus 2:5–6, 10); and Moses's wife Zipporah (Exodus 2:16–21). How did these women further God's plan? How do their experiences remind us of Jesus Christ's mission? You could also gather pictures of female relatives and ancestors and share stories about them. How have we been blessed by righteous women? President Russell M. Nelson's message "A Plea to My Sisters" (*Ensign* or *Liahona,* Nov. 2015, 95–98) could add to your discussion.

**Exodus 3:1–6.** When Moses approached the burning bush, the Lord told him to remove his shoes as a sign of reverence. How can we show reverence for sacred places? For example, what can we do to make our home a sacred place where the Lord's Spirit can dwell? How can we show more reverence in other sacred places?

**Exodus 4:1–9.** The Lord gave Moses power to perform three miracles as signs to show the children of Israel that He had sent Moses. What do these signs teach us about Jesus Christ?

**Exodus 5:2.** What might it mean for us to "know" the Lord? How do we come to know Him? (for example, see Alma 22:15–18). How does our relationship with Him affect our desire to obey Him? (see also John 17:3; Mosiah 5:13).

For more ideas for teaching children, see this week's outline in *Come, Follow Me—For Primary.*

Suggested song: "Reverence Is Love," *Children's Songbook,* 31.

### Improving Personal Study

**Keep a study journal.** You might find it helpful to use a journal or notebook to write down thoughts, ideas, questions, or impressions that come while you study.

*Moses Found in the Bulrushes by Pharaoh's Daughter,* by George Soper

Illustration of Moses and Aaron in the court of Pharaoh, by Rober T. Barrett

# Exodus 7–13

"REMEMBER THIS DAY, IN WHICH YE CAME OUT FROM EGYPT"

As you read and ponder Exodus 7–13, record the impressions that come to you. As you do this regularly, your ability to recognize the whisperings of the Holy Ghost will grow.

RECORD YOUR IMPRESSIONS

Plague after plague afflicted Egypt, but Pharaoh still refused to release the Israelites. And yet God continued to demonstrate His power and give Pharaoh opportunities to accept "that I am the Lord" and "there is none like me in all the earth" (Exodus 7:5; 9:14). Meanwhile, Moses and the Israelites must have watched with awe at these manifestations of God's power in their behalf. Surely these continued signs confirmed their faith in God and strengthened their willingness to follow God's

prophet. Then, after nine terrible plagues had failed to free the Israelites, it was the tenth plague—the death of the firstborn, including Pharaoh's firstborn—that finally ended the captivity. This seems fitting because in every case of spiritual captivity, there truly is only one way to escape. No matter what else we may have tried in the past, it is with us as it was with the children of Israel. It is only the sacrifice of Jesus Christ, the Firstborn—the blood of the Lamb without blemish—that will save us.

# Ideas for Personal Scripture Study

### EXODUS 7–11

## I can choose to soften my heart.

Hopefully your will is never as dramatically opposed to God's will as Pharaoh's was. Still, we all have times when our hearts aren't as soft as they should be, so there is something to learn from Pharaoh's actions recorded in Exodus 7–10. As you read about the plagues in these chapters, what stands out to you about Pharaoh's responses? Do you notice any similar tendencies toward hard-heartedness in yourself? Ponder what you learn from these chapters about what it means to have a soft heart.

Note that the Joseph Smith Translation of Exodus 7:3, 13; 9:12; 10:1, 20, 27; 11:10 clarifies that the Lord did not harden Pharaoh's heart—Pharaoh hardened his own heart (see the footnotes for each verse).

What do you learn from the following scriptures about developing a soft heart? 1 Nephi 2:16; Mosiah 3:19; Alma 24:7–8; 62:41; Ether 12:27.

See also Michael T. Ringwood, "An Easiness and Willingness to Believe," *Ensign* or *Liahona,* Nov. 2009, 100–102.

### EXODUS 12:1–42

## The Passover symbolizes Jesus Christ's Atonement.

The only way for the Israelites to be spared from the tenth plague, described in Exodus 11:4–5, was to precisely follow the instructions the Lord gave to Moses in Exodus 12, a ritual known as the Passover. The Passover teaches us through symbols that just as the Lord delivered the Israelites from bondage in Egypt, He can also deliver us from the bondage of sin. What do you find in the instructions and symbols of the Passover that remind you of Jesus Christ and His Atonement? What do these symbols and instructions suggest to you about how to receive the blessings of His Atonement? For example, what could putting lamb's blood on the door posts represent? (verse 7). What does it mean to you to have "your shoes on your feet, and your staff in your hand"? (verse 11).

See also Doctrine and Covenants 89:21.

The sacrament helps us remember our Deliverer, Jesus Christ.

### EXODUS 12:14–17, 24–27; 13:1–16

## The sacrament helps me remember my deliverance through Jesus Christ.

The Savior wanted the Israelites to always remember that He had delivered them, even after their captivity became a distant memory. This is why He commanded them to observe the Passover feast each year. As you read His instructions in Exodus 12:14–17, 24–27; 13:1–16, think about what you are doing to remember God's blessings to you. How can you preserve that remembrance "throughout your generations"? (see Exodus 12:14, 26–27).

What similarities do you see between the purposes of the feast of the Passover and the sacrament? How does reading about the Passover remind you of the sacrament and bring more meaning to that ordinance? Consider what you can do to "always remember" Jesus Christ (Moroni 4:3; 5:2; see also Luke 22:7–8, 19–20).

You might also ponder other things the Lord wants you to remember; see, for example, Helaman 5:6–12; Moroni 10:3; Doctrine and Covenants 3:3–5, 10; 18:10; 52:40.

See also John 6:54; "Always Remember Him" (video), ChurchofJesusChrist.org; "The Sacrament of the Lord's Supper," in *Teachings of Presidents of the Church: Howard W. Hunter* (2015), 197–206.

# Ideas for Family Scripture Study and Home Evening

**Exodus 7–12.** Perhaps after reading about the plagues the Lord sent to the Egyptians as signs of His power, your family could share ways the Lord is demonstrating His power today.

**Exodus 8:28, 32; 9:27–28, 34–35.** These verses can be used to start a discussion about the importance of keeping our word. Maybe family members could share experiences when they have seen others doing what they agreed to do.

**Exodus 12:1–42.** After reading Exodus 12:1–42 together, you could write on pieces of paper things you can do as a family to remember Jesus Christ's Atonement. Because the lamb's blood on the door posts (see verse 23) represented the Savior, you could place these papers around a doorway in your home. You could also eat some of the foods from the Passover, such as unleavened bread (crackers or tortillas) or bitter herbs (parsley or horseradish), and discuss how the Passover helps us remember how God delivered His people. For example, the unleavened bread reminded them that there was not time for their bread to rise before they fled from captivity. The bitter herbs reminded them of the bitterness of captivity.

**Exodus 12:14, 24–27.** Perhaps you could review these verses as a family before your next sacrament meeting. How do these verses relate to the sacrament? How can we more fully make the sacrament a "memorial" of what the Savior has done for us?

For more ideas for teaching children, see this week's outline in *Come, Follow Me—For Primary.*

Suggested song: "In Memory of the Crucified," *Hymns,* no. 190.

## Improving Our Teaching

**Share object lessons.** Invite family members to find objects that help them understand the principles in the scriptures you are reading. For instance, soft and hard objects could help family members discuss the difference between having a soft heart and a hard heart.

Illustration of a Passover supper, by Brian Call

# Exodus 14–17

"STAND STILL, AND SEE THE SALVATION OF THE LORD"

God commanded Moses to write about his experiences "for a memorial in a book, and rehearse it" to Joshua (Exodus 17:14). Similarly, recording your spiritual experiences will help you and your loved ones remember the Lord's goodness.

RECORD YOUR IMPRESSIONS

The Israelites were trapped. The Red Sea was on one side, and the army of Pharaoh was advancing on the other. Their escape from Egypt, it seemed, would be short-lived. But God had a message for the Israelites that He wanted them to remember for generations: "Fear ye not. . . . The Lord shall fight for you" (Exodus 14:13–14).

Since that time, when God's people have needed faith and courage, they have often turned to this account of Israel's miraculous deliverance. When Nephi wanted to inspire his brothers, he said, "Let us be strong like unto Moses; for he truly spake unto the waters of the Red Sea and they divided hither and thither, and our fathers came through, out of captivity, on dry ground" (1 Nephi 4:2). When King Limhi wanted his captive people to "lift up [their] heads, and rejoice," he reminded them of this same story (Mosiah 7:19). When Alma wanted to testify to his son of God's power, he also referred to this story (see Alma 36:28). And when we need deliverance—when we need a little more faith, when we need to "stand still, and see the salvation of the Lord"—we can remember how "the Lord saved Israel that day out of the hand of the Egyptians" (Exodus 14:13, 30).

# Ideas for Personal Scripture Study

**EXODUS 14**

## God has the power to deliver me.

As you read Exodus 14:1–10, imagine how the Israelites might have felt as they saw Pharaoh's army closing in. Perhaps you feel that you need a miracle to survive a difficult challenge you are facing. What do you learn from Exodus 14:13–31 that can help you seek God's deliverance in your life? What have you learned about the ways God provides deliverance from adversity? Ponder how you have seen His delivering power in your life.

See also Doctrine and Covenants 8:2–3; L. Tom Perry, "The Power of Deliverance," *Ensign* or *Liahona,* May 2012, 94–97; Bible Maps, no. 2, "Israel's Exodus from Egypt and Entry into Canaan."

**EXODUS 15:22–27**

## The Lord can make bitter things sweet.

As you read in Exodus 15:22–27 about Israel's journeyings toward the promised land, think about things in your life that have seemed "bitter" like the waters of Marah. Consider the following questions as you ponder these verses: How can the Lord make bitter things in your life sweet? What value have these experiences had in your life? What do verses 26 and 27 suggest about how the Lord blesses us when we hearken to His voice?

**EXODUS 15:23–27; 16:1–15; 17:1–7**

## I can trust the Lord, even during difficult times.

It's tempting to be critical of the Israelites because they murmured or complained when their circumstances became difficult, even after everything God had done for them. But as you read Exodus 15:23–27; 16:1–15; 17:1–7, consider whether you have ever done the same thing. What do you learn from the Israelites' experiences that can help you murmur less and trust more completely in God? For example, what differences do you notice about the way the Israelites responded to difficulties and the way Moses responded? What do these verses teach you about God?

See also 1 Nephi 2:11–12; "Sin of Murmuring" (video), ChurchofJesusChrist.org.

Manna from God fed Israel physically; we also need daily spiritual nourishment. Fresco by Leopold Bruckner

**EXODUS 16**

## I should seek daily spiritual nourishment.

There are many spiritual lessons we can learn from the miracle of the manna, found in Exodus 16. Notice the detailed instructions the Israelites were given about how to gather, use, and preserve the manna (see Exodus 16:16, 19, 22–26). What do you find in these instructions that applies to you as you daily seek spiritual nourishment?

See also John 6:31–35, 48–58 and the videos "Daily Bread: Pattern," "Daily Bread: Experience," and "Daily Bread: Change" (ChurchofJesusChrist.org).

EXODUS 17:1–7

## Jesus Christ is my spiritual rock and living water.

Think about the Savior as you read Exodus 17:1–7. How is Jesus Christ like a rock to you? (see Psalm 62:6–7; Helaman 5:12). How is He like water? (see John 4:10–14; 1 Corinthians 10:1–4; 1 Nephi 11:25).

# Ideas for Family Scripture Study and Home Evening

**Exodus 14:13–22.** Your family members might enjoy trying to "divide" the water in a bowl or a bathtub, as Moses divided the Red Sea. Help them understand that the Red Sea could not be divided without the power of God. How have we seen God's power in our lives and the lives of our ancestors?

**Exodus 15:1–21.** After miraculously crossing the Red Sea, the Israelites sang a song of praise known as the song of Moses, found in Exodus 15:1–21. As a family, search these verses for phrases that testify of what God did for the Israelites and other meaningful phrases. Then you could sing a hymn that reminds your family of what God has done for you.

**Exodus 16:1–5, 17:1–7.** Reading Exodus 16:1–5 and 17:1–7 could lead to a discussion about the Savior as the Bread of Life, as Living Water, and as our Rock. How do these stories remind us of what Jesus Christ does for us? As part of your discussion, you might read John 4:10–14; 6:29–35, 48–51; Helaman 5:12; Doctrine and Covenants 20:77, 79.

**Exodus 17:8–16.** You might act out the story of Aaron and Hur holding up the hands of Moses and discuss how this could symbolize how we sustain those whom God has called to lead us. You might also contrast the example of Aaron and Hur with the Israelites' murmuring against Moses (described throughout chapters 15–17). What are some ways we can help and sustain our leaders? What blessings come to us and our leaders as we do?

For more ideas for teaching children, see this week's outline in *Come, Follow Me—For Primary.*

Suggested song: "Redeemer of Israel," *Hymns,* no. 6.

## Improving Personal Study

**Seek your own spiritual insights.** In your personal and family study, do not limit yourself to the verses highlighted in these study outlines. The Lord likely has messages for you in these chapters that are not emphasized here. Prayerfully seek for inspiration.

Illustration of Moses parting the Red Sea, by Robert T. Barrett

APRIL 11–17

# Easter

"HE WILL SWALLOW UP DEATH IN VICTORY"

As you read about and ponder the Savior's Atonement this week, consider recording your thoughts and feelings about His sacrifice in your journal or in the space provided in this outline.

RECORD YOUR IMPRESSIONS_____

_____

_____

The life of Jesus Christ "is central to all human history" ("The Living Christ: The Testimony of the Apostles," ChurchofJesusChrist.org). What does that mean? In part, it surely means that the Savior's life influences the eternal destiny of every human being who has ever lived or will ever live. You might also say that the life and mission of Jesus Christ, culminating in His Resurrection on that first Easter Sunday, connects all of God's people throughout history: Those who were born before Christ looked forward to Him with faith (see Jacob 4:4), and those born after look back on Him with faith. As we read Old Testament accounts and prophecies, we don't ever see the name Jesus Christ, but we do see the evidence of the ancient believers' faith in and longing for their Messiah and Redeemer. So we who are invited to *remember* Him can feel a connection with those who *looked forward* to Him. For truly Jesus Christ has borne "the iniquity of us *all*" (Isaiah 53:6; italics added), and "in Christ shall *all* be made alive" (1 Corinthians 15:22; italics added).

# Ideas for Personal Scripture Study

## The Old Testament testifies of the Savior's atoning sacrifice.

Many passages in the Old Testament point to the Savior's ministry and atoning sacrifice. The table below lists some of these passages. As you read these verses, what impressions come to you about the Savior?

| Old Testament | New Testament |
|---|---|
| Zechariah 9:9 | Matthew 21:1–11 |
| Zechariah 11:12–13 | Matthew 26:14–16 |
| Isaiah 53:4 | Matthew 8:16–17; 26:36–39 |
| Isaiah 53:7 | Mark 14:60–61 |
| Psalm 22:16 | John 19:17–18; 20:25–27 |
| Psalm 22:18 | Matthew 27:35 |
| Psalm 69:21 | Matthew 27:34, 48 |
| Psalm 118:22 | Matthew 21:42 |
| Isaiah 53:9, 12 | Matthew 27:57–60; Mark 15:27–28 |
| Isaiah 25:8 | Mark 16:1–6; Luke 24:6 |
| Daniel 12:2 | Matthew 27:52–53 |

Prophecies and teachings about the Savior are even more abundant and clear in the Book of Mormon. Consider how your faith is strengthened by passages like these: 1 Nephi 11:31–33; 2 Nephi 25:13; Mosiah 3:2–11.

## I can find peace and joy through the Savior's Atonement.

Throughout time, Jesus Christ, through His atoning sacrifice, has offered peace and joy to all who come unto Him (see Moses 5:9–12). Consider studying the following scriptures that testify of the peace and joy He offers, and as you do, think about how you can receive the peace and joy He brings: Psalms 16:8–11; 30:2–5; Isaiah 12; 25:8–9; 40:28–31; John 14:27; 16:33; Alma 26:11–22.

See also Dallin H. Oaks, "Strengthened by the Atonement of Jesus Christ," *Ensign* or *Liahona,* Nov. 2015, 61–64; Sharon Eubank, "Christ: The Light That Shines in Darkness," *Ensign* or *Liahona,* May 2019, 73–76; "I Stand All Amazed," *Hymns,* no. 193.

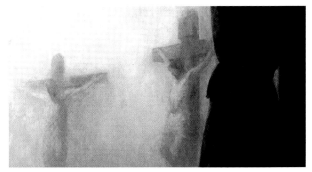

*Grey Day Golgotha,* by J. Kirk Richards

## Through His Atonement, Jesus Christ has power to help me overcome sin, death, trials, and weaknesses.

Throughout the scriptures, prophets have testified of Jesus Christ's power to deliver us from sin and death and to help us overcome our trials and weaknesses. How has Christ made a difference in your life? Why is He important to you? Ponder these questions as you read these verses, and record your thoughts and feelings about the Savior:

- Isaiah 61:1–3
- Ezekiel 36:26–28
- Matthew 11:28–30
- Luke 1:46–55
- Romans 8:35–39
- Alma 7:10–13

- Alma 11:42–45
- Alma 58:11
- Moroni 10:32–33
- Doctrine and Covenants 19:15–19
- Moses 5:9–12

See also Walter F. González, "The Savior's Touch," *Ensign* or *Liahona,* Nov. 2019, 90–92.

## Ideas for Family Scripture Study and Home Evening

**Exodus 12:1–28.** As you celebrate Easter, your family could review what you learned about the Passover earlier this month. Why is it significant that the Savior's sacrifice occurred at the same time as Passover?

For a summary of what happened during the last week of the Savior's life, see "Holy Week" at ComeuntoChrist.org/2016/easter/easter-week. For scriptures about the events of the Savior's final week, see "The Last Week: Atonement and Resurrection" in Harmony of the Gospels (in the Bible appendix).

**Isaiah 53.** Reading the prophecies about Jesus Christ in Isaiah 53 could help family members understand the Savior's atoning sacrifice. Which verses or phrases does your family find especially powerful? Consider having a family testimony meeting in which you share your personal testimonies of the Savior's Atonement.

**"Special Witnesses of Christ."** The Gospel Library app and ChurchofJesusChrist.org have a collection of videos called "Special Witnesses of Christ," in which each member of the First Presidency and Quorum of the Twelve Apostles shares his witness of Jesus Christ. Perhaps your family could watch some of these videos and talk about what you learn about Jesus Christ from His chosen servants. As a family, talk about ways you can share your witness of Christ. For example, you might invite someone to worship with you at church this Easter Sunday.

**Hymns and songs.** Music is a powerful way to remember the Savior and invite the Spirit into our homes. Family members could share and sing together hymns or songs about Easter or about Jesus Christ, such as "Christ the Lord Is Risen Today" (*Hymns,* no. 200) or "Did Jesus Really Live Again?" (*Children's Songbook,* 64). To find other hymns or children's songs, look in the topical index of *Hymns* and *Children's Songbook.*

For more ideas for teaching children, see this week's outline in *Come, Follow Me—For Primary.*

Suggested song: "Did Jesus Really Live Again?" *Children's Songbook,* 64.

### Improving Our Teaching

**Live the gospel of Jesus Christ.** "To be a Christlike teacher [in your home], perhaps the most important thing you can do is to . . . live the gospel with all your heart. . . . This is the principal way to qualify for the companionship of the Holy Ghost. You don't have to be perfect, just diligently trying—and seeking forgiveness through the Savior's Atonement whenever you stumble" (*Teaching in the Savior's Way,* 13).

*For This Purpose I Have Come,* by Yongsung Kim

# Exodus 18–20

"ALL THAT THE LORD HATH SPOKEN WE WILL DO"

Sister Michelle Craig taught, "As [Jesus Christ's] faithful disciple, you can receive personal inspiration and revelation, consistent with His commandments, that is tailored to you" ("Spiritual Capacity," *Ensign* or *Liahona,* Nov. 2019, 21). Record and act on the inspiration you receive as you read Exodus 18–20.

RECORD YOUR IMPRESSIONS_____

_____

_____

The Israelites' journey from Egypt to the foot of Mount Sinai was filled with miracles—undeniable manifestations of the Lord's matchless power, love, and mercy. However, the Lord had blessings in store for them that went beyond freeing them from Egypt and satisfying their physical hunger and thirst. He wanted them to become His covenant people, His "peculiar treasure," and a "holy nation" (Exodus 19:5–6). Today, the blessings of this covenant extend beyond just one nation or people. God wants all of His children to become His covenant people, to "obey [His] voice indeed, and keep [His] covenant" (Exodus 19:5), for He shows His mercy "unto thousands of them that love [Him], and keep [His] commandments" (Exodus 20:6).

# Ideas for Personal Scripture Study

### EXODUS 18:13–26

## I can help "bear the burden" of doing the Lord's work.

As you read the counsel Moses received from his father-in-law, Jethro, ponder how you can be like the "men of truth" (sometimes translated as "trustworthy" men) described in verse 21. How can you help "bear the burden" of your Church leaders? (verse 22). For instance, how might this counsel apply to your ministering efforts?

You might also consider whether you, at times, are like Moses, trying to do too much. How might Jethro's counsel apply to you?

See also Mosiah 4:27; Henry B. Eyring, "The Caregiver," *Ensign* or *Liahona,* Nov. 2012, 121–24.

Ministering to others is one way we can take part in the Lord's work.

### EXODUS 19:3–6

## The Lord's covenant people are a treasure to Him.

Consider what it means to you to be "a peculiar treasure" of the Lord (Exodus 19:5). President Russell M. Nelson offered one explanation of this phrase: "In the Old Testament, the Hebrew term from which *peculiar* was translated is *segullah,* which means 'valued property,' or 'treasure.' . . . For us to be identified by servants of the Lord as his *peculiar* people is a compliment of the highest order" ("Children of the Covenant," *Ensign,* May 1995, 34). How does knowing that keeping your covenants makes you a "peculiar treasure" influence the way you live?

See also Gerrit W. Gong, "Covenant Belonging," *Ensign* or *Liahona,* Nov. 2019, 80–83.

### EXODUS 19:10–11, 17

## Sacred experiences require preparation.

The Lord told Moses that the children of Israel needed to be prepared before they could "meet with God" (Exodus 19:10–11, 17) and keep a covenant with Him (see Exodus 19:5). What do you do to prepare for sacred experiences in your life, such as attending the temple or partaking of the sacrament? What can you do to more fully prepare for these experiences? Think of other spiritual activities that require preparation, and ponder how your preparation can affect the kind of experience you have.

### EXODUS 20

## God is merciful.

As you read Exodus 20, consider noting which of the Ten Commandments you feel you are obeying and which you feel you could obey more faithfully. You could choose one commandment to work on and then study it in more detail by reading related scriptures (see the Guide to the Scriptures at scriptures.ChurchofJesusChrist.org) or conference messages (see the topics section of conference.ChurchofJesusChrist.org). Consider including in your study the blessings that come to those who obey the commandment. How do these blessings show God's mercy and love for you?

See also Carole M. Stephens, "If Ye Love Me, Keep My Commandments," *Ensign* or *Liahona,* Nov. 2015, 118–20.

EXODUS 20:1–7

## It is important to put the Lord first in my life.

Reading Exodus 20:1–7 might prompt you to think about the priorities in your life—you could even write them down in a list. What are some possible "gods" or "graven image[s]" (Exodus 20:3–4) that you might be tempted to put before God? How can putting the Lord first help you with the other important things in your life? What are you inspired to do to increase your focus on Heavenly Father and Jesus Christ?

See also Dallin H. Oaks, "No Other Gods," *Ensign* or *Liahona,* Nov. 2013, 72–75.

# Ideas for Family Scripture Study and Home Evening

**Exodus 18:8–12.** What effect did Moses's testimony of God's deliverance have on Jethro? What great things has the Lord done for our family? Who can we share our experiences with? How can we preserve those experiences for future generations?

**Exodus 18:13–26.** These verses might inspire your family to think about the service of your local Church leaders, such as the bishop, youth leaders, or Primary teachers. What responsibilities do they have that may seem "too heavy" (Exodus 18:18) for one person to carry alone? What can we do to help lift their burdens?

**Exodus 20:3–17.** Think of a meaningful way to discuss the Ten Commandments as a family. For instance, you might write the commandments in Exodus 20:3–17 on ten strips of paper. Family members could then sort them into two categories: (1) honoring God and (2) loving others (see also Matthew 22:36–40). Consider choosing a commandment or two each day this week and discussing it together in more detail. For example, how does obeying this commandment strengthen our family? How did the Savior obey it?

**Exodus 20:12.** To better understand Exodus 20:12, it might help if your family looked up definitions of the word "honor." Then family members could make a list of things we can do that would honor our parents. You might sing a song about honoring parents, like "Quickly I'll Obey" (*Children's Songbook,* 197), and then use some of the ideas in your list to write new verses to the song.

For more ideas for teaching children, see this week's outline in *Come, Follow Me—For Primary.*

Suggested song: "Keep the Commandments," *Children's Songbook,* 146–47.

### Improving Personal Study

**Find a time that works for you.** It is often easier to learn from the scriptures when you can study them without being interrupted. Find a time that works for you, and do your best to consistently study at that time each day.

Illustration of Moses holding the Ten Commandments, by Sam Lawlor

Illustration of Jehovah appearing to Moses and 70 elders of Israel by Jerry Harston

# Exodus 24; 31–34

"MY PRESENCE SHALL GO WITH THEE"

Not every meaningful principle in the scriptures can be highlighted in these outlines. Listen to the Spirit to help you focus on the truths you need.

RECORD YOUR IMPRESSIONS _____

_____

_____

There was reason to be hopeful that the children of Israel would remain true to God after He revealed His law to them (see Exodus 20–23). Even though they had murmured and wavered in the past, when Moses read the law at the foot of Mount Sinai, they made this covenant: "All that the Lord hath said will we do, and be obedient" (Exodus 24:7). God then called Moses onto the mountain, telling him to build a tabernacle so "that I may dwell among them" (Exodus 25:8; see chapters 25–30).

But while Moses was at the top of the mountain learning how the Israelites could have God's presence among them, the Israelites were at the bottom of the mountain making a golden idol to worship instead. They had just promised to "have no other gods," yet they "turned aside quickly" from God's commandments (Exodus 20:3; 32:8; see also Exodus 24:3). It was a surprising turn, but we know from experience that faith and commitment can sometimes be overcome by impatience, fear, or doubt. As we seek the Lord's presence in our lives, it is encouraging to know that the Lord did not give up on ancient Israel and He will not give up on us—for He is "merciful and gracious, longsuffering, and abundant in goodness and truth" (Exodus 34:6).

## Ideas for Personal Scripture Study

### EXODUS 24:1–11

### My covenants show my willingness to obey God's law.

As you read in Exodus 24:3–8 about the Israelites covenanting to obey God's law, your thoughts may turn to the covenants you have made with God. Israel's covenant included rituals that are different from what God requires today, but you may notice some similarities, especially if you consider the eternal truths symbolized by these rituals.

For example, verses 4, 5, and 8 mention an altar, animal sacrifices, and blood. What could these things represent, and how do they relate to your covenants? How can your covenants help you do "all that the Lord hath said"? (verse 7).

See also Moses 5:4–9; Becky Craven, "Careful versus Casual," *Ensign* or *Liahona,* May 2019, 9–11.

### EXODUS 32–34

### Sin is turning away from God, but He offers a way back.

By pondering how the Israelites so quickly "corrupted themselves" (Exodus 32:7) by breaking their covenants, we can avoid similar mistakes. As you read Exodus 32:1–8, try to put yourself in the Israelites' place—you're in the wilderness, Moses has been gone for 40 days, you don't know if or when he will come back, and a confrontation with the Canaanites over the promised land is in your future (see also Exodus 23:22–31). Why do you think the Israelites wanted a golden idol? Why was the Israelites' sin so serious? These verses might prompt you to ponder ways you might be tempted to put your trust in someone or something other than the Savior. Is there anything you feel inspired to do so

that you can more completely put God first in your life? What inspires you about Moses's plea to the Lord in Exodus 33:11–17?

While the Israelites' sin was serious, this story also includes a message of God's mercy and forgiveness. What does Exodus 34:1–10 teach you about the Savior? How do Moses's actions on behalf of the Israelites remind you of what Jesus Christ did for all people? (see Exodus 32:30–32; Mosiah 14:4–8; 15:9; Doctrine and Covenants 45:3–5).

### JOSEPH SMITH TRANSLATION, EXODUS 34:1–2 (IN THE BIBLE APPENDIX)

### What was the difference between the two sets of stone tables Moses made?

When Moses came down from the mountain, he brought the law written on stone tables. After finding that the Israelites had broken their covenant, Moses broke the tables (see Exodus 31:18; 32:19). Later, God commanded Moses to make another set of stone tables and take them back to the mountain (see Exodus 34:1–4). Joseph Smith Translation, Exodus 34:1–2 (in the Bible appendix) clarifies that the first set of stone tables included the ordinances of God's "holy order," or the Melchizedek Priesthood. The second set included "the law of a carnal commandment." This was a lesser law administered by the "lesser priesthood" (see Doctrine and Covenants 84:17–27), which was meant to prepare the Israelites for the higher law and higher priesthood so they could more fully enter into God's presence.

## Ideas for Family Scripture Study and Home Evening

**Exodus 31:12–13, 16–17.** After reading these verses, perhaps your family could discuss President

Russell M. Nelson's question about our behavior on the Sabbath: "What sign will you give to the Lord to show your love for Him?" ("The Sabbath Is a Delight," *Ensign* or *Liahona,* May 2015, 130). Your family could make some signs to place around your home to remind you how you will show love for the Lord on the Sabbath. (See also the video collection "Sabbath Day—At Home" [ChurchofJesusChrist.org].)

By honoring the Sabbath, we show our love for the Lord.

**Exodus 32:1–8.** To help your family discuss how the Israelites turned away from God, consider creating a path on the floor (or find one near your home). While walking on the path, family members could talk about temptations we face to turn aside "out of the way which [the Lord] commanded." How can we remain on the path? If we have strayed, how can we return to it? How does the Savior help us?

**Exodus 32:26.** After the Israelites were found worshipping an idol, Moses asked, "Who is on the Lord's side?" How do we show we are on the Lord's side?

**Exodus 33:14–15.** Family members could share experiences when they have felt what God promised Moses: "My presence shall go with thee, and I will give thee rest." You could sing a hymn about our dependence on God, such as "Abide with Me!" (*Hymns,* no. 166).

For more ideas for teaching children, see this week's outline in *Come, Follow Me—For Primary.*

Suggested song: "Who's on the Lord's Side?" *Hymns,* no. 260.

## Improving Our Teaching

**Invite the Spirit.** Consider how sacred music, artwork, and expressions of love influence the spiritual atmosphere in your home as you teach your family (see *Teaching in the Savior's Way,* 15).

*Worship of the Calf,* by W. C. Simmonds

# The Tabernacle and Sacrifice

As we read the Old Testament, we sometimes find long passages about things that were clearly important to the Lord but may not feel immediately relevant to us today. Exodus 25–30; 35–40; Leviticus 1–9; 16–17 are examples. These chapters describe in detail Israel's tabernacle in the wilderness and the animal sacrifices to be performed there.[1] The tabernacle was a portable temple, the Lord's dwelling place among His people.

Our modern temples share similarities with Israel's tabernacle, but they certainly don't match its description in Exodus. And we don't kill animals in our temples—the Savior's Atonement ended animal sacrifice over 2,000 years ago. Yet despite these differences, there is great value today in reading about ancient Israel's forms of worship, especially if we see them the way God's people in the Book of Mormon did—as a way "to strengthen their faith in Christ" (Alma 25:16; see also Jacob 4:5; Jarom 1:11). When we understand the symbolism of the tabernacle and animal sacrifice, we can gain spiritual insights that will also strengthen our faith in Christ.

Illustration of Israelites bringing a lamb to the tabernacle, by Robert T. Barrett

## The Tabernacle Strengthens Faith in Jesus Christ

When God commanded Moses to build a tabernacle in the camp of the Israelites, He stated its purpose: "that I may dwell among them" (Exodus 25:8). Within the tabernacle, the presence of God was represented by the ark of the covenant—a wooden box, covered with gold, containing the written record of God's covenant with His people (see Exodus 25:10–22). The ark was kept in the holiest, innermost room, separated from the rest of the tabernacle by a veil. This veil symbolizes our separation from the presence of God because of the Fall.

Other than Moses, we know of only one person who could enter that "most holy place" (Exodus 26:34)—the high priest. Like the other priests, he first had to be washed and anointed (see Exodus 40:12–13) and dressed in sacred clothing symbolic of his office (see Exodus 28). Once a year, on a day called the Day of Atonement, the high priest would offer sacrifices on behalf of the people before entering alone into the tabernacle. At the veil, he would burn incense (see Leviticus 16:12). The scented smoke ascending to heaven represented the prayers of the people ascending to God (see Psalm 141:2). Then the high priest, carrying blood from an animal sacrifice, would pass through the veil and approach the throne of God, symbolized by the ark of the covenant (see Leviticus 16:14–15).

Knowing what you know about Jesus Christ and His role in Heavenly Father's plan, can you see how the tabernacle points us to the Savior? Just as the tabernacle, and the ark within it, represented God's presence among His people, Jesus Christ *was* God's presence among His people (see John 1:14). Like the high priest, Jesus Christ is the Mediator between us and God the Father. He passed through the veil to make intercession for us by virtue of the blood of His own sacrifice (see Hebrews 8–10).

Some aspects of Israel's tabernacle may sound familiar to you, especially if you have been to the temple to receive your own ordinances. Like the tabernacle's most holy place, the temple's celestial room represents the presence of God. To enter, we must first be washed and anointed. We wear sacred clothing. We pray at an altar from which prayers ascend to God. And we finally pass through a veil into God's presence.

Perhaps the most important similarity between modern temples and the ancient tabernacle is that both, if understood correctly, strengthen our faith in Jesus Christ and fill us with gratitude for His atoning sacrifice. God wants all of His children to enter into His presence; He wants "a kingdom of priests" and priestesses (Exodus 19:6). But our sins prevent us from obtaining that blessing, for "no unclean thing can dwell with God" (1 Nephi 10:21). So God the Father sent Jesus Christ, our "high priest of good things to come" (Hebrews 9:11). He parts the veil for us and empowers *all* of God's people to "come boldly unto the throne of grace, that we may obtain mercy" (Hebrews 4:16).

Today, the purpose of temples is more than obtaining exaltation for ourselves. After receiving our own ordinances, we can stand in the place of our ancestors, vicariously receiving ordinances in their behalf. In a sense, we can become something like the ancient high priest—and the Great High Priest—opening the way to God's presence for others.

## Sacrifice Strengthens Faith in Jesus Christ

The principles of atonement and reconciliation are taught powerfully in the ancient practice of animal sacrifice, which existed long before the law of Moses. Because of the restored gospel, we know that Adam and Eve offered sacrifice, understood its symbolic reference to the Savior's sacrifice, and taught this to their children (see Moses 5:4–12; see also Genesis 4:4).

The symbolism of animal sacrifice may have seemed especially poignant on ancient Israel's Day of Atonement ("Yom Kippur" in Hebrew). The need for this annual ceremony was expressed in Leviticus 16:30: "On that day shall the priest make an atonement for you, to cleanse you, that ye may be clean from all your sins before the Lord." Thus God's presence could remain among the people. This atonement was accomplished through a variety of ceremonies. In one of these, a goat was killed as an offering for the sins of the people, and the high priest took the goat's blood into the most holy place. Later, the high priest laid his hands on a live goat and confessed the sins of the children of Israel—symbolically transferring those sins to the goat. The goat was then driven out of the camp of Israel.

In this ritual, the goats symbolized Jesus Christ, taking the place of the sinful people. Sin must not be allowed in God's presence. But rather than destroy or drive out the sinners, God provided another way—a goat would be killed or driven out instead. "And the goat shall bear upon him all their iniquities" (Leviticus 16:22).

The symbolism of these rituals pointed to the way God has provided to bring us back into His presence—Jesus Christ and His Atonement. The Savior has "borne our griefs, and carried our sorrows," even "the iniquity of us all" (Isaiah 53:4, 6). He stood in our place, gave His life to pay the penalty of sin, and then conquered death through His Resurrection (see Mosiah 15:8–9). The sacrifice of Jesus Christ was the "great and last sacrifice; yea, not a sacrifice of man, neither of beast" but rather "an infinite and eternal sacrifice" (Alma 34:10). He was the fulfillment of everything the ancient sacrifices pointed toward.

For this reason, after His sacrifice was complete, He said, "Ye shall offer up unto me no more the shedding of blood; yea, your sacrifices . . . shall be done away. . . . And ye shall offer for a sacrifice unto me a broken heart and a contrite spirit" (3 Nephi 9:19–20).

So when you find passages in the Old Testament about sacrifices and the tabernacle (or later, the temple)—and you'll find a lot of them—remember that the primary purpose of it all is to strengthen your faith in the Messiah, Jesus Christ. Let your heart and your mind turn to Him. Ponder what He has done to bring you back into God's presence— and what you will do to follow Him.

---

**Note**

1. Exodus 33:7–11 mentions a "tabernacle of the congregation," where Moses communicated with the Lord, but this was not the setting for the sacrifices described in Exodus and Leviticus. Those sacrifices were performed in the tabernacle described in Exodus 25–30, which God commanded Moses to build and which the children of Israel built (see Exodus 35–40). This tabernacle, where Aaron and his sons performed animal sacrifices, was also often referred to as the "tabernacle of the congregation" (see, for example, Exodus 28:43; 38:30; Leviticus 1:3).

# Exodus 35–40; Leviticus 1; 16; 19

"HOLINESS TO THE LORD"

As you study the scriptures, pay attention to spiritual impressions you receive about ways you can become more like Heavenly Father and Jesus Christ.

RECORD YOUR IMPRESSIONS

Leaving Egypt—as important and miraculous as that was—didn't fully accomplish God's purposes for the children of Israel. Even future prosperity in the promised land wasn't God's ultimate objective for them. These were only steps toward what God really wanted for His people: "Ye shall be holy: for I the Lord your God am holy" (Leviticus 19:2). How did God seek to make His people holy when they had known nothing but captivity for generations? He commanded them to create a place of holiness to the Lord—a tabernacle in the wilderness. He gave them covenants and laws to guide their actions and, ultimately, to change their hearts. And when they fell short in their efforts to keep those laws,

He commanded them to make animal sacrifices to symbolize atonement for their sins. All of this was meant to point their minds, their hearts, and their lives toward the Savior and the redemption He offers. He is the true path to holiness, for the Israelites and for us. We have all spent some time in the captivity of sin, and we are all invited to repent—to leave sin behind and follow Jesus Christ, who has promised, "I am able to make you holy" (Doctrine and Covenants 60:7).

For an overview of the book of Leviticus, see "Leviticus" in the Bible Dictionary.

## Ideas for Personal Scripture Study

### EXODUS 35–40; LEVITICUS 19

### The Lord wants me to become holy as He is.

Exodus 25–31 records the Lord's instructions to the Israelites about how to build a tabernacle, where sacred ordinances would help them become a holy people. Exodus 35–40 describes the Israelites' efforts to obey these instructions. As you read chapters 35–40, look for the things the Lord asked His people to place in the tabernacle, and ponder what these items could represent and what they suggest to you about increasing in holiness. Especially consider how these items turn your thoughts toward the Savior. A table like this might help you:

| What object did you find? | What can this represent? |
|---|---|
| Ark of the covenant (Exodus 37:1–9; 40:20–21) | God's presence; His covenants and commandments |
| Altar of incense (Exodus 40:26–27; see also Exodus 30:1, 6–8) | Prayers rising to the Lord |
| Candlestick or lampstand (Exodus 37:17–24) | |
| Altar of sacrifice (Exodus 38:1–7; see also Exodus 27:1; 29:10–14) | |
| Laver (basin) of water (Exodus 30:17–21) | |
| | |
| | |

If you have participated in temple ordinances, what do you learn about the tabernacle from Exodus 35–40 that reminds you of your experience there? (see also "Thoughts to Keep in Mind: The Tabernacle and Sacrifice"). Ponder how temple covenants help you become more holy like Heavenly Father and Jesus Christ.

Of course, simply being in holy places doesn't make us holy. Leviticus 19 describes laws and commandments the Lord gave to help the Israelites increase in holiness. What do you find in these commandments that could help you become more holy? What do you feel impressed to do to more fully live these principles?

See also Carol F. McConkie, "The Beauty of Holiness," *Ensign* or *Liahona,* May 2017, 9–12; "The Tabernacle" (video), ChurchofJesusChrist.org; Bible Dictionary, "Holiness"; temples.ChurchofJesusChrist.org.

### EXODUS 35:4–36:7

### The Lord asks me to make my offerings with a willing heart.

In the year after leaving Egypt, the relationship of the children of Israel with Jehovah could be described as inconsistent. And yet, as you read Exodus 35:4–36:7, notice how the Israelites responded to the commandment to build the tabernacle. What do you learn from the Israelites that could help you better serve the Lord?

President Bonnie L. Oscarson taught: "Each member should know how much he or she is needed. Each person has something important to contribute and has unique talents and abilities that help move this important work along" ("Young Women in the Work," *Ensign* or *Liahona,* May 2018, 37). As you read Exodus 36:1–4, ponder what the Lord has "put" into you. Consider asking Heavenly Father what He has given you so that you can participate in His work.

The children of Israel gave offerings for the tabernacle with "a willing heart" (Exodus 35:5). Illustration by Corbert Gauthier, © Lifeway Collection/licensed from goodsalt.com

### LEVITICUS 1:1–9; 16

## Through the Atonement of Jesus Christ, I can be forgiven.

Much of the book of Leviticus may seem strange to us—animal sacrifices, rituals involving blood and water, and laws governing minute details of life. But these rituals and laws were meant to teach principles that are familiar—repentance, holiness, and the Savior's Atonement. To find these principles as you read Leviticus 1:1–9; 16, consider questions like these: What can I learn from these sacrifices about Jesus Christ and His atoning sacrifice? How am I like those making these sacrifices? You might consider reviewing "Thoughts to Keep in Mind: The Tabernacle and Sacrifice" in this resource and "Sacrifice" in Guide to the Scriptures (scriptures.ChurchofJesusChrist.org).

# Ideas for Family Scripture Study and Home Evening

**Exodus 36:1–7.** In Exodus 36:1–7, what do we learn from the way the Israelites responded to the command to build the tabernacle? As a family, you could think of ways the Lord has invited us to participate in His work. How can we follow the Israelites' example?

**Exodus 40.** As you read Exodus 40 together, you could invite family members to raise their hands each time they hear a phrase like "as the Lord commanded." What do we learn from this chapter about obedience to the Lord?

**Exodus 40:1–34.** As you read about the assembling of the tabernacle in Exodus 40, you could work together to identify the different parts of the tabernacle, using the picture that accompanies this outline. To connect this discussion with temple worship in our day, you could review together "Why Latter-day Saints Build Temples" (temples.ChurchofJesusChrist.org) or watch the video "Temples" (ChurchofJesusChrist.org).

**Leviticus 19.** Family members could each find a verse in this chapter that they feel will help them "be holy" (Leviticus 19:2) and share it with the family.

For more ideas for teaching children, see this week's outline in *Come, Follow Me—For Primary*.

Suggested song: "More Holiness Give Me," *Hymns,* no. 131.

### Improving Personal Study

**Look for Jesus Christ.** All scriptures, even the Old Testament, testify of Jesus Christ. As you read the Old Testament, consider what the symbols, people, and events can teach you about the Savior.

*The Ancient Tabernacle,* by Bradley Clark

# Numbers 11–14; 20–24

"REBEL NOT YE AGAINST THE LORD, NEITHER FEAR"

This outline highlights some of the many valuable principles in the book of Numbers. Be open also to others the Spirit may help you see.

RECORD YOUR IMPRESSIONS_____

_____

_____

Even on foot, it wouldn't normally take 40 years to travel from the wilderness of Sinai to the promised land in Canaan. But that's how long the children of Israel needed, not to cover the geographical distance but to cover the spiritual distance: the distance between who they were and who the Lord needed them to become as His covenant people.

The book of Numbers describes some of what happened during those 40 years, including lessons the children of Israel needed to learn before entering the promised land. They learned about being faithful to the Lord's chosen servants (see Numbers 12). They learned about trusting the

Lord's power, even when the future seems hopeless (see Numbers 13–14). And they learned that being faithless or untrusting brings spiritual harm, but they could repent and look to the Savior for healing (see Numbers 21:4–9).

We're all like the Israelites in some ways. We all know what it's like to be in a spiritual wilderness, and the same lessons they learned can help us prepare to enter our own promised land: eternal life with our Heavenly Father.

For an overview of the book of Numbers, see "Numbers" in the Bible Dictionary.

## Ideas for Personal Scripture Study

### NUMBERS 11:11–17, 24–29; 12

### Revelation is available to all, but God guides His Church through His prophet.

In Numbers 11:11–17, 24–29, notice the problem Moses faced and the solution God proposed. What do you think Moses meant when he said he wished "that all the Lord's people were prophets"? (verse 29). As you ponder these verses, consider these words of President Russell M. Nelson: "Does God really *want* to speak to you? Yes! . . . Oh, there is so much more that your Father in Heaven wants you to know" ("Revelation for the Church, Revelation for Our Lives," *Ensign* or *Liahona,* May 2018, 95).

However, saying that everyone can be a prophet doesn't mean they all can lead God's people the way Moses did. The incident recorded in Numbers 12 makes this clear. As you read this chapter, what cautions do you find? What do you feel the Lord wants you to understand about personal revelation and following the prophet?

See also 1 Nephi 10:17; Doctrine and Covenants 28:1–7; Dallin H. Oaks, "Two Lines of Communication," *Ensign* or *Liahona,* Nov. 2010, 83–86.

### NUMBERS 13–14

### With faith in the Lord, I can have hope for the future.

As you read Numbers 13–14, try to put yourself in the place of the Israelites. Why do you think they wanted to "return into Egypt"? (Numbers 14:3). Are you ever like those who were pessimistic about entering the promised land? How would you describe the other "spirit" Caleb had? (Numbers

14:24). What impresses you about the faith of Caleb and Joshua, and how might you apply their examples to situations you face?

See also *Teachings of Presidents of the Church: Gordon B. Hinckley* (2016), 75–76.

### NUMBERS 21:4–9

### If I look to Jesus Christ in faith, He can heal me spiritually.

Book of Mormon prophets knew the story recorded in Numbers 21:4–9 and understood its spiritual significance. What do 1 Nephi 17:40–41; Alma 33:18–22; and Helaman 8:13–15 add to your understanding of this story? As you study these passages, think about the spiritual healing you hope for. The Israelites had to "[behold] the serpent of brass" (Numbers 21:9) to be healed. What do you feel inspired to do to more fully "look upon the Son of God with faith"? (Helaman 8:15).

See also John 3:14–15; Doctrine and Covenants 6:36; Dale G. Renlund, "Abound with Blessings," *Ensign* or *Liahona,* May 2019, 70–73.

The Israelites were healed by looking upon the brass serpent.

### NUMBERS 22–24

### I can follow God's will, even if others try to persuade me not to.

When Balak, the king of Moab, learned that the Israelites were approaching, he called for Balaam, a man known for pronouncing blessings and curses.

Balak wanted him to weaken the Israelites by cursing them. Notice how Balak tried to persuade Balaam (see Numbers 22:5–7, 15–17), and think about temptations you face to go against God's will. What impresses you about Balaam's responses in Numbers 22:18, 38; 23:8, 12, 26; 24:13?

Sadly, it seems that Balaam eventually gave in to pressure and betrayed Israel (see Numbers 31:16; Jude 1:11). Ponder how you can remain faithful to the Lord despite pressure from others.

# Ideas for Family Scripture Study and Home Evening

**Numbers 11:4–6.** Is our attitude ever similar to the attitude the Israelites expressed in Numbers 11:4–6? How can the counsel in Doctrine and Covenants 59:15–21 help?

**Numbers 12:3.** How did Moses show that he was "very meek" in Numbers 12 or in other scripture passages you've read? You might review Elder David A. Bednar's explanation of meekness in his message "Meek and Lowly of Heart" (*Ensign* or *Liahona,* May 2018, 30–33) or in "Meek, Meekness" in Guide to the Scriptures (scriptures .ChurchofJesusChrist.org). What do we learn about

how we can become more meek? What blessings can come as we do so?

**Numbers 13–14.** Two (or more) members of your family could pretend to "spy out" (Numbers 13:17) another part of your home as if it were the promised land. Then they could each give a report based on Numbers 13:27–33 or Numbers 14:6–9. What do we learn about faith from the two different reports in these verses? How can we be more like Caleb and Joshua?

**Numbers 21:4–9.** After reading Numbers 21:4–9, along with 1 Nephi 17:40–41; Alma 33:18–22; and Helaman 8:13–15, your family could make a serpent out of paper or clay and write on it or on paper some simple things you can do to "look upon the Son of God with faith" (Helaman 8:15).

For more ideas for teaching children, see this week's outline in *Come, Follow Me—For Primary.*

Suggested song: "Jesus, the Very Thought of Thee," *Hymns,* no. 141.

## Improving Our Teaching

**Help your family develop spiritual self-reliance.** "Rather than simply imparting information, help [your family members] discover gospel truths for themselves in the scriptures and the words of the prophets" (*Teaching in the Savior's Way,* 28).

*Moses and the Brass Serpent,* by Judith A. Mehr

MAY 16–22

# Deuteronomy 6–8; 15; 18; 29–30; 34

"BEWARE LEST THOU FORGET THE LORD"

Moses commanded the children of Israel to teach the words of the Lord to their children (see Deuteronomy 6:7). As you study Deuteronomy this week, find ways to share what you learn with members of your family.

RECORD YOUR IMPRESSIONS

Moses's earthly ministry began on a mountain, when God spoke to him from a burning bush (see Exodus 3:1–10). It also ended on a mountain, more than 40 years later, when God gave Moses a glimpse of the promised land from the top of Mount Nebo (see Deuteronomy 34:1–4). Moses had spent his life preparing the children of Israel to enter that promised land, and the book of Deuteronomy records his final instructions, reminders, exhortations, and pleadings with the Israelites. Reading his words makes it clear that the real object of Moses's ministry—the preparation the people needed—wasn't about wilderness survival, conquering nations, or building a community. It was about learning to love God, obey Him, and remain loyal to Him. That's the preparation we all need in order to enter the promised land of eternal life. So while Moses never set foot in the "land flowing with milk and honey" (Exodus 3:8), because of his faith and faithfulness, he did enter the promised land that God has prepared for all those who follow Him.

For an overview of Deuteronomy, see "Deuteronomy" in the Bible Dictionary.

# Ideas for Personal Scripture Study

**DEUTERONOMY 6:4–7; 8:2–5, 11–17; 29:18–20; 30:6–10, 15–20**

## The Lord wants me to love Him with all my heart.

In his final teachings, Moses reminded the children of Israel, "These forty years the Lord thy God hath been with thee; thou hast lacked nothing," even while in the wilderness (Deuteronomy 2:7). Now that the Israelites were entering the promised land, with "cities, which [they] buildedst not, and houses full of all good things, which [they] filledst not" (Deuteronomy 6:10–11), Moses feared that they would harden their hearts and forget the Lord.

Consider the condition of your own heart as you read Moses's counsel. You may want to focus on the following verses and write down your impressions:

- Deuteronomy 6:4–7: _____
- Deuteronomy 8:2–5: _____
- Deuteronomy 8:11–17: _____
- Deuteronomy 29:18–20: _____
- Deuteronomy 30:6–10: _____
- Deuteronomy 30:15–20: _____

What can you do to keep your heart from hardening and to love the Lord with all your heart? What connection do you see between Deuteronomy 6:5–6 and Matthew 22:35–40? (see also Leviticus 19:18).

See also Dieter F. Uchtdorf, "A Yearning for Home," *Ensign* or *Liahona,* Nov. 2017, 21–24.

**DEUTERONOMY 6:4–12, 20–25**

## "Beware lest thou forget the Lord."

Much of the generation of Israelites who would enter the promised land had not witnessed the plagues in Egypt or crossed the Red Sea. Moses knew that they—and future generations—would need to remember God's miracles and God's laws if they were to remain God's people.

What counsel does Moses give in Deuteronomy 6:4–12, 20–25 that could help you remember the great things God has done for you? What are you inspired to do so that the word of the Lord will daily "be in thine heart"? (verse 6).

How will you pass your faith on to future generations?

See also Deuteronomy 11:18–21; Gerrit W. Gong, "Always Remember Him," *Ensign* or *Liahona,* May 2016, 108–11; Bible Dictionary, "Frontlets or phylacteries."

**DEUTERONOMY 15:1–15**

## Helping the needy involves generous hands and willing hearts.

Deuteronomy 15:1–15 gives counsel about helping the poor and the needy, including some specific practices that aren't followed today. But notice what these verses teach about why we should help the poor and how our attitudes about helping them matter to the Lord. What do you feel the Lord wants you to learn from these verses about serving others?

See also Russell M. Nelson, "The Second Great Commandment," *Ensign* or *Liahona,* Nov. 2019, 96–100.

**DEUTERONOMY 18:15–19**

## Jesus Christ is the Prophet who would be raised up like unto Moses.

Peter, Nephi, Moroni, and the Savior Himself all commented on the prophecy in Deuteronomy 18:15–19 (see Acts 3:20–23; 1 Nephi 22:20–21; Joseph

Smith—History 1:40; 3 Nephi 20:23). What do you learn about the Savior from these verses? How is the Savior "like unto" Moses? (Deuteronomy 18:15).

Jesus Christ is the prophet like unto Moses.

### DEUTERONOMY 34:5–8

## What happened to Moses?

Even though Deuteronomy 34:5–8 says that Moses died, latter-day understanding clarifies that he was translated, or changed so that he would not suffer pain or death until being resurrected (see Alma 45:18–19; Bible Dictionary, "Moses"; Guide to the Scriptures, "Translated Beings," scriptures .ChurchofJesusChrist.org). It was necessary for Moses to be translated because he needed to have a physical body in order to give priesthood keys to Peter, James, and John on the Mount of Transfiguration (see Matthew 17:1–13).

# Ideas for Family Scripture Study and Home Evening

**Deuteronomy 6:10–15.** These verses might prompt your family members to think of ways your family

has been blessed. How can we follow the counsel to "beware lest thou forget the Lord"? (Deuteronomy 6:12). You may want to record your feelings about your blessings, perhaps in a journal or on FamilySearch.

**Deuteronomy 6:13, 16; 8:3.** These verses helped the Savior during an important moment in His life; to see how, read together Matthew 4:1–10. What scripture passages have helped us in times of need?

**Deuteronomy 7:6–9.** Do something to help your family members feel special, such as preparing a favorite food. Then you could read Deuteronomy 7:6–9 and discuss what you feel it means to be "a special people" (verse 6) to the Lord.

**Deuteronomy 29:12–13.** Talking about Deuteronomy 29:12–13 provides an opportunity for your family members to discuss covenants they will make or have made with Heavenly Father. What does it mean to be God's people? How do our covenants "establish [us] . . . for a people unto [God]"? (verse 13).

For more ideas for teaching children, see this week's outline in *Come, Follow Me—For Primary.*

Suggested song: "I Want to Live the Gospel," *Children's Songbook,* 148.

### Improving Personal Study

**Seek your own spiritual insights.** This outline suggests passages and principles to focus on, but don't let that limit your study. As you study, you might learn about a principle that is not mentioned here. Let the Spirit guide you to what you need to learn.

*The Lord Shewed Him All the Land,* by Walter Rane

# The Historical Books in the Old Testament

The books of Joshua through Esther are tradition-ally known as the "historical books" of the Old Testament. This doesn't mean that other books in the Old Testament don't have historical value. Rather, the historical books are called that because the main objective of their writers was to show God's hand in the history of the people of Israel. The purpose was not to outline the law of Moses, as Leviticus and Deuteronomy do. It was not to ex-press praise or lament in poetic form, as the Psalms and Lamentations do. And it was not to record the words of prophets, as the books of Isaiah and Ezekiel do. Instead, the historical books tell a story.

## A Matter of Perspective

Naturally, that story is told from a certain point of view—really, certain *points* of view. Just as it's impossible to look at a flower, rock, or tree from more than one angle at a time, it's inevitable that a historical account will reflect the perspective of the person or group of people writing it. This perspec-tive includes the writers' national or ethnic ties and their cultural norms and beliefs. Knowing this can help us understand that the writers and compilers of the historical books focused on certain details while leaving out others.[1] They made certain assumptions that others might not have made. And they came to conclusions based on those details and assumptions. We can even see different perspectives across the

books of the Bible (and sometimes within the same book).[2] The more we're aware of these perspectives, the better we can understand the historical books.

One perspective common to all the Old Testament historical books is the perspective of the children of Israel, God's covenant people. Their faith in the Lord helped them see His hand in their lives and His intervention in the affairs of their nation. While secular history books don't tend to see things this way, this spiritual perspective is part of what makes the Old Testament historical books so valuable to those who are seeking to build their own faith in God.

## Context for the Rest of the Old Testament

The historical books begin where the book of Deuteronomy leaves off, with the Israelites' years of wandering in the wilderness about to end. The book of Joshua shows the children of Israel ready to enter Canaan, their promised land, and describes how they took it over. The books that follow, Judges through 2 Chronicles, depict Israel's experience in the promised land, from the time they settled it until the time they were conquered by Assyria and Babylon. The books of Ezra and Nehemiah tell of the return of several groups of Israelites to their capital, Jerusalem, decades later. Finally, the book of Esther relates a story of Israelites living in exile under Persian rule.

And that's where the chronology of the Old Testament ends. Some first-time Bible readers are surprised to find that they've actually finished reading the *story* of the Old Testament before they've read much more than half its pages. After Esther, we don't get much information about the history of the Israelites. Instead, the books that follow—especially the books of the prophets—fit *within* the timeline that the historical books presented.[3] The ministry of the prophet Jeremiah, for example, took place during the events recorded in 2 Kings 22–25 (and the parallel account in 2 Chronicles 34–36). Knowing this can influence the way you read both the historical narratives and the prophetic books.

Some scripture passages may be like puzzle pieces that we don't know how to fit with the rest of the puzzle.

## When Something Doesn't Fit

When reading the Old Testament, as with any history, you're likely to read about people doing or saying things that, to modern eyes, seem strange or even troubling. We should expect this—Old Testament writers saw the world from a perspective that was, in some ways, quite different from ours. Violence, ethnic relations, and the roles of women are just some of the issues that ancient writers might have seen differently than we do today.

So what should we do when we come across passages in the scriptures that seem troubling? First, it might help to consider each passage in a broader context. How does it fit in God's plan of salvation? How does it fit with what you know about the nature of Heavenly Father and Jesus Christ? How does it fit with revealed truths in other scriptures or with the teachings of living prophets? And how does it fit with the whisperings of the Spirit to your own heart and mind?

In some cases, the passage may not seem to fit well with any of these. Sometimes the passage may be like a puzzle piece that doesn't look like it has a place among the other pieces you've already assembled. Trying to force the piece to fit isn't the best approach. But neither is giving up on the entire puzzle. Instead, you may need to set the piece aside for now. As you learn more and put together more of the puzzle, you may be able to better see how the pieces fit together.

It can also help to remember that in addition to being limited to a particular perspective, scriptural histories are subject to human error (see Articles of Faith 1:8). For example, over the centuries "many plain and precious things [were] taken away from the [Bible]," including important truths about doctrine and ordinances (1 Nephi 13:28; see also verses 29, 40). At the same time, we should be willing to admit that our own perspectives are also limited: there will always be things we don't fully understand and questions we can't yet answer.

## Finding the Gems

But in the meantime, unanswered questions need not keep us from the precious gems of eternal truth that are found in the Old Testament—even if those gems are sometimes hidden in the rocky ground of troubling experiences and poor choices made by imperfect people. Perhaps the most precious of these gems are the stories and passages that testify of God's love—especially those that point our minds toward the sacrifice of Jesus Christ. Viewed from any angle, gems like these shine just as brightly today as they did back then. And because these accounts tell of the covenant people of God—men and women who had human weaknesses and yet loved and served the Lord—gems of truth abound in the historical books of the Old Testament.

### Notes

1. The historical narratives of the Bible we have today are primarily the work of many unnamed writers and compilers, who sometimes worked many years, even centuries, after the time periods they describe. They relied on a variety of historical sources and made decisions about what to include in their accounts and what to exclude.

2. For example, although 1–2 Chronicles covers roughly the same period as 1 Samuel 31 through the end of 2 Kings, 1–2 Chronicles emphasizes different details and presents a different perspective. Unlike 1 Samuel–2 Kings, 1–2 Chronicles focuses almost solely on the Southern Kingdom of Judah and often omits negative stories about David and Solomon (compare, for example, 2 Samuel 10–12 with 1 Chronicles 19–20 and 1 Kings 10–11 with 2 Chronicles 9). *Come, Follow Me* emphasizes studying the account in 1 and 2 Kings, though there is value in comparing that account with 1 and 2 Chronicles. It might be helpful to know that work on 1 Samuel–2 Kings likely began before the Babylonian empire conquered Judah and was completed during the exile in Babylon. The record that became 1–2 Chronicles, on the other hand, was compiled after the Jews returned to Jerusalem from their exile. As you read, you might consider how these different circumstances could have affected the perspectives of the compilers of the different accounts.

3. *Come, Follow Me—For Individuals and Families* includes a timeline that shows how the ministry of each prophet fits into the history of Israel (as well as can be determined). You'll notice that most of the prophetic books of the Old Testament fall near the end of that timeline—just before and just after the children of Israel were conquered, exiled, and scattered by their enemies.

Illustration of Moses ordaining Joshua, by Darrell Thomas.

# Joshua 1–8; 23–24

"BE STRONG AND OF A GOOD COURAGE"

As you study the book of Joshua, consider how the things you learn about the Israelites can increase your faith in Jesus Christ.

RECORD YOUR IMPRESSIONS

It had taken several generations, but the Lord's promise was about to be fulfilled: the children of Israel were on the verge of inheriting the promised land. But in their way stood the Jordan River, the walls of Jericho, and a wicked but mighty people who had rejected the Lord (see 1 Nephi 17:35). On top of that, their beloved leader Moses was gone. The situation may have made some Israelites feel weak and fearful, but the Lord said, "Be strong and of a good courage." Why should they feel this way?

Not because of their own strength—or even Moses's or Joshua's—but because "the Lord thy God is with thee whithersoever thou goest" (Joshua 1:9). When we have our own rivers to cross and walls to bring down, wonderful things can happen in our lives, because it is "the Lord [who] will do wonders among [us]" (Joshua 3:5).

For an overview of the book of Joshua, see "Joshua, book of" in the Bible Dictionary.

# Ideas for Personal Scripture Study

### JOSHUA 1:1–9

## God will be with me if I am faithful to Him.

Imagine what it might have been like for Joshua to be called to replace Moses. Notice what the Lord said in Joshua 1:1–9 to encourage him. Think about the difficult challenges you face; what in these verses gives you courage?

It may be interesting to note that the name Joshua (*Yehoshua* or *Yeshua* in Hebrew) means "Jehovah saves." And the name *Jesus* comes from *Yeshua.* So as you read about Joshua, consider how his mission to lead the children of Israel into the promised land reminds you of the Savior's mission.

See also Ann M. Dibb, "Be of a Good Courage," *Ensign* or *Liahona,* May 2010, 114–16.

### JOSHUA 2

## Both faith and works are necessary for salvation.

Early Christians saw Rahab as an example of the power of both faith and works (see Hebrews 11:31; James 2:25). As you read Joshua 2, consider the role of Rahab's faith and works in saving herself, her family, and the Israelite scouts. What does this teach you about how your faith in Christ and your works can influence yourself and others?

You may be interested to know that Rahab was the ancestor of both King David and Jesus Christ (see Matthew 1:5). What possible lessons can we learn from this?

Rahab at her window. *Waiting for the Promise,* by Elspeth Young.

### JOSHUA 3–4

## I can experience God's "wonders" if I have faith in Jesus Christ.

The Lord desires that "all the people of the earth might know the hand of the Lord, that it is mighty" (Joshua 4:24). As you read Joshua 3–4, ponder how you know the hand of the Lord is mighty. How has the Lord done "wonders" in your life? (Joshua 3:5). How can you experience—or recognize—those wonders more often? (for example, see Joshua 3:17).

Why do you think the Israelites needed to sanctify themselves before they crossed the Jordan River? What significance do you find in the fact that the river parted only after "the feet of the priests . . . were dipped in the brim of the water"? (Joshua 3:13, 15).

For other significant events that happened at the Jordan River, see 2 Kings 2:6–15; 5:1–14; and Mark 1:9–11. As you ponder these scriptures, what connections do you see between these events?

See also Gérald Caussé, "Is It Still Wonderful to You?" *Ensign* or *Liahona,* May 2015, 98–100; "Exercise Faith in Christ" (video), ChurchofJesusChrist.org.

### JOSHUA 6–8

## Obedience brings God's power into my life.

These chapters deal with battles over the lands of Jericho and Ai. As you read them, consider how you battle temptation in your own life (for example, see Joshua 7:10–13). What do you learn about how God can help you and what you need to do to access His power? For example, what impresses you about the Lord's instructions for taking Jericho? (see Joshua 6:1–5). Perhaps the account in Joshua 7 will inspire you to determine if "there is an accursed thing" in your life that you need to remove (Joshua 7:13).

### JOSHUA 23–24

## "Cleave unto the Lord your God."

After dividing the promised land among the twelve tribes of Israel (see Joshua 13–21), Joshua gave them his final teachings. As you read these teachings in Joshua 23–24, you might keep a list of the warnings, counsel, and promised blessings you find. Considering everything the Israelites had been through, why do you think Joshua chose to tell them these things at the end of his life? What do you find that inspires you to "cleave unto the Lord"? (Joshua 23:8).

# Ideas for Family Scripture Study and Home Evening

**Joshua 1:8.** What does this verse suggest about how we should approach our scripture study, both individually and as a family? How have the scriptures made our "way prosperous" and brought us "good success"?

**Joshua 4:3, 6–9.** After reading what the Lord wanted the Israelites to do with stones from the Jordan River, your family could talk about some of the great things the Lord has done for you. Then you could give each family member a stone and invite them to write or draw on it something the Lord has done for them.

**Joshua 6:2–5.** Your family might have fun acting out the instructions the Lord gave to the Israelites in order to conquer Jericho. What might the Lord want us to learn from this story?

**Joshua 24:15.** After reading this verse, family members could share experiences in which they chose to serve the Lord even though it was difficult. Why is it important to make the choice to serve Him "this day" instead of waiting to decide until a situation arises? How can we support members of our "house" as we strive to "serve the Lord"?

For more ideas for teaching children, see this week's outline in *Come, Follow Me—For Primary.*

Suggested song: "Choose the Right," *Hymns,* no. 239.

## Improving Our Teaching

**Bear your testimony often.** Your sincere witness of truth can powerfully influence your family. It need not be eloquent or lengthy. A testimony is most powerful when it is direct and heartfelt. (See *Teaching in the Savior's Way,* 11.)

The Lord caused the walls of Jericho to fall. © Providence Collection/licensed from goodsalt.com

MAY 30–JUNE 5

# Judges 2–4; 6–8; 13–16

"THE LORD RAISED UP A DELIVERER"

The scriptures testify of Jesus Christ. Ponder how the stories you read in Judges help you come closer to Him.

RECORD YOUR IMPRESSIONS

We all know what it's like to make a mistake, feel bad about it, and then repent and resolve to change our ways. But in some cases we forget our earlier resolve, and, when we face temptation, we may find ourselves making the mistake again. This tragic pattern is typical of the Israelites' experiences described in the book of Judges. Influenced by the beliefs and worship practices of the Canaanites—whom they were supposed to drive out of the land—the Israelites broke their covenants with the Lord and turned away from worshipping Him. As a result, they lost His protection and fell into captivity. And yet each time this happened, the Lord gave them the chance to repent and raised up a deliverer, a military leader called a "judge." Not all of the judges in the book of Judges were righteous, but some of them exercised great faith in delivering the children of Israel and restoring them to their covenant relationship with the Lord. These stories remind us that no matter what has led us away from Jesus Christ, He is the Redeemer of Israel and is always willing to deliver us and welcome us back to Him.

For an overview of the book of Judges, see "Judges, book of" in the Bible Dictionary.

# Ideas for Personal Scripture Study

### JUDGES 2:1–19; 4:1–16

## The Lord offers deliverance when I stray.

The book of Judges can serve as a warning to us: even after we experience the Lord's power in our lives, it is always possible to fall away. The book can also provide encouragement to those who do fall away, for the Lord offers a way back. For instance, as you read Judges 2:1–19, look for actions that led the Israelites away from the Lord and how the Lord delivered them. What do these verses teach you about the Lord? What can you do to remain more consistently faithful to Him?

You will find the pattern of rebelliousness, sorrow, and deliverance repeated throughout Judges (see specifically chapters 3, 4, 6, and 13). As you read the book of Judges, ponder what the judges did to deliver Israel and how the Savior helps you when you need deliverance.

One noteworthy example of someone who helped deliver Israel is Deborah. Read about her in Judges 4:1–16, and note the influence she had on people around her. What words or actions of Deborah show you that she had faith in the Lord? What do you feel Deborah meant by her question in verse 14: "Is not the Lord gone out before thee?"

See also Alma 7:13; Doctrine and Covenants 84:87–88.

### JUDGES 2:13

## Who were Baal and Ashtaroth?

Baal was the Canaanite storm god, and Ashtaroth was the Canaanite fertility goddess. The worship of these two gods indicates how important the fertility of the land and of the people was to the Canaanites. The ways the people worshipped these and other false gods—including, at times, sexual immorality and the sacrifice of children—were especially offensive to the Lord.

### JUDGES 6–8

## The Lord can work miracles when I trust in His ways.

To receive the Lord's miracles in our lives, we must trust in His ways, even when His ways seem unusual. The story of Gideon, found in Judges 6–8, is a good example of this. How did the Lord work an unlikely miracle when Gideon's army defeated the Midianites? What do you feel the Lord is trying to teach you? How have you seen the Lord do His work in ways that seem unlikely?

See also Russell M. Nelson, "With God Nothing Shall Be Impossible," *Ensign,* May 1988, 33–35.

### JUDGES 13–16

## Strength comes from faithfulness to my covenants with God.

Samson lost both his physical strength and his spiritual strength because he violated his covenants with God, including those that applied specifically to Nazarites (for information about the Nazarites, see Numbers 6:1–6; Judges 13:7). As you read Samson's story in Judges 13–16, ponder each covenant you have made. How have you been blessed with strength because you have kept those covenants? What do you learn from Samson's story that inspires you to stay true to your covenants with God?

*Samson Puts Down the Pillars,* by James Tissot and others

# Ideas for Family Scripture Study and Home Evening

**Judges 2:10.** After Joshua died, the next generation of Israelites "knew not the Lord." Talk with your family about how they know the Lord and "the works which he [has] done" for them. How will you ensure that this knowledge will be preserved for future generations?

**Judges 3:7–10.** These verses summarize a pattern that occurs often throughout the book of Judges. As your family members read these verses, they could identify what Israel did to stray from the Lord and what the Lord did to deliver them. What might lead us to forget the Lord? How can He deliver us? How can we be more consistently faithful to Him?

**Judges 6:13–16, 25–30.** Gideon showed great courage in obeying the Lord, even though his actions were not popular. What has the Lord asked us to do that others might not agree with? How can the Lord's words to Gideon in verses 13–16 inspire us to do the right thing?

**Judges 7.** Could you use a role play or other creative activity to help your family learn from the experience of Gideon's army described in this chapter? How can the Lord's words in this chapter (see, for example, verses 2 and 15) apply to our lives?

**Judges 13:5.** Samson's covenants with the Lord gave him strength, just as our covenants give us strength. Your family might enjoy doing some physical exercises and discussing how those exercises can help make us strong. What can we do to help us become spiritually stronger? For some ideas, family members could read Mosiah 18:8–10; Doctrine and Covenants 20:77, 79. How does keeping our covenants give us spiritual strength?

For more ideas for teaching children, see this week's outline in *Come, Follow Me—For Primary.*

Suggested song: "Redeemer of Israel," *Hymns,* no. 6.

## Improving Personal Study

**Act on what you learn.** As you study, ask yourself how you can apply what you are learning, and then commit to do it. Let the Spirit guide you. (See *Teaching in the Savior's Way,* 35.)

*Gideon's Army,* by Daniel A. Lewis

# Ruth; 1 Samuel 1–3

"MY HEART REJOICETH IN THE LORD"

As you study the lives of Ruth, Naomi, Hannah, and others this week, listen closely to the Spirit and record any impressions you receive. What are you inspired to do?

RECORD YOUR IMPRESSIONS

Sometimes we imagine that our lives should follow a clear path from beginning to end. The shortest distance between two points is a straight line, after all. And yet life is often full of delays and detours that take us in unexpected directions. We may find that our lives are quite different from what we thought they should be.

Ruth and Hannah surely understood this. Ruth was not an Israelite, but she married one, and when her husband died, she had a choice to make. Would she return to her family and her old, familiar life, or would she embrace the Israelite faith and a new home with her mother-in-law? (see Ruth 1:4–18). Hannah's plan for her life was to bear children, and

her inability to do so left her "in bitterness of soul" (see 1 Samuel 1:1–10). As you read about Ruth and Hannah, consider the faith they must have had to put their lives in the Lord's hands and travel their unexpected paths. Then you might think about your own journey. It will look different from Ruth's and Hannah's—and anyone else's. But throughout the trials and surprises between here and your eternal destination, you can learn to say with Hannah, "My heart rejoiceth in the Lord" (1 Samuel 2:1).

For an overview of the books of Ruth and 1 Samuel, see "Ruth" and "Samuel, books of" in the Bible Dictionary.

# Ideas for Personal Scripture Study

### RUTH

## Christ can turn tragedy into triumph.

When Ruth's husband died, the tragedy had consequences for her that were even more severe than a widow today might face. In Israelite culture at that time, a woman without a husband or sons had no right to property and practically no way to earn a living. As you read Ruth's story, notice how the Lord turned tragedy into great blessings. What do you notice about Ruth that might have helped her? What was Boaz's role in redeeming Ruth from her desperate situation? (see Ruth 4:4–7). What Christlike characteristics do you see in both Ruth and Boaz?

### RUTH; 1 SAMUEL 1

## I can trust that God will guide and help me regardless of my situation.

Can you see yourself in the stories of Ruth, Naomi, and Hannah? Perhaps you have suffered a great loss, as Ruth and Naomi did (see Ruth 1:1–5). Or maybe, like Hannah, you long for blessings you have not yet received (see 1 Samuel 1:1–10). Ponder what messages you can learn from the examples of these faithful women. How did Ruth and Hannah show faith in God? What blessings did they receive? How can you follow their examples? Consider how you have "come to trust" the Lord (Ruth 2:12) even when life feels difficult.

See also Reyna I. Aburto, "Thru Cloud and Sunshine, Lord, Abide with Me!" *Ensign* or *Liahona,* Nov. 2019, 57–60.

*For This Child I Prayed,* by Elspeth Young

### 1 SAMUEL 2:1–10

## My heart can rejoice in the Lord.

After Hannah took young Samuel to the temple, she spoke beautiful words of praise to the Lord, recorded in 1 Samuel 2:1–10. These words are even more moving when you consider that a short time earlier, "she was in bitterness of soul, . . . and wept sore" (1 Samuel 1:10). As you study these verses, what messages do you find that increase your feelings of praise and gratitude to the Lord? Perhaps Hannah's song will inspire you to find a creative way to express your gratitude to the Lord—a song, a painting, an act of service, or anything that communicates your feelings toward Him.

Of course, not all fervent prayers are answered the way that Hannah's was. What do you find in President Dieter F. Uchtdorf's message "Grateful in Any Circumstances" that can help you when your prayers aren't answered in the way you hope? (*Ensign* or *Liahona,* May 2014, 70–77).

### 1 SAMUEL 3

## I can hear and obey the voice of the Lord.

Like all of us, Samuel had to learn how to recognize the voice of the Lord. As you study 1 Samuel 3, what do you learn from this young boy about hearing and obeying the Lord's voice? What experiences have you had with hearing His voice? What opportunities do you have, like Eli, to help others recognize when the Lord is speaking to them? (see 1 Samuel 3:7).

See also John 14:14–21; David P. Homer, "Hearing His Voice," *Ensign* or *Liahona,* May 2019, 41–43.

## Ideas for Family Scripture Study and Home Evening

**Ruth 1:16–18; 2:5–8, 11–12.** Your family could look for examples of kindness and loyalty in these verses. How do we show kindness to our family and others and loyalty to Jesus Christ? The chapter "Ruth and Naomi" (in *Old Testament Stories*) could help your family learn from Ruth's example.

**1 Samuel 1:15.** Maybe you could pour something out of a container to help family members visualize what Hannah meant when she said, "I . . . have poured out my soul before the Lord." Why is this a good way to describe what our prayers should be like? How can we improve our personal and family prayers?

**1 Samuel 2:1–10.** Hannah's poem of praise to the Lord may lead you to think of songs that you use to praise the Lord. You could sing some together. Your family members might also think of other ways to express their feelings for Jesus Christ. For example, they could draw pictures that show why they love the Savior.

**1 Samuel 3:1–11.** It might be fun to act out the story of the Lord calling to Samuel, or your family could watch the video "Samuel and Eli" (ChurchofJesusChrist.org). Family members could talk about times when they have felt the Lord speaking to them and how they acted on His words.

For more ideas for teaching children, see this week's outline in *Come, Follow Me—For Primary.*

Suggested song: "There Is Sunshine in My Soul Today," *Hymns,* no. 227.

### Improving Personal Study

**Let the Spirit guide your study.** Pray that the Holy Ghost will guide you to the things you need to learn. Be sensitive to His whisperings, even if this leads you to read about a topic you weren't expecting or to study in a different way.

Illustration of Samuel hearing the Lord, by Sam Lawlor

David and Goliath, by Steve Nethercott

# 1 Samuel 8–10; 13; 15–18

"THE BATTLE IS THE LORD'S"

The suggestions in this outline can help you identify some of the important principles in these chapters. You may find other principles as you study.

RECORD YOUR IMPRESSIONS

Ever since the tribes of Israel had settled in the promised land, the Philistines had been an ongoing threat to their safety. Many times in the past, the Lord had delivered the Israelites from their enemies. But now the elders of Israel demanded, "We will have a king . . . [to] go out before us, and fight our battles" (1 Samuel 8:19–20). The Lord relented, and Saul was anointed king. And yet when the menacing giant Goliath hurled his challenge to the armies of Israel, Saul—like the rest of his army—was "greatly afraid" (1 Samuel 17:11). On that day, it wasn't King Saul who saved Israel but a humble shepherd boy named David, who was wearing no armor but was clothed with impenetrable faith in the Lord. This battle proved to Israel, and to anyone who has

spiritual battles to fight, that "the Lord saveth not with sword and spear" and that "the battle is the Lord's" (1 Samuel 17:47).

## Ideas for Personal Scripture Study

### 1 SAMUEL 8

### Jesus Christ is my King.

As you read 1 Samuel 8, notice how the Lord felt about the Israelites' desire for a king other than

Himself. What does it mean to choose the Lord to "reign over [you]"? (1 Samuel 8:7). You might also consider ways you are tempted to follow the unrighteous trends of the world instead of following the Lord. How can you show that you want Jesus Christ to be your Eternal King?

See also Judges 8:22–23; Mosiah 29:1–36; Neil L. Andersen, "Overcoming the World," *Ensign* or *Liahona,* May 2017, 58–62.

### 1 SAMUEL 9:15–17; 10:1–12; 16:1–13
## God calls people by prophecy to serve in His kingdom.

God chose Saul and David to be kings through prophecy and revelation (see 1 Samuel 9:15–17; 10:1–12; 16:1–13). This is also how He calls men and women to serve in His Church today. What do you learn from these accounts about what it means to "be called of God, by prophecy"? (Articles of Faith 1:5). What blessings come from being called and set apart by the Lord's authorized servants?

Illustration of Samuel anointing Saul, © Lifeway Collection/licensed from goodsalt.com

### 1 SAMUEL 13:5–14; 15
## "To obey is better than sacrifice."

Although Saul was physically tall, he felt "little in [his] own sight" when he became king (1 Samuel 15:17). However, as he was blessed with success, he began to trust himself more and the Lord less. What evidence do you see of this in 1 Samuel 13:5–14; 15? If you had been with Saul then, what would you have said to him that might have helped him overcome his "rebellion" and "stubbornness"? (1 Samuel 15:23).

See also 2 Nephi 9:28–29; Helaman 12:4–5; Doctrine and Covenants 121:39–40; Thomas S. Monson, "Ponder the Path of Thy Feet," *Ensign* or *Liahona,* Nov. 2014, 86–88.

### 1 SAMUEL 16:7
## "The Lord looketh on the heart."

What are some ways people judge others "on the outward appearance"? What does it mean to look "on the heart," as the Lord does? (1 Samuel 16:7). Consider how you can apply this principle to the way you see others—and yourself. How might doing so affect your interactions or relationships with others?

### 1 SAMUEL 17
## With the help of the Lord, I can overcome any challenge.

As you read 1 Samuel 17, ponder the words of various people in this chapter (see the list below). What do their words reveal about them? How do David's words show his courage and faith in the Lord?

- Goliath: verses 8–10, 43–44

- Eliab: verse 28

- Saul: verse 33

- David: verses 26, 32, 34–37, 39, 45–47

Ponder the personal battles you are facing. What can you find in 1 Samuel 17 that strengthens your faith that the Lord can help you?

See also Gordon B. Hinckley, "Overpowering the Goliaths in Our Lives," *Ensign,* May 1983, 46, 51–52.

## Ideas for Family Scripture Study and Home Evening

**1 Samuel 9:15–21; 16:7.** Reading these verses along with the following words from Elder Dieter F. Uchtdorf could inspire a discussion about why the Lord chose Saul and David: "If we look at ourselves only through our mortal eyes, we may not see ourselves as good enough. But our Heavenly Father sees us as who we truly are and who we can become" ("It Works Wonderfully!" *Ensign* or *Liahona,* Nov. 2015, 23). Perhaps family members could take turns talking about what good qualities they see in each other's hearts (see 1 Samuel 16:7).

**1 Samuel 10:6–12.** When have we seen God bless someone with spiritual power to fulfill an assignment or calling like He blessed Saul? What experiences can we share when "God gave [us] another heart" or "the Spirit of God came upon [us]" in His service? (verses 9–10).

**1 Samuel 17:20–54.** Your family might enjoy reading together the story of David and Goliath ("David and Goliath" in *Old Testament Stories* could help) or watching the video "The Lord Will Deliver Me" (ChurchofJesusChrist.org). This could lead to a

discussion about challenges we face that may feel like "Goliaths" to us. You could even write some of these challenges on a target or a drawing of Goliath and take turns throwing objects (like balls of paper) at it.

It might also be interesting to read about the armor and weapons Goliath had (see verses 4–7). What did David have? (see verses 38–40, 45–47). What has the Lord provided to help us defeat our Goliaths?

**1 Samuel 18:1–4.** How were David and Jonathan good friends to each other? How have good friends blessed us? What can we do to be good friends—including to our family members?

For more ideas for teaching children, see this week's outline in *Come, Follow Me—For Primary.*

Suggested song: "I Will Be Valiant," *Children's Songbook,* 162.

### Improving Our Teaching

**Bear your testimony often.** "Your simple, sincere witness of spiritual truth can have a powerful influence on [your family]. A testimony is most powerful when it is direct and heartfelt. It need not be eloquent or lengthy" (*Teaching in the Savior's Way,* 11).

Illustration of David, by Dilleen Marsh

*King David Enthroned, by Jerry Miles Harston*

# 2 Samuel 5–7; 11–12; 1 Kings 3; 8; 11

"THY KINGDOM SHALL BE ESTABLISHED FOR EVER"

"All scripture is given by inspiration of God, and is profitable for doctrine, for reproof, for correction, for instruction in righteousness" (2 Timothy 3:16).

RECORD YOUR IMPRESSIONS

King David's reign started out with so much promise. His undaunted faith in defeating Goliath was legendary. As king, he secured Jerusalem as his capital and united Israel (see 2 Samuel 5). The kingdom had never been stronger. And yet David gave in to temptation and lost his spiritual power.

The reign of David's son Solomon likewise started out with so much promise. His divinely received wisdom and discernment were legendary. As king, he extended Israel's borders and built a magnificent temple to the Lord. The kingdom had never been stronger. And yet Solomon foolishly allowed his heart to be turned away to other gods.

What can we learn from these tragic stories? Perhaps one lesson is that regardless of our past experiences, our spiritual strength depends on the choices we make today. We can also see in these accounts that it isn't our own strength or courage or wisdom that will save us—it is the Lord's. These stories show us that Israel's true hope—and ours—is not in David, Solomon, or any other mortal king, but in another "son of David": Jesus Christ (Matthew 1:1), the Eternal King who will "forgive the sin of [His] people" if we "turn again to [Him]" (1 Kings 8:33–34).

For an overview of the books of 2 Samuel and 1 Kings, see "Samuel, books of" and "Kings, books of" in the Bible Dictionary.

## Ideas for Personal Scripture Study

### 2 SAMUEL 5:17–25

### The Lord can give me direction.

Once David was able to unite Israel (see 2 Samuel 5:1–5), he had to defend his people from the Philistines. As you read 2 Samuel 5:17–25, consider how David's example can help you in the challenges you face (see also 1 Samuel 23:2, 10–11; 30:8; 2 Samuel 2:1). How are you seeking the Lord's direction in your life? How are you being blessed by acting on the revelation you receive?

See also 1 Chronicles 12; Richard G. Scott, "How to Obtain Revelation and Inspiration for Your Personal Life," *Ensign* or *Liahona,* May 2012, 45–47.

### 2 SAMUEL 7

### What is the "house" the Lord promised to David?

When David offered to build a house, meaning a temple, for the Lord (see 2 Samuel 7:1–3), the Lord responded that in fact David's *son* would build it (see verses 12–15; see also 1 Chronicles 17:1–15). The Lord also said that He in turn would build David a "house," meaning a posterity, and that his throne would last forever (see 2 Samuel 7:11, 16, 25–29; Psalm 89:3–4, 35–37). This promise was fulfilled in Jesus Christ, our Eternal King, who was a descendant of David (see Matthew 1:1; Luke 1:32–33; John 18:33–37).

### 2 SAMUEL 11; 12:1–14

### I should always be on guard against sin.

David's faithfulness to the Lord in the past did not make him immune to temptation when he "walked upon the roof of the king's house" and "saw a woman washing herself" (2 Samuel 11:2). Consider what lessons you can learn from his experiences. Questions like these might help you study this account:

- What choices did David make that led him down an increasingly sinful path? What righteous choices could he have made instead?

- How might the adversary be trying to lead you down sinful paths in your own life? What choices could you make now to return to safety?

See also 2 Nephi 28:20–24; "To Look Upon" (video), ChurchofJesusChrist.org.

### 1 KINGS 3:1–15

### The gift of discernment helps me distinguish between right and wrong.

If the Lord said to you, "Ask what I shall give thee" (1 Kings 3:5), what would you ask for? What impresses you about Solomon's request? Ponder why "an understanding heart" to "discern between good and bad" (verse 9) is a valuable gift. What can you do to seek this gift?

See also 2 Chronicles 1; Moroni 7:12–19; David A. Bednar, "Quick to Observe," *Ensign,* Dec. 2006, 30–36.

Barranquilla Colombia Temple

### 1 KINGS 8:12–61

## The temple is the house of the Lord.

For hundreds of years, God's presence was represented by the portable tabernacle that Moses built. Although David had wanted to build God a more permanent dwelling place, God instead chose David's son Solomon to build the temple of the Lord. As you read Solomon's prayer and the words he spoke to his people upon completing the temple, notice how he felt about the Lord and His house. You could also make a list of the blessings Solomon asked for in his prayer. What do you notice about these blessings? How are you blessed by the Lord's house in our day?

See also 2 Chronicles 6.

# Ideas for Family Scripture Study and Home Evening

**2 Samuel 5:19, 23.** When have we "inquired of the Lord" for guidance and direction? How has He answered us?

**2 Samuel 7:16.** When the Lord told David, "Thy throne shall be established forever," He was referring to a future king in David's family line who would reign forever: Jesus Christ. Perhaps your family would enjoy creating homemade crowns while discussing why you are grateful that Jesus Christ is your Eternal King.

**2 Samuel 11.** Reading about David's tragic sins might be a good opportunity to discuss the dangers of pornography, unclean thoughts, and immorality. The following resources could be useful in your discussion: the October 2019 issue of the *Ensign* or *Liahona,* the Church's Addressing Pornography resources (ChurchofJesusChrist.org/addressing-pornography), and the videos "What Should I Do When I See Pornography?" and "Watch Your Step" (ChurchofJesusChrist.org). Family members could make a plan about what they will do when they encounter pornography.

**1 Kings 11:9–11.** What are some "other gods" (verse 10) that could turn our hearts away from the Lord? How can we keep our hearts centered on Heavenly Father and Jesus Christ?

For more ideas for teaching children, see this week's outline in *Come, Follow Me—For Primary.*

Suggested song: "More Holiness Give Me," *Hymns,* no. 131.

### Improving Our Teaching

**Focus on principles that will bless your family.** As you prayerfully study the word of God, ask yourself, "What do I find here that will be especially meaningful to my family?" (see *Teaching in the Savior's Way,* 17).

Illustration of Solomon's temple, by Sam Lawlor

# 1 Kings 17–19

"IF THE LORD BE GOD, FOLLOW HIM"

When you read the scriptures, you are exercising faith, which prepares your heart and mind to hear the "still small voice" of the Spirit (1 Kings 19:12).

RECORD YOUR IMPRESSIONS

The house of Israel was in disarray. The unity and prosperity achieved under David and Solomon were long past, and the nation's covenant relationship with the Lord was, for many people, a distant memory. The Kingdom of Israel had divided, with ten tribes forming the Northern Kingdom of Israel and two tribes forming the Southern Kingdom of Judah. Both kingdoms were unstable spiritually, led by kings who violated their covenants with the Lord and influenced others to do likewise (see 1 Kings 11–16). But the apostasy was especially severe in the Northern Kingdom, where King Ahab encouraged Israel to worship the false god Baal.

It was in this setting that the prophet Elijah was called to preach. The account of his ministry makes clear that personal faith in the Lord can thrive among the righteous even in a wicked environment. Sometimes the Lord responds to such faith with impressive, public miracles, like fire falling from heaven. But He also works quiet, private miracles, like meeting the personal needs of a faithful widow and her son. And most often His miracles are so individual that they are known only to you—for example, when the Lord reveals Himself and His will through "a still small voice" (1 Kings 19:12).

For more about Elijah, see "Elijah" in the Bible Dictionary.

# Ideas for Personal Scripture Study

## 1 KINGS 17:1–16

### An invitation to sacrifice is an opportunity to exercise my faith.

At first it might seem hard to understand why the prophet Elijah asked the widow in Zarephath to give him food and water before feeding herself and her starving son. But Elijah's request could also be seen as a blessing for this small family. They needed the Lord's blessings, and sacrifice often brings blessings—including the blessing of stronger faith.

As you read this story, put yourself in the place of this remarkable widow. What impresses you about her? Consider the opportunities you have to exercise your faith—including opportunities to sacrifice. How can you be more like this widow?

See also Matthew 6:25–33; Luke 4:24–26; Lynn G. Robbins, "Tithing—a Commandment Even for the Destitute," *Ensign* or *Liahona*, May 2005, 34–36.

## 1 KINGS 18

### "If the Lord be God, follow him."

The Israelites may have felt they had good reasons to worship Baal despite the Lord's command, "Thou shalt have no other gods before me" (Exodus 20:3). Baal was known as the god of storms and rain, and after three years of drought, they desperately needed a storm. And Baal worship was socially accepted and endorsed by the king and queen. As you read 1 Kings 18, consider any situations in your life that could be compared to the situation the Israelites were in. Do you ever find yourself indecisive about following the Lord because the alternatives seem reasonable and compelling? (see 1 Kings 18:21). In the events found in this chapter, what do you think the Lord was trying to teach the people about

Himself and about Baal? What experiences have taught you similar truths?

It might be interesting to note things Elijah said and did in this chapter that demonstrate his faith in the Lord. What do you learn from Elijah about faith?

See also Joshua 24:15; 2 Nephi 2:26–28; D. Todd Christofferson, "Choice and Commitment" (worldwide devotional for young adults, Jan. 12, 2020), ChurchofJesusChrist.org.

A symbolic depiction of 1 Kings 19:11–12. *The Prophet,* © Robert Booth Charles/Bridgeman Images

## 1 KINGS 19:1–18

### The Lord often speaks in quiet, simple ways.

When Queen Jezebel heard about what had happened to her priests on Mount Carmel, she wasn't converted—she was enraged. Fearing for his life, Elijah fled to the wilderness and sought refuge in a cave. There, struggling with loneliness and discouragement, he had an experience with the Lord that was very different from what had happened on Mount Carmel. What does Elijah's experience in 1 Kings 19:1–18 teach you about how the Lord communicates with you in your times of need? Ponder times in your life when you have experienced His voice. What do you need to do to receive His guidance more often?

Ponder the words and phrases used in the following verses to describe how the Lord communicates with us: Helaman 5:30; 3 Nephi 11:3–7; Doctrine and Covenants 6:22–23; 8:2–3; 9:8–9; 11:12–14; 36:2.

See also Psalm 46:10; 1 Nephi 17:45; Russell M. Nelson, "Hear Him," *Ensign* or *Liahona,* May 2020, 88–92.

### 1 KINGS 19:19–21

## Serving the Lord takes priority over worldly concerns.

The fact that Elisha owned 12 yoke of oxen indicates he was probably a wealthy man. What impresses you about his actions recorded in 1 Kings 19:19–21? How can you follow Elisha's example?

See also Matthew 4:18–22.

# Ideas for Family Scripture Study and Home Evening

**1 Kings 17:1–16.** The video "Elijah and the Widow of Zarephath" (ChurchofJesusChrist.org) and the picture in this outline could help your family visualize the account in 1 Kings 17:1–16. After reading the verses and looking at these resources, each family member could list inspiring qualities the widow had. What is the Lord asking us to do to demonstrate our faith?

**1 Kings 18.** "Elijah and the Priests of Baal" (in *Old Testament Stories*) can help your family learn the story in 1 Kings 18. Are there things that are keeping us from being fully committed to the Lord? How can we show our willingness to choose Him? (see verse 21).

**1 Kings 19:11–12.** What would help your family understand the importance of listening to the "still small voice"? You could read 1 Kings 19:11–12 together in a soft voice or quietly sing a song about the Spirit, such as "The Holy Ghost" (*Children's Songbook,* 105). You might add some distracting noises to illustrate how Satan tries to keep us from hearing the still, small voice. Family members could share what they do to be sensitive to promptings of the Spirit.

For more ideas for teaching children, see this week's outline in *Come, Follow Me—For Primary.*

Suggested song: "The Holy Ghost," *Children's Songbook,* 105.

### Improving Personal Study

**Record your impressions.** When you sense the Spirit speaking to you, consider writing down what you feel He is telling you. The thought it takes to put these impressions into words can help you ponder and treasure them.

*Widow of Zarephath,* by Rose Datoc Dall

JULY 4–10

# 2 Kings 2–7

"THERE IS A PROPHET IN ISRAEL"

As you read the scriptures, the Holy Ghost may bring to your attention certain phrases or passages. Consider writing down why those passages are meaningful to you.

RECORD YOUR IMPRESSIONS

A prophet's main mission is to teach and testify of the Savior Jesus Christ. Our record of the prophet Elisha, however, doesn't include much of his teaching or testifying. What the record does include is the miracles Elisha performed, including raising a child from the dead (see 2 Kings 4:18–37), feeding a multitude with a small quantity of food (see 2 Kings 4:42–44), and healing a leper (see 2 Kings 5:1–14). So while we don't have Elisha's words bearing witness of Christ, we do have, throughout Elisha's ministry, powerful manifestations of the Lord's life-giving, nourishing, and healing power. Such manifestations are more plentiful in our lives than we sometimes realize. To see them, we need to seek the miracle Elisha sought when he prayed on behalf of his fearful young servant, "Lord, I pray thee, open his eyes, that he may see" (2 Kings 6:17).

For more information about 2 Kings, see "Kings, books of" in the Bible Dictionary.

# Ideas for Personal Scripture Study

### 2 KINGS 2–6
## God can work miracles in my life.

Miracles often help us overcome the difficulties of mortality—in Elisha's time, a barren land needed pure water and a lost ax needed to be recovered (see 2 Kings 2:19–22; 6:4–7). But miracles also turn our hearts to the Lord and teach us spiritual lessons. As you read 2 Kings 2–6, consider making a list of the miracles you find, and ponder the spiritual lessons you learn from each one. What do these miracles teach you about the Lord and what He can do in your life?

See also 2 Nephi 26:12–13; 27:23; Mormon 9:7–21; Moroni 7:35–37; Donald L. Hallstrom, "Has the Day of Miracles Ceased?" *Ensign* or *Liahona,* Nov. 2017, 88–90.

### 2 KINGS 4:8–17; 7:1–16
## The words of the Lord through His prophets will be fulfilled.

As recorded in 2 Kings 4:8–17; 7:1–16, the Lord inspired Elisha to prophesy of things to come—things that seemed, from the perspective of others, unlikely to occur. As you read these verses, think about how you respond to the word of the Lord through His prophets today. What teachings, prophecies, or promises have you heard from living prophets? What are you doing to act in faith on those promises?

See also 3 Nephi 29:6; Doctrine and Covenants 1:37–38.

### 2 KINGS 5
## If I am humble and obedient, Jesus Christ can heal me.

Sometimes it's easier to find personal meaning in the scriptures when you compare physical things in a story with spiritual things. For example, while reading 2 Kings 5, you might compare Naaman's leprosy with a spiritual challenge you are facing. Like Naaman, perhaps you have hoped that the Lord would "do some great thing" (verse 13) to help you. What does Naaman's experience teach you? In your life, what would be the equivalent of following the simple counsel to "wash, and be clean"?

Note how Naaman's experience affected his faith in the God of Israel (see verse 15). What experiences have strengthened your faith in God?

See also Luke 4:27; 1 Peter 5:5–7; Alma 37:3–7; Ether 12:27; L. Whitney Clayton, "Whatsoever He Saith unto You, Do It," *Ensign* or *Liahona,* May 2017, 97–99; "Naaman and Elisha" (video), ChurchofJesusChrist.org.

### 2 KINGS 6:8–23
## "They that be with us are more than they that be with them."

Have you ever felt outnumbered and fearful, wondering, as Elisha's young servant did, "How shall we do?" (see 2 Kings 6:8–23). What inspires you about Elisha's answer? How does this account change the way you think and feel about your trials, your responsibilities, or your efforts to live the gospel?

As you ponder, consider President Henry B. Eyring's words: "Like that servant of Elisha, there are more with you than those you can see opposed to you. Some who are with you will be invisible to your mortal eyes. The Lord will bear you up and will at times do it by calling others to stand with you" ("O Ye That Embark," *Ensign* or *Liahona,* Nov. 2008, 58).

See also Psalm 121; Doctrine and Covenants 84:88.

## Ideas for Family Scripture Study and Home Evening

**2 Kings 2:1–14.** Think about the people who saw that Elisha "took up" Elijah's mantle (or cloak—a symbol of his prophetic calling). How might this have affected the way they responded to Elisha's ministry? (See also 1 Kings 19:19.) Maybe family members could take turns wearing a "mantle" and testifying of ways they have seen the Lord support and strengthen those called to serve in His Church.

**2 Kings 4.** You could invite family members to read about one of the miracles in 2 Kings 4 (see verses 1–7, 14–17, 32–35, 38–41, 42–44) and write a clue to help other family members guess which miracle he or she is describing. What do we learn about the Lord and His miracles from this chapter? What miracles—big or small—have we seen in our lives?

**2 Kings 5:1–15.** As you read these verses and ponder the simple thing Naaman was asked to do, consider the simple things our prophet has asked us to do. How can our family better follow his counsel?

Your family could also watch the video "Naaman and Elisha" (ChurchofJesusChrist.org) or read "Elisha Heals Naaman" (in *Old Testament Stories*).

**2 Kings 5:20–27.** How might Gehazi have benefited from reading "Honesty and Integrity" in *For the Strength of Youth*? (page 19). How does dishonesty harm us? How are we blessed for being honest?

**2 Kings 6:13–17.** Family members might enjoy drawing a picture of the experience of Elisha and his servant described in these verses. How can these verses help us when we feel alone or overwhelmed?

For more ideas for teaching children, see this week's outline in *Come, Follow Me—For Primary*.

Suggested song: "Dearest Children, God Is Near You," *Hymns,* no. 96.

### Improving Our Teaching

**Encourage questions.** Questions from children are an indication that they are ready to learn. If you don't know the answers to their questions, look for answers with them. (See *Teaching in the Savior's Way,* 25–26.)

Illustration of Naaman being healed of leprosy, by Paul Mann

# "Jesus Will Say to All Israel, 'Come Home'"

In the desert of Sinai, Moses gathered the children of Israel at the foot of a mountain. There the Lord declared that He wanted to turn this group of recently liberated slaves into a mighty people. "Ye shall be unto me," He said, "a kingdom of priests, and an holy nation" (Exodus 19:6). He promised that they would flourish and prosper, even when surrounded by much larger and more powerful enemies (see Deuteronomy 28:1–14).

All this would happen not because the Israelites were numerous or strong or skillful. It would happen, the Lord explained, "if ye will obey my voice indeed, and keep my covenant" (Exodus 19:5). It was God's power, not their own, that would make them mighty.

Yet the Israelites didn't always obey His voice, and over time they stopped keeping His covenant. Many started worshipping other gods and adopting the practices of the cultures around them. They rejected the very thing that made them a nation, distinct from everyone else—their covenant relationship with the Lord. Without God's power protecting them (see 2 Kings 17:6–7), there was nothing to stop their enemies (see 2 Chronicles 36:12–20).

## The Scattering

Several times between about 735 and 720 BC, the Assyrians invaded the Northern Kingdom of Israel, home to ten of the twelve tribes, and carried thousands of the Israelites away captive into various parts of the Assyrian Empire (see 2 Kings 17:1–7).[1] These Israelites became known as "the lost tribes," in part because they were removed from their homeland and scattered among other nations. But they were also lost in a deeper sense:

over time they lost their sense of identity as God's covenant people.

Because the Southern Kingdom of Judah was, at times, more righteous than the Northern Kingdom, it lasted longer.[2] But eventually the people there also turned away from the Lord. The Assyrians attacked and conquered most of the Southern Kingdom; only Jerusalem was miraculously preserved (see 2 Kings 19; Isaiah 10:12–13). Later, between 597 and 580 BC, the Babylonians destroyed Jerusalem, including the temple, and carried away captive many of the city's inhabitants (see 2 Kings 24–25; 2 Chronicles 36; Jeremiah 39; 52). About 70 years later, a remnant of Judah was allowed to return to Jerusalem and rebuild the temple. Many, however, stayed in Babylon.[3]

As the generations passed, Israelites from all the tribes were "scattered . . . with a whirlwind among all the nations whom they knew not" (Zechariah 7:14; see also Amos 9:8–9). Some had been led away by the Lord to other lands (see 2 Nephi 1:1–5; Omni 1:15–16). Others had left Israel to escape capture (see 2 Kings 25:22–26; Jeremiah 42:13–19; 43:1–7) or for political or economic reasons.[4]

We call these events the scattering of Israel. And it's important to know about the scattering for several reasons. For one thing, it's a major topic of the Old Testament: Many Old Testament prophets were witnesses to the spiritual downward spiral that led to the scattering of Israel. They foresaw that scattering and warned about it, and some of them even lived through it.[5] That's helpful to remember when you read the books of Isaiah, Jeremiah, Amos, and many of the other books in the latter part of the Old Testament. With this context in mind, when you read their prophecies about Assyria and Babylon, idolatry and captivity, desolation and eventual restoration, you will know what they're talking about.

Understanding the scattering of Israel will help you understand the Book of Mormon better too, because the Book of Mormon is a record of a branch of scattered Israel (see 1 Nephi 15:12). This record begins with Lehi's family fleeing Jerusalem in about 600 BC, just before the Babylonians attacked. Lehi was one of those prophets who prophesied about the scattering of Israel.[6] And his family helped fulfill that prophecy, taking their branch of the house of Israel and planting it on the other side of the world, in the Americas.

*The Destruction of Jerusalem by Nebuzar-adan,* by William Brassey Hole, © Providence Collection/licensed from goodsalt.com

## The Gathering

The scattering of Israel, however, is only half of the story. The Lord doesn't forget His people, nor does He fully forsake them, even when they have forsaken Him. The many prophecies that Israel would be scattered were accompanied by many promises that God would one day gather them.[7]

That day is today—our day. The gathering has already begun. In 1836, thousands of years after Moses gathered the children of Israel at the foot of Mount Sinai, Moses appeared in the Kirtland Temple to commit to Joseph Smith "the keys of the gathering of Israel from the four parts of the earth" (Doctrine and Covenants 110:11). Now, under the direction of those who hold these keys, the tribes of Israel are being gathered from every nation where the Lord's servants are able to go.

President Russell M. Nelson has called this gathering "the most important thing taking place on earth today. Nothing else compares in magnitude, nothing else compares in importance, nothing else compares in majesty. And if you choose to, if you want to, you can be a big part of it."[8]

How do you do it? What does it mean to gather Israel? Does it mean restoring the twelve tribes back to the land they once inhabited? Actually, it means something much greater, much more eternal. As President Nelson explained:

"When we speak of the *gathering,* we are simply saying this fundamental truth: every one of our Heavenly Father's children, on both sides of the veil, deserves to hear the message of the restored gospel of Jesus Christ. . . .

"*Anytime* you do *anything* that helps *anyone*—on either side of the veil—take a step toward making covenants with God and receiving their essential baptismal and temple ordinances, you are helping to gather Israel. It is as simple as that."[9]

This happens, as Isaiah said, "one by one" (Isaiah 27:12) or, as Jeremiah predicted, "one of a city, and two of a family" (Jeremiah 3:14).

Gathering Israel means bringing God's children back to Him. It means restoring them to their covenant relationship with Him. It means reestablishing the "holy nation" He proposed to establish so long ago (Exodus 19:6).

## Come Home

As a covenant keeper, you are part of the house of Israel.[10] You have been gathered, and you are a gatherer. The centuries-long epic story that began with a covenant between God and Abraham is building to its climax, and you are a key player. Now is the time when "Jesus will say to all Israel, 'Come home.'"[11]

This is the message of the gatherers: Come home to the covenant. Come home to Zion. Come home to Jesus Christ, the Holy One of Israel, and He will bring you home to God, your Father.

---

**Notes**

1. The ten tribes that were taken captive by Assyria were Reuben, Simeon, Issachar, Zebulun, Dan, Naphtali, Gad, Asher, Ephraim, and Manasseh. Members of the tribe of Levi were spread throughout the other tribes' territories in order to perform their priestly responsibilities.

2. The Southern Kingdom consisted primarily of the tribes of Judah and Benjamin. However, members of several other tribes lived there too (see 2 Chronicles 11:14–17). For example, Lehi, who lived in Jerusalem, was of the tribe of Manasseh.

3. See Ezra 1; 7; Nehemiah 2. The Babylonian Empire had been conquered by the Persian Empire. It was the Persian king, Cyrus, who allowed several groups of exiled Jews to return to Jerusalem.

4. In AD 70, Jerusalem and its temple were again destroyed, this time by the Romans, and the remaining Jews were scattered throughout many nations of the earth.

5. See Jeremiah 29:18; Ezekiel 22:15; Hosea 9:17; Amos 9:9; 1 Nephi 1:13.

6. See 1 Nephi 1:13, 18–20; 10:12–14.

7. See Isaiah 5:26; 27:12; 54; Jeremiah 16:14–15; 29:14; 31:10; Ezekiel 11:17; 34:12; 37:21–28; Zechariah 10:8; 1 Nephi 10:14; 22:25; 3 Nephi 16:1–5; 17:4.

8. Russell M. Nelson and Wendy W. Nelson, "Hope of Israel" (worldwide youth devotional, June 3, 2018), supplement to the *New Era* and *Ensign,* 8, ChurchofJesusChrist.org.

9. Russell M. Nelson and Wendy W. Nelson, "Hope of Israel," 15, ChurchofJesusChrist.org.

10. See 2 Nephi 30:2.

11. "Now Let Us Rejoice," *Hymns,* no. 3.

# 2 Kings 17–25

"HE TRUSTED IN THE LORD GOD OF ISRAEL"

When Josiah heard the words from the book of the law, he responded in faith. How can you respond in faith to what you read in 2 Kings 17–25?

RECORD YOUR IMPRESSIONS

Despite the prophet Elisha's impressive ministry, the spirituality of the Northern Kingdom of Israel kept declining. Wicked kings promoted idolatry, and war and apostasy abounded. Finally the Assyrian Empire conquered and scattered the ten tribes of Israel.

Meanwhile, the Southern Kingdom of Judah wasn't doing much better; idolatry was also widespread there. But amid all this spiritual decay, the scriptural accounts mention two righteous kings who, for a time, turned their people back to the Lord. One was Hezekiah. During his reign, the Assyrians, fresh from their victory in the north, conquered much of the south. But Hezekiah and his people showed faith in the Lord, who delivered Jerusalem in a miraculous way. Later, after another period of apostasy, Josiah

began to reign. Inspired in part by a rediscovery of the book of the law, Josiah brought reforms that revived the religious life of many of his people.

What do we learn from these two bright spots in the otherwise dark years of Judah's history? Among other things, you might ponder the power of faith and of the word of God in your life. Like Israel and Judah, we all make both good and bad choices. And when we sense that reforms are needed in our lives, perhaps the examples of Hezekiah and Josiah can inspire us to "trust in the Lord our God" (2 Kings 18:22).

See also 2 Chronicles 29–35; the "Thoughts to Keep in Mind" section "Jesus Will Say to All Israel, 'Come Home.'"

# Ideas for Personal Scripture Study

### 2 KINGS 18–19

## I can stay true to the Lord during challenging times.

Most of us have experienced times that challenge our faith. For Hezekiah and his people, one of those times came when the Assyrian army invaded Judah, destroyed many cities, and approached Jerusalem. As you read 2 Kings 18–19, imagine that you lived in Jerusalem during this time. How might you have felt, for example, to hear the taunts of the Assyrians as recorded in 2 Kings 18:28–37 and 19:10–13? What do you learn from what Hezekiah did in response? (see 2 Kings 19:1–7, 14–19). How did the Lord sustain Hezekiah? (see 2 Kings 19:35–37). Ponder how He has sustained you in challenging times.

You might also ponder the description of Hezekiah in 2 Kings 18:5–7. What do these verses suggest about why Hezekiah was able to remain faithful when challenges came? How can you follow his example?

See also 3 Nephi 3–4; D. Todd Christofferson, "Firm and Steadfast in the Faith of Christ," *Ensign* or *Liahona,* Nov. 2018, 30–33.

### 2 KINGS 19:20–37

## All things are in the Lord's hands.

Sennacherib, the king of Assyria, had good reason to believe that his army would conquer Jerusalem. Assyria had defeated many nations, including Israel—why should Jerusalem be any different? (see 2 Kings 17; 18:33–34; 19:11–13). But the Lord had a message for Sennacherib, given through the prophet

Isaiah, and it's recorded in 2 Kings 19:20–34. How would you summarize this message? What truths do you find in these verses that help you have faith in the Lord and His plan?

See also Helaman 12:4–23; Doctrine and Covenants 101:16.

### 2 KINGS 21–23

## The scriptures can turn my heart to the Lord.

Have you ever felt that you were lacking something spiritually? Maybe you felt that your relationship with God could be a lot stronger. What helped you turn back to Him? Ponder these questions as you read about how the Kingdom of Judah fell away from the Lord under King Manasseh (see 2 Kings 21) and how King Josiah helped them recommit themselves to Him (see 2 Kings 22–23). What inspired Josiah and his people? This account might inspire you to renew your commitment to "walk after the Lord . . . with all [your] heart and all [your] soul" (2 Kings 23:3).

As you read these chapters, consider also studying chapter 6 in *Teachings of Presidents of the Church: Spencer W. Kimball* ([2006], 59–68), in which President Kimball suggested that the story of King Josiah "is one of the finest stories in all of the scriptures" (page 62). Why might President Kimball have felt that way? What do you find in President Kimball's words, especially his comments about King Josiah, that helps you apply 2 Kings 22–23 to your life?

See also Alma 31:5; Takashi Wada, "Feasting upon the Words of Christ," *Ensign* or *Liahona,* May 2019, 38–40; "Josiah and the Book of the Law" (video), ChurchofJesusChrist.org.

The scriptures can help turn our hearts to the Lord.

## Ideas for Family Scripture Study and Home Evening

**2 Kings 19:14–19.** What can we learn from Hezekiah's example that can help us when we have difficult problems or questions? How has the Lord answered our prayers for help? Perhaps each family member could make something to display in the home that reminds them to turn to the Lord.

**2 Kings 22:3–7.** The workers described in 2 Kings 22:3–7 were trusted with the money used to rebuild the temple "because they dealt faithfully" (verse 7). After reading these verses, you could ask family members to name things they have been entrusted with. How can we be trustworthy like the workers in these verses?

**2 Kings 22:8–11, 19; 23:1–3.** What impresses us about how Josiah and his people responded to the word of God? How do we respond to God's word in the scriptures? Members of your family could share scripture passages or stories that have increased their desire to follow Heavenly Father and Jesus Christ.

**2 Kings 23:25.** What stands out to us about the description of Josiah in this verse? Your family could draw on paper hearts things they can do this week to turn to the Lord with all their heart.

For more ideas for teaching children, see this week's outline in *Come, Follow Me—For Primary.*

Suggested song: "As I Search the Holy Scriptures," *Hymns,* no. 277.

### Improving Personal Study

**Look for inspiring words and phrases.** As you read, the Spirit may bring certain words or phrases to your attention. They may inspire and motivate you; they may even seem to be written just for you.

Illustration of a scribe bringing a scroll of scripture to King Josiah, by Robert T. Barrett

Illustration of the temple of Zerubbabel, by Sam Lawlor

JULY 18–24

# Ezra 1; 3–7; Nehemiah 2; 4–6; 8

"I AM DOING A GREAT WORK"

President Ezra Taft Benson taught, "The word of God . . . has the power to fortify the Saints and arm them with the Spirit so they can resist evil, hold fast to the good, and find joy in this life" (*Teachings of Presidents of the Church: Ezra Taft Benson* [2014], 118).

RECORD YOUR IMPRESSIONS

The Jewish people had been held captive in Babylonia for about 70 years. They had lost Jerusalem and the temple, and many had forgotten their commitment to God's law. But God had not forgotten them. In fact, He had declared through His prophet, "I will visit you, and perform my good word toward you, in causing you to return" (Jeremiah 29:10). True to this prophecy, the Lord did make a way for the Jews to return, and He raised up servants who accomplished "a great work" for His people (Nehemiah 6:3). These servants included a governor named Zerubbabel, who oversaw the rebuilding of the house of the Lord; Ezra, a priest

and scribe who turned the hearts of the people back to the Lord's law; and Nehemiah, a later governor of Judah who led the work of rebuilding the protective walls around Jerusalem. They met opposition, of course, but also received assistance from unexpected sources. Their experiences can inform and inspire ours, because we too are doing a great work. And like theirs, our work has much to do with the house of the Lord, the law of the Lord, and the spiritual protection we find in Him.

For an overview of the books of Ezra and Nehemiah, see "Ezra" and "Nehemiah" in the Bible Dictionary.

# Ideas for Personal Scripture Study

## EZRA 1

### The Lord inspires people to bring about His purposes.

After Persia conquered Babylonia, the Persian king, Cyrus, was inspired by the Lord to send a group of Jews to Jerusalem to rebuild the temple. As you read Ezra 1, note what Cyrus was willing to do to support the Jews in this important work. How do you see the Lord working through men and women around you, including those who are not members of His Church? What does this suggest to you about the Lord and His work?

See also Isaiah 44:24–28.

## EZRA 3:8–13; 6:16–22

### Temples can bring me joy.

When the Babylonians invaded Jerusalem, they plundered the temple and burned it to the ground (see 2 Kings 25:1–10; 2 Chronicles 36:17–19). How do you think you might have felt if you had been among the Jews who witnessed this? (see Psalm 137). Notice how the Jews felt, decades later, when they were allowed to return and rebuild the temple (see Ezra 3:8–13; 6:16–22). Ponder your own feelings about the temple. Why are temples a source of joy? How can you demonstrate your gratitude to the Lord for temples?

For modern examples of rejoicing at the building of temples, see the videos "Practice, Celebration, Dedication: Temple Blessings in El Salvador" and "The Laie Hawaii Temple Youth Cultural Celebration" (ChurchofJesusChrist.org).

The temple can be a source of joy in our lives.

## EZRA 4–6; NEHEMIAH 2; 4; 6

### I can help the work of God advance despite opposition.

The Lord's work rarely goes unopposed, and this was certainly true of the efforts led by Zerubbabel and Nehemiah. In both cases, the "adversaries of Judah" (Ezra 4:1) were Samaritans—descendants of Israelites who had mixed with the Gentiles. Reading about their opposition to building the temple (see Ezra 4–6) might lead you to ponder the opposition God's work faces today and how you might respond when opposition comes.

Similarly, reading about Nehemiah's work repairing Jerusalem's walls (see Nehemiah 2; 4; 6) might cause you to reflect on work that God wants you to do. What do you learn from Nehemiah's example?

See also Dieter F. Uchtdorf, "We Are Doing a Great Work and Cannot Come Down," *Ensign* or *Liahona*, May 2009, 59–62.

## EZRA 7; NEHEMIAH 8

### I am blessed when I study the scriptures.

Even after the temple was rebuilt, the people of Jerusalem struggled spiritually, in part because, for generations, they had limited access to "the book of the law of Moses" (Nehemiah 8:1). Ezra the scribe received permission from the king of Persia to go to Jerusalem, where he "brought the law before the congregation" (Nehemiah 8:2). How can you follow

Ezra's example as described in Ezra 7:10? As you read Nehemiah 8, which gives the account of Ezra reading the law to the people, what thoughts do you have about the power of the word of God in your life?

See also *Teachings: Ezra Taft Benson,* 115–24.

## Ideas for Family Scripture Study and Home Evening

**Ezra 3:8–13; 6:16–22.** How did the Jews show their joy for the temple as it was being rebuilt and then as it was dedicated? What are we doing to show our joy for the temple? Perhaps your family could look at pictures of temples and talk about how temples bring you joy (see temples.ChurchofJesusChrist.org).

**Ezra 7:6, 9–10, 27–28.** Several times in these verses, Ezra wrote that the hand of the Lord was upon him as he traveled to Jerusalem. What might this phrase mean? How have we felt the Lord's hand upon us? Perhaps family members could share examples from their lives.

**Nehemiah 2; 4; 6.** The story of Nehemiah can inspire family members when they face opposition as they do "a great work" (Nehemiah 6:3). Family members could build a wall from objects you have around your home as you read together key passages (such as Nehemiah 2:17–20; 4:13–18; 6:1–3). What do we learn from Nehemiah about facing opposition? What great work does the Lord want us to do? How has the Lord strengthened us to overcome opposition to this work?

**Nehemiah 8:1–12.** In Nehemiah 8, Ezra read the law of Moses to a people who were eager to hear God's word. Reading verses 1–12 could help deepen your family's appreciation for the word of God. How did the people feel about God's law? How can we help each other "understand the reading"? (verse 8).

For more ideas for teaching children, see this week's outline in *Come, Follow Me—For Primary.*

Suggested song: "I Love to See the Temple," *Children's Songbook,* 95.

### Improving Our Teaching

**Share scriptures as a family.** During your family scripture study, allow family members to share passages from their personal study that are particularly meaningful to them.

Illustration of Ezra reading scriptures to the people at Jerusalem, by H. Willard Ortlip, © Providence Collection/licensed from goodsalt.com

*Esther*, by James Johnson

# Esther

"THOU ART COME . . . FOR SUCH A TIME AS THIS"

As you read Esther, seek inspiration from the Spirit that is tailored to you, and record impressions you receive.

RECORD YOUR IMPRESSIONS

Many events in the book of Esther might seem like luck or coincidence. How else do you explain how an orphaned Jewish girl became the queen of Persia at just the right time to save her people from being slaughtered? What are the chances that Esther's cousin Mordecai would just happen to overhear a plot to assassinate the king? Were these coincidences, or were they part of a divine plan? Elder Ronald A. Rasband noted: "What may appear to be a random chance is, in fact, overseen by a loving Father in Heaven. . . . The Lord is in the small details of our lives" ("By Divine Design," *Ensign* or *Liahona,* Nov. 2017, 56). We may not always recognize the Lord's influence in these "small details." But we learn from Esther's experience that He can guide our path and prepare us "for such a time" (Esther 4:14) when we can be instruments in His hands to fulfill His purposes.

For an overview of the book of Esther, see "Esther, book of" in the Bible Dictionary.

# Ideas for Personal Scripture Study

## ESTHER

### The Lord can make me an instrument to bless others.

Sister Anne C. Pingree taught: "To become an instrument in the hands of God is a great privilege and sacred responsibility. Wherever we live, whatever our circumstances, no matter our marital status or age, the Lord needs *each one* of us to fulfill [our] unique part in building His kingdom in this final dispensation" ("Knowing the Lord's Will for You," *Ensign* or *Liahona,* Nov. 2005, 112).

As you read the story of Esther, ponder how this statement applies to her. Look for ways the Lord made it possible for her to save the Jews (see, for example, Esther 2:21–23; 3:10–14; 4:14–16). Then ponder how He has guided your life in ways that allow you to bless others. What are some circumstances or relationships that you feel He has guided you to "for such a time as this"? (Esther 4:14). If you have a patriarchal blessing, consider reading it to learn more about the work the Lord has for you to do.

### ESTHER 3; 5:9–14; 7

### Pride and anger can lead to downfall.

In the book of Esther, we learn from the faithfulness of Esther and Mordecai as well as from the pride and anger of Haman. As you read Esther 3; 5:9–14, consider noting Haman's feelings, words, and actions. What do they reveal about him and his motivations? What consequences did he face? (see Esther 7). Reading about Haman may prompt you to evaluate what motivates your feelings and actions. Are you inspired to make any changes? How can you turn to Heavenly Father for help?

See also Proverbs 16:32; Alma 5:28.

### ESTHER 3–4; 5:2–3; 8:11–12

### Fasting demonstrates my dependence on the Lord.

Notice the conditions that led Esther and the rest of the Jews to fast (see Esther 3:13; 4:1–3, 10–17). How was fasting a blessing to them? (see Esther 5:2–3; 8:11–12). Why does the Lord ask us to fast? (see Gospel Topics, "Fasting and Fast Offerings," topics.ChurchofJesusChrist.org). Consider what you can do to make fasting a greater blessing in your life.

See also Isaiah 58:6–12; Matthew 4:1–4; 17:14–21; "Fasting: Young Single Adult Ward, Amanda" (video), ChurchofJesusChrist.org.

### ESTHER 3:1–11; 4:10–17; 5:1–4

### Doing the right thing often requires great courage.

When Mordecai and Esther stood up for their beliefs, they put their lives at stake. Our choices have consequences that might be less severe, but doing the right thing can still require courage. What do you learn from Esther 3:1–4; 4:10–17 about having courage to do the right thing? Note the different consequences Mordecai and Esther experienced after showing courage (see Esther 3:5–11; 5:1–4). What would a person need to know about God in order to make the choices Esther and Mordecai made—to do what's right regardless of the consequences?

The next time you consider the consequences of doing what is right, you might apply Esther's courageous words in Esther 4:16 to your own situation. For instance, you might say to yourself, "When I choose the right, if I [lose friends], I [lose friends]."

See also Thomas S. Monson, "May You Have Courage," *Ensign* or *Liahona,* May 2009, 123–27.

*Esther before the King,* by Minerva K. Teichert

# Ideas for Family Scripture Study and Home Evening

**Esther 1–10.** After reviewing the story of Esther (see "Queen Esther," in *Old Testament Stories,* or the video "For Such a Time as This," ChurchofJesusChrist.org), your family might enjoy making simple puppets of some of the characters (see this week's activity page in *Come, Follow Me—For Primary*). They could then use them to retell the story. You could also sing a song about being brave and true, such as "Dare to Do Right" (*Children's Songbook,* 158) or "Do What Is Right" (*Hymns,* no. 237). What words in the song remind us of Esther?

**Esther 2:5–7.** What can we learn from Mordecai's example about helping family members in times of trial? Who in our family needs our support? Make a plan to help them.

**Esther 4:15–17.** Esther's bravery could inspire your family to discuss how to develop courage to stand for the truth in situations they face. What did Esther mean by "If I perish, I perish"? How do her words apply to us when we need to be brave? The video "Courage" (ChurchofJesusChrist.org) gives some examples.

**Esther 9:26–32.** The Jewish feast of Purim was established to remember the story of Esther. At mealtime this week, consider sharing stories of when your family members, including ancestors, blessed others by standing for the right as Esther did.

For more ideas for teaching children, see this week's outline in *Come, Follow Me—For Primary.*

Suggested song: "Dare to Do Right," *Children's Songbook,* 158.

## Improving Our Teaching

**Emulate the Savior's life.** "The Savior's power to teach and lift others came from the way He lived and the kind of person He was. The more diligently you strive to *live* like Jesus Christ, the more you will be able to *teach* like Him" (*Teaching in the Savior's Way,* 13).

*Queen Esther,* by Minerva K. Teichert, © William and Betty Stokes

# Reading Poetry in the Old Testament

In the Old Testament books that come before the book of Job, we find mostly stories—narrative accounts that describe historical events from a spiritual perspective. Noah built an ark, Moses delivered Israel, Hannah prayed to have a son, and so on. Beginning with Job, we find a different writing style, as Old Testament writers turned to poetic language to express deep feelings or monumental prophecies in a memorable way.

We have already seen a few examples of poetry sprinkled throughout the historical books of the Old Testament. And from the book of Job forward, we will see a lot more of it. The books of Job, Psalms, and Proverbs are almost entirely poetry, as are parts of the writings of prophets like Isaiah, Jeremiah, and Amos. Because reading poetry is different from reading a story, understanding it often requires a different approach. Here are some thoughts that could make your reading of Old Testament poetry more meaningful.

## Getting to Know Hebrew Poetry

First, it may help you to keep in mind that Hebrew poetry in the Old Testament isn't based on rhyme, like some other kinds of poetry. And although rhythm, wordplay, and repetition of sounds are common features of ancient Hebrew poetry, they are typically lost in translation. One feature you will notice, however, is the repetition of thoughts or ideas, sometimes called "parallelism." This verse from Isaiah contains a simple example:

> Put on thy strength, O Zion;

> put on thy beautiful garments, O Jerusalem (Isaiah 52:1).

The 29th Psalm has many parallel lines—here is one example:

> The voice of the Lord is powerful;

> the voice of the Lord is full of majesty (Psalm 29:4).

And here's an instance in which knowing that the second line is parallel to the first actually makes the passage easier to understand:

> I also have given you cleanness of teeth in all your cities,

> and want of bread in all your places (Amos 4:6).

In these examples, an idea is repeated with slight differences. This technique can emphasize the repeated idea while using the differences to more fully describe or develop it.

In other cases, the two parallel phrases use similar language to convey contrasting ideas, as in this example:

> A soft answer turneth away wrath:

> but grievous words stir up anger (Proverbs 15:1).

This parallelism didn't happen by accident. The writers did it intentionally. It allowed them to express spiritual feelings or truths in a way that seemed to them both powerful and beautiful. So when you notice parallelism in Old Testament writing, ask yourself how it helps you understand the writer's message. For example, what might Isaiah have been trying to say by relating "strength" with "beautiful garments" and "Zion" with "Jerusalem"? (Isaiah 52:1). What can we infer about the phrase "a soft answer" if we know that "grievous words" is its opposite? (Proverbs 15:1).

*He Restoreth My Soul,* by Walter Rane

## Hebrew Poetry as a New Friend

It may be helpful for you to compare reading poetry to meeting a new person. For example, you might compare reading Old Testament poetry to meeting someone from a distant country and foreign culture who doesn't speak the same language we do—and who happens to be over two thousand years old. This person will probably say things we don't understand at first, but that doesn't mean he or she has nothing valuable to tell us. With some patience and some compassion, our new acquaintance can eventually become a dear friend. We just need to spend some time together, trying to see things from his or her point of view. We may even find that in our hearts we actually understand each other quite well.

So the first time you read a passage from Isaiah, for example, consider it your first introduction to a new acquaintance. Ask yourself, "What's my general impression?" How does the passage make you feel—even if you don't understand every word? Then read it again, several times if possible. Some people find added meaning by reading the passages out loud. Notice specific words Isaiah chose, especially words that paint a picture in your mind. How do those pictures make you feel? What does the imagery suggest about how Isaiah felt? The more you study the

words of these Old Testament poets, the more you will find that they deliberately chose their words and techniques to express a deep spiritual message.

Poems can be wonderful friends because they help us understand our feelings and experiences. Old Testament poems are especially precious, because they help us understand our most important feelings and experiences—those that have to do with our relationship with God.

As you study the poetry in the Old Testament, remember that scripture study is most valuable when it leads us to Jesus Christ. Look for symbols, imagery, and truths that build your faith in Him. Listen for promptings from the Holy Ghost as you study.

### Wisdom Literature

One category of Old Testament poetry is what scholars call "wisdom literature." Job, Proverbs, and Ecclesiastes fall into this category. While psalms express feelings of praise, mourning, and worship, wisdom literature focuses on timeless advice or deep, philosophical questions. The book of Job, for example, explores the justice of God and the reasons behind human suffering. Proverbs offers counsel on how to live well, including wise sayings collected and passed down from earlier generations. And Ecclesiastes calls into question the purpose of life itself—when everything seems fleeting and random, where do we find true meaning? You might think of wisdom literature as thoughtful conversations with inspired mentors who want to share some observations about God and the world He created—and maybe help you understand these things a little better than you did before.

*The Judgments of Job,* by Joseph Brickey

AUGUST 1–7

# Job 1–3; 12–14; 19; 21–24; 38–40; 42

"YET WILL I TRUST IN HIM"

As you read about Job, the Spirit will guide you to discover important truths relevant to you. Write down what you discover, and ponder how these truths apply to you.

RECORD YOUR IMPRESSIONS _____

It's natural to wonder why bad things happen to good people—or for that matter, why good things happen to bad people. Why would God, who is just, allow that? Questions like these are explored through the experience of Job, one of those good people to whom bad things happened. Because of Job's trials, his friends wondered if he was really good after all. Job asserted his own righteousness and wondered if God is really just after all. But despite his suffering and wondering, Job maintained his integrity and faith in Jesus Christ. In the book of

Job, faith is questioned and tested but never completely abandoned. That doesn't mean that all of the questions are answered. But the book of Job teaches that until they are answered, questions and faith can coexist, and regardless of what happens in the meantime, we can say of our Lord, "Yet will I trust in Him" (Job 13:15).

For an overview of the book of Job, see "Job" in Guide to the Scriptures (scriptures.ChurchofJesusChrist.org).

# Ideas for Personal Scripture Study

### JOB 1–3; 12–13

## My trust in Heavenly Father and Jesus Christ can help me remain faithful in all circumstances.

The opening chapters of Job are intended to emphasize Satan's role as our adversary or accuser, not to describe how God and Satan really interact. As you read Satan's claims about Job (see Job 1:9–11; 2:4–5), you might ponder if the same could be said about you. You might ask yourself, What are my reasons for remaining faithful to God? Ponder the trials Job was given and his responses (see Job 1:20–22; 2:9–10). What do you learn from him that might help you respond to your challenges?

Even though Job was trying to stay faithful, his trials and his suffering continued (note his laments in chapter 3). In fact, his suffering seemed to intensify, and his friends suggested that God was punishing him (see Job 4–5; 8; 11). As you read part of Job's response in chapters 12–13, consider what Job knew about God that enabled him to continue trusting, despite his suffering and unanswered questions. What do you know about God that helps you face challenges? How have you come to know these truths, and how have they strengthened your faith?

### JOB 19

## Jesus Christ is my Redeemer.

Sometimes the most important truths are revealed to us in the midst of our deepest anguish. Ponder the trials Job described in Job 19:1–22 and the truths he proclaimed in Job 19:23–27. Then ponder how you know that your Redeemer lives. What difference does this knowledge make when you experience difficult trials?

See also Doctrine and Covenants 121:1–12; 122.

*Job,* by Gary L. Kapp

### JOB 21–24

## "When he hath tried me, I shall come forth as gold."

As you read more of the debate between Job and his friends about the reasons behind Job's suffering, you might ponder how you would answer the question at the heart of their debate: Why do the righteous sometimes suffer and the wicked sometimes go unpunished? Think about this as you read Job 21–24. What do you know about Heavenly Father and His plan that can help provide answers? See, for example, 2 Nephi 2:11–13; Mosiah 23:21–23; 24:10–16; Abraham 3:22–26; Dallin H. Oaks, "Opposition in All Things," *Ensign* or *Liahona,* May 2016, 114–17.

See also L. Todd Budge, "Consistent and Resilient Trust," *Ensign* or *Liahona,* Nov. 2019, 47–49.

### JOB 38; 40; 42

## God's perspective is greater than mine.

Frustrated with the accusations of his friends (see Job 16:1–5; 19:1–3), Job repeatedly cried to God seeking an explanation for his suffering (see Job 19:6–7; 23:1–9; 31). Elder Neal A. Maxwell observed that "when we are unduly impatient with an omniscient God's timing," as Job seemed to be, "we really are suggesting that we know what is best. Strange, isn't it—we who wear wristwatches seek to counsel Him who oversees cosmic clocks and calendars" ("Hope through the Atonement of Jesus Christ," *Ensign,* Nov. 1998, 63). Ponder these words as you read God's response to Job in chapters 38 and 40. What truths was He teaching Job? Why are these truths important for us to know as we struggle with adversity and questions here in mortality? What impresses you about Job's response in Job 42:1–6?

## Ideas for Family Scripture Study and Home Evening

**Job 1:20–22.** To understand how Job might have felt, as described in these verses, your family could read "Job" in *Old Testament Stories* or act out Job 1:13–22. What can we learn from Job's example?

**Job 14:14.** How would we answer Job's question in this verse? How could Alma 11:42–44 help us? (See also the video "He Lives—Celebrate Easter Because Jesus Christ Lives," ChurchofJesusChrist.org.)

**Job 16:1–5.** Are we ever like Job's friends, who judged and criticized Job when he needed comfort? (see Job 16:1–4; see also John 7:24). How can our words strengthen others in their grief? (see Job 16:5).

**Job 19:23–27.** After reading these verses, family members could share how they know that our Redeemer lives. You might work together to put your words of testimony (or children's drawings of the Savior) in a book, such as a family journal (see verse 23). You could also sing a song that testifies of the Savior, such as "I Know That My Redeemer Lives" (*Hymns,* no. 136), and share phrases that strengthen your faith in Him.

**Job 23:8–11.** What does it mean to "come forth" from our trials "as gold"? (see also the video "The Refiner's Fire," ChurchofJesusChrist.org). Who do we know who has done this? Children might enjoy making something with the words from verse 10 written on it. You might also discuss how Jesus Christ overcame His trials (see Luke 22:41–44; Doctrine and Covenants 19:16–19).

For more ideas for teaching children, see this week's outline in *Come, Follow Me—For Primary.*

Suggested song: "My Redeemer Lives," *Hymns,* no. 135.

### Improving Personal Study

**Imagine.** Meaningful insights can come as we try to put ourselves into the scriptures. For instance, putting yourself in Job's situation could help you ponder your relationship with Heavenly Father and Jesus Christ.

*Job and His Friends,* by Ilya Repin

*The Lord Is My Shepherd*, by Yongsung Kim, havenlight.com

# Psalms 1–2; 8; 19–33; 40; 46

"THE LORD IS MY SHEPHERD"

Don't feel limited to the selection of Psalms or the principles suggested in this outline. Let the Spirit guide you to truths that help you feel closer to the Lord.

RECORD YOUR IMPRESSIONS

We don't know for certain who wrote the Psalms. Some have been attributed to King David, but for most of them, the writers remain anonymous. Yet after reading the Psalms, we may feel as if we know the hearts of the Psalmists, even if we don't know their names. What we do know is that the Psalms were an important part of worship among the Israelites, and we know that the Savior quoted them often. In the Psalms, we get a window into the soul of God's ancient people. We see how they felt about God, what they worried about, and how they found peace. As believers today, all over the world, we still use these words in our worship of God. The writers of the Psalms seem to have had a window into *our* souls and seem to have found a way to express how we feel about God, what we worry about, and how we find peace.

For an overview of the book of Psalms, see "Psalms" in the Bible Dictionary.

## Ideas for Personal Scripture Study

### PSALMS 1; 23; 26–28; 46
### The Psalms teach us to trust the Lord.

You might notice as you read the Psalms how often the writers express fear, sorrow, or anxiety. Such feelings are normal, even for people of faith. But what makes the Psalms inspiring is the solutions they offer, including complete trust in the Lord. Consider these inspiring messages as you read Psalms 1; 23; 26–28; 46. Watch for the following, and write down what you discover:

- Invitations to trust the Lord: _____ _____

- Words that describe the Lord: _____ _____

- Words that describe the peace, strength, and other blessings He provides: _____ _____

- Words that describe those who trust Him: _____ _____

### PSALMS 2; 22
### The Psalms point our minds to the life and ministry of Jesus Christ.

Several of the Psalms point to the mortal life of Jesus Christ. Christians in New Testament times saw these connections too—for example, they recognized in Psalm 2 a reference to Jesus's trials before King Herod and Pontius Pilate (see Acts 4:24–30). Consider reading Psalms 2 and 22 along with Matthew 27:35–46; Luke 23:34–35; and John 19:23–24. Look for connections between the words in these psalms and the life of the Savior, and keep looking for similar connections as you study the book of Psalms throughout the next few weeks.

Imagine that you were a Jew in Jesus's time who was familiar with the Psalms and saw connections to the Savior's life. How might this knowledge have been a blessing to you?

See also Psalms 31:5; 34:20; 41:9; Luke 24:44; Hebrews 2:9–12.

### PSALMS 8; 19; 33
### "The earth is full of the goodness of the Lord."

Reading Psalms 8; 19; and 33 may inspire you to consider the Lord's many wonderful creations. Pay attention to your thoughts and feelings as you do. How do the Lord's creations "declare the glory of God" to you? (Psalm 19:1).

### PSALMS 19:7–11; 29
### The word of the Lord is powerful, "rejoicing the heart."

In the Psalms, words like *testimony, statutes, commandment,* and *judgments* can refer to the word of the Lord. Keep that in mind as you read Psalm 19:7–11. What do these verses suggest to you about the word of the Lord? What does Psalm 29 teach you about His voice? In your experience, how has the word or voice of the Lord matched these descriptions?

### PSALMS 24; 26–27
### Entering the Lord's presence requires purity.

Because the temple at Jerusalem was built on a hill, the phrase "hill of the Lord" (Psalm 24:3) may refer to the temple or to the presence of God. What does this add to your understanding of Psalm 24? What does it mean to you to have "clean hands, and a pure heart"? (Psalm 24:4).

What do Psalms 26 and 27 teach you about the house of the Lord?

See also Psalm 15; David A. Bednar, "Clean Hands and a Pure Heart," *Ensign* or *Liahona,* Nov. 2007, 80–83.

We must be spiritually clean and pure to enter the Lord's presence.

# Ideas for Family Scripture Study and Home Evening

**Psalm 22.** While one family member reads this psalm, others could look for similarities in Matthew 27:35–46. Then they could share their feelings about Jesus Christ and His sacrifice for us.

**Psalm 23.** Psalm 23 was the inspiration for several hymns, such as "The Lord Is My Shepherd" and "The Lord My Pasture Will Prepare" (*Hymns,* nos. 108, 109). Perhaps your family would like to sing one of these hymns and identify words in the psalm that might have inspired the lyrics. Or they might enjoy drawing pictures of something they find in the psalm or the hymn and letting family members guess the verses or lyrics that go with the pictures. How is the Lord like a shepherd to us?

**Psalm 24:3–5.** To emphasize the importance of having clean hands and a pure heart, you could read Psalm 24:3–5 while family members wash their hands. What might hands represent in this psalm? What could the heart symbolize? What can we do to spiritually cleanse our hands and purify our hearts?

**Psalm 30:5, 11.** Psalm 30:5 contains the promise that "weeping may endure for a night, but joy cometh in the morning." How has the Lord turned our sadness into joy? Some family members might enjoy acting out what verse 11 describes.

**Psalm 33.** Note how many times the word *all* is used in this psalm. What do we learn about the Lord from the repeated use of this word, especially in verses 13–15?

**Psalm 46:10.** You might do something together that requires family members to "be still." How can being still help us come to know God? What opportunities do we have to be still and come to know God?

For more ideas for teaching children, see this week's outline in *Come, Follow Me—For Primary.*

Suggested song: "The Lord Is My Shepherd," *Hymns,* no. 108.

## Improving Personal Study

**Be creative.** Scriptures like the Psalms often inspire people to praise the Lord in creative ways. If you feel moved to express your devotion through music, poetry, visual art, or some other way, act on those feelings. Consider sharing what you create to help others build faith in Heavenly Father and Jesus Christ.

*The Good Shepherd,* by Ken Spencer

*Saving That Which Was Lost, by Michael T. Malm*

# Psalms 49–51; 61–66; 69–72; 77–78; 85–86

"I WILL DECLARE WHAT HE HATH DONE FOR MY SOUL"

This outline identifies some of the doctrinal topics addressed in these psalms. As you study, certain words, images, or ideas may stand out to you. What do you feel the Lord is trying to teach you?

RECORD YOUR IMPRESSIONS

The writers of the Psalms shared deeply personal feelings in their poetry. They wrote about feeling discouraged, afraid, and remorseful. At times, they even seemed to feel abandoned by God, and some psalms carry a tone of frustration or desperation. If you've ever had feelings like these, reading the Psalms can help you know that you aren't the only one. But you'll also find psalms that can encourage you when you're having such feelings, because the psalmists also praised the Lord for His goodness, marveled at His power, and rejoiced in His mercy. They knew that the world is burdened by evil and sin but that the Lord is "good, and ready to forgive" (Psalm 86:5). They understood that having faith in the Lord doesn't mean that you'll never struggle with anxiety, sin, or fear. It means that you know Who to turn to when you do.

# Ideas for Personal Scripture Study

## PSALMS 49; 62:5–12

### Redemption comes only through Jesus Christ.

Psalm 49 has a message for "both low and high, rich and poor" (verse 2). What would you say this message is? What do you feel Psalm 62:5–12 adds to that message?

Reading these psalms may prompt you to ponder the ways that some people put their trust in something other than God for redemption (see Psalm 49:6–7). How is your life influenced by your testimony that "God will redeem [your] soul from the power of the grave"? (verse 15).

See also Proverbs 28:6; Alma 34:8–17.

## PSALMS 51; 85–86

### Because of the Savior's mercy, I can be forgiven of my sins.

The pleas for mercy in Psalm 51 are attributed to King David, who was guilty of adultery and murder (see 2 Samuel 11). Even when our sins are less serious, we can relate to the need for mercy expressed in this psalm. We can also learn something about what it means to repent. For example, what words or phrases in Psalm 51 teach you about the attitude we need in order to repent? What do you learn about the effect the Savior's Atonement can have in your life?

You might ask the same questions as you read Psalms 85–86. You could also look for phrases that describe the Lord. How do these phrases strengthen your faith that He will forgive you? (see, for example, Psalm 86:5, 13, 15).

See also Alma 36; Russell M. Nelson, "We Can Do Better and Be Better," *Ensign* or *Liahona,* May 2019,

67–69; Carole M. Stephens, "The Master Healer," *Ensign* or *Liahona,* Nov. 2016, 9–12.

## PSALMS 51:13–15; 66:16–17; 71:15–24

### My testimony of Jesus Christ can help others come unto Him.

Ponder how you gained your testimony of Jesus Christ and His atoning power. Then, as you study Psalms 51:13–15; 66:16–17; 71:15–24, think about how you can invite others to "come and see the works of God" (Psalm 66:5). What does it mean to you to "talk of [His] righteousness all the day long"? (Psalm 71:24). How will you tell others "what he hath done for [your] soul"? (Psalm 66:16).

See also Mosiah 28:1–4; Alma 26.

We can share with others our testimonies of what the Lord has done for us.

## PSALMS 63; 69; 77–78

### The Lord will help me in my time of urgent need.

Several psalms describe, in vivid language, what it's like to feel distant from God and to desperately need His help. You might consider looking for such descriptions in Psalms 63:1, 8; 69:1–8, 18–21; 77:1–9. What do you find in Psalms 63; 69; 77–78 that gave these psalmists reassurance?

When you are distressed, how does it help you to "remember the works of the Lord" and His "wonders of old"? (Psalm 77:11). Some of those wonders are described in Psalm 78. As you read about them, ponder what helps you "set [your] hope in God" (verse 7). What experiences from your family history inspire you?

# Ideas for Family Scripture Study and Home Evening

**Psalm 51:17.** Consider how you might teach your family what it means to have a broken heart. For example, family members could take turns breaking open something that has a hard shell, like an egg or a nut. How are our hearts sometimes like that shell? How can we open our hearts to the Lord? Reading Psalm 51 together might provide some ideas.

**Psalm 61:2–3.** Family members might enjoy drawing pictures of the symbols in these verses and discussing how Jesus Christ is like a high "rock," "a shelter for [us]," and "a strong tower."

**Psalms 71:17; 78:5–7.** What does the Lord want you to "make . . . known to [your] children"? (Psalm 78:5). Perhaps each family member could share an example of the Lord's "wondrous works," such as a scripture story, an experience, or a personal testimony, that helps them "set their hope in God" (Psalms 71:17; 78:7).

**Psalm 72.** Psalm 72 was written by David about his son Solomon, but much of it can also apply to Jesus Christ. As your family reads this psalm, they could hold up a picture of the Savior when they find verses that remind them of Jesus Christ. How can we help fulfill the desire that "the whole earth be filled with his glory"? (Psalm 72:19; see also Doctrine and Covenants 65:2).

**Psalm 85:11.** This verse could inspire a discussion about events of the Restoration of the gospel—how the Book of Mormon is truth that "[sprang] out of the earth" and how heavenly messengers came "down from heaven" (see also Moses 7:62). The video "Preparation of Joseph Smith: Tutored by Heaven" (ChurchofJesusChrist.org) depicts some of these events.

For more ideas for teaching children, see this week's outline in *Come, Follow Me—For Primary.*

Suggested song: "I Need Thee Every Hour," *Hymns,* no. 98.

## Improving Our Teaching

**Use variety.** "Look for ways you can add variety to your efforts to teach the gospel. Doing so will add richness and beauty to the experience. . . . Consider how using music, stories, pictures, and other forms of art can invite the Spirit" (*Teaching in the Savior's Way,* 22).

*Doubt Not, Thomas,* by J. Kirk Richards

*Every Knee Shall Bow, by J. Kirk Richards*

# Psalms 102–103; 110; 116–119; 127–128; 135–139; 146–150

"LET EVERY THING THAT HATH BREATH PRAISE THE LORD"

Psalm 119:105 teaches that the word of God is "a light unto [your] path." As you read Psalms, record phrases and ideas that inspire you and help illuminate your path back to Heavenly Father.

RECORD YOUR IMPRESSIONS_____

_____

_____

The traditional Jewish name for the book of Psalms is a Hebrew word that means "praises." That word, *Tehillim,* is also related to the exclamation "halle-lujah" (meaning "praise Jehovah" or "praise the Lord"). If you had to choose one word to sum up the main message of the Psalms, "praise" would be a good choice. Some of the Psalms contain the direct invitation to "praise ye the Lord" (see especially Psalms 146–50), and all of them can inspire a feeling of worship and praise. The Psalms invite us to reflect on the Lord's power, on His mercy, and on the great things He has done. We can never repay Him for any of this, but we can praise Him for it. That praise may take different forms for different people—it may involve singing, praying, or bearing testimony. It often leads to a deeper commitment to the Lord and to following His teachings. Whatever "praise ye the Lord" means in your life, you can find more inspiration to do it as you read and ponder the Psalms.

# Ideas for Personal Scripture Study

## PSALMS 102–3; 116

### The Lord can comfort me in my suffering.

Note how Psalm 102:1–11 describes feelings of anxiety and isolation that often come during afflictions. Maybe you've experienced such feelings, and these descriptions help you understand your experiences better. Or these verses might help you understand the feelings of others who are suffering.

As you read Psalms 102:12–28; 103; 116, look for phrases that give you confidence that you can "call upon the name of the Lord" in your trials (Psalm 116:13). You may want to mark, memorize, or share with others the phrases that give you hope in Him.

See also Isaiah 25:8; 2 Corinthians 1:3–7; Hebrews 2:17–18; Alma 7:11–13; Evan A. Schmutz, "God Shall Wipe Away All Tears," *Ensign* or *Liahona,* Nov. 2016, 116–18.

*Healing,* by J. Kirk Richards

## PSALMS 110; 118

### The Psalms can point me to the Savior.

The Psalms contain passages that point toward the life and ministry of Jesus Christ. Here are a few examples:

- Psalm 110:1–4 (see Matthew 22:41–45; Hebrews 5:4–10; 6:20)
- Psalm 118:22 (see Matthew 21:42; Acts 4:10–11; 1 Peter 2:7)
- Psalm 118:25–26 (see Matthew 21:9)

What truths do these verses teach you about Jesus Christ? How does knowing these truths bless you?

As you read the Psalms this week, continue to make note of other passages that teach you about the Savior. You might also read or listen to some of your favorite hymns that help you think about Him.

## PSALM 119

### God's word will keep me on His path.

This psalm contains many phrases that compare our lives to a journey back to Heavenly Father. As you read, look for words like *walk, path, way, feet,* and *wander.* Ponder your own life's journey—where you've been, where you are now, and what direction you are headed. What do you learn from this psalm about your journey back home? According to this psalm, what has God provided to help you stay on the right path?

You might be interested to know that in the original Hebrew, the first eight verses in Psalm 119 begin with the first letter in the Hebrew alphabet. The next eight verses begin with the next letter, and so on through the end of the alphabet.

See also Isaiah 42:16; 2 Nephi 31:17–21; Alma 7:19–20.

## PSALMS 134–36

### The Lord is more powerful than any idol.

Notice the reasons given in Psalm 135:15–18 about why it is foolish to trust in false gods. What might you be tempted to trust in that is similar to the idols described in these verses?

155

You might make a list of the powerful things the Lord can do, as described in Psalms 134–36. What powerful things has He done for you?

### PSALMS 146–50

## "Praise ye the Lord."

As you read these final psalms of praise, think about reasons you have to praise the Lord. Why is it important to praise Him? What are ways you can praise Him?

# Ideas for Family Scripture Study and Home Evening

**Psalm 119:105.** Perhaps your family could create a path and walk along it in the dark, using a light to illuminate the way ahead. As you walk, you could ask questions like "What in our lives is like this darkness?" or "How is the word of God like a light?" Singing a song about God's light, such as "Teach Me to Walk in the Light" (*Children's Songbook,* 177), can help you reinforce the principle taught in Psalm 119:105.

**Psalms 127–28.** What does it mean for the Lord to help us "build [our] house"? (Psalm 127:1). How can we better involve Him in our efforts to create a righteous home? To help your family answer this question, you might draw a house on a piece of

paper and cut it into puzzle pieces. On the back of each piece, family members could write or draw ways to make the Lord part of your home. Then you could put the puzzle together. What else do we find in these psalms that inspires us to walk in the Lord's ways?

**Psalm 139.** After reading verses 1–4, family members could talk about how they have come to know that God knows them personally (see also verses 14–15, 23–24).

**Psalms 146–50.** You might invite your family to read a few verses of Psalms 146–50 out loud, trying to convey the feelings of the writer. How can we express our praise to the Lord? Family members might enjoy writing their own psalms of praise and sharing them with each other.

For more ideas for teaching children, see this week's outline in *Come, Follow Me—For Primary.*

Suggested song: "Teach Me to Walk in the Light," *Children's Songbook,* 177.

## Improving Our Teaching

**Use audio recordings.** As you teach your family, consider listening to the audio version of the scriptures, found on ChurchofJesusChrist.org or in the Gospel Library app. Listening to psalms can be particularly powerful because they were meant to be recited aloud.

"Make me to go in the path of thy commandments; for therein do I delight" (Psalm 119:35).

# Proverbs 1–4; 15–16; 22; 31; Ecclesiastes 1–3; 11–12

"THE FEAR OF THE LORD IS THE BEGINNING OF WISDOM"

Consider how your study of Proverbs and Ecclesiastes can help you "incline thine ear unto wisdom, and apply thine heart to understanding" (Proverbs 2:2).

RECORD YOUR IMPRESSIONS

In the first chapter of the book of Proverbs, we find these words: "My son, hear the instruction of thy father, and forsake not the law of thy mother" (Proverbs 1:8). Proverbs can be seen as a collection of wise sayings from a loving parent, whose main message is that blessings of peace and prosperity come to those who seek wisdom—particularly the kind of wisdom God offers. But Proverbs is followed by the book of Ecclesiastes, which seems to say, "It's not that simple." The Preacher quoted in Ecclesiastes observed that he "gave [his] heart to know wisdom" but still found "vexation of spirit" and "much grief" (Ecclesiastes 1:17–18). In a variety of ways, the book asks, "Can there be real meaning in a world where everything seems vain, temporary, and uncertain?"

And yet, while the two books look at life from different perspectives, they teach similar truths. Ecclesiastes declares: "Let us hear the conclusion of the whole matter: Fear God, and keep his commandments: for this is the whole duty of man" (Ecclesiastes 12:13). This is the same principle found throughout Proverbs: "Trust in the Lord with all thine heart. . . . Be not wise in thine own eyes: fear the Lord" (Proverbs 3:5, 7). No matter what life holds, even when it seems confusing and random, it is always better when we trust in the Lord Jesus Christ.

For an overview of these books, see "Proverbs, book of" and "Ecclesiastes" in the Bible Dictionary.

## Ideas for Personal Scripture Study

### PROVERBS 1–4; 15–16

### "Incline thine ear unto wisdom."

The book of Proverbs is filled with insights about wisdom. Consider marking the word "wisdom" and related words, like "knowledge" and "understanding," as you find them in chapters 1–4 and 15–16. How do these chapters affect the way you think about wisdom? Based on what you find, how would you describe the wisdom that "the Lord giveth"? (Proverbs 2:6). Consider how you are seeking the Lord's help to be "wise in heart" (Proverbs 16:21). What blessings come from God's wisdom?

See also Proverbs 8–9; Matthew 7:24–27; 25:1–13.

### PROVERBS 1:7; 2:5; 16:6; 31:30; ECCLESIASTES 12:13

### What is the "fear of the Lord"?

Elder David A. Bednar explained: "Unlike worldly fear that creates alarm and anxiety, godly fear is a source of peace, assurance, and confidence. . . . [It] encompasses a deep feeling of reverence, respect, and awe for the Lord Jesus Christ; obedience to His commandments; and anticipation of the Final Judgment and justice at His hand. . . . Godly fear is loving and trusting in Him" ("Therefore They Hushed Their Fears," *Ensign* or *Liahona,* May 2015, 48–49).

See also Proverbs 8:13.

### PROVERBS 4

### "Ponder the path of thy feet."

Proverbs 4 describes wisdom and righteousness as a "path" or a "way" (see also Proverbs 3:5–6). As you read this chapter, you might find passages that help you ponder "the path of thy feet" (verse 26) and how your steps are drawing you closer to the Lord. For example, what do verses 11–12 and 18–19 teach about the blessings of following the right path? What do verses 26 and 27 mean to you?

See also 2 Nephi 31:18–21.

### PROVERBS 15:1–2, 4, 18, 28; 16:24–32

### "A soft answer turneth away wrath."

Some of the proverbs in chapters 15 and 16 may inspire you to improve the way you communicate with others, especially loved ones. For example, think about specific times when you could have used "a soft answer" rather than "grievous words" (Proverbs 15:1). How does the counsel in Proverbs 16:24–32 help you think about the words you use?

Consider this insight from Elder W. Craig Zwick: "A 'soft answer' consists of a reasoned response—disciplined words from a humble heart. It does not mean we never speak directly or that we compromise doctrinal truth. Words that may be firm in information can be soft in spirit" ("What Are You Thinking?" *Ensign* or *Liahona,* May 2014, 42).

*Who Can Find a Virtuous Woman? II,* by Louise Parker

### PROVERBS 31:10–31

### "A woman that feareth the Lord, she shall be praised."

Proverbs 31:10–31 describes "a virtuous woman," or a woman of great spiritual strength, capability, and influence. You might try summarizing in your own words what each of these verses says about her. What are some of her traits that you can emulate?

ECCLESIASTES 1–3; 12

### Mortal life is temporary.

Why is it valuable for you to remember that much in this world, as Ecclesiastes 1–2 asserts, is "vanity" (or temporary and often unimportant)? What do you find in chapter 12 that gives life eternal value?

## Ideas for Family Scripture Study and Home Evening

**Proverbs.** Your family might enjoy creating your own "book of Proverbs"—a collection of wise counsel from the scriptures and latter-day prophets.

**Proverbs 1:7; 2:5; 16:6; Ecclesiastes 12:13–14.** To help family members understand Proverbs 1:7; 2:5; 16:6; Ecclesiastes 12:13, it might help to substitute the word *fear* with words like *reverence, love,* or *obedience* (see also Hebrews 12:28). How does this affect the way we think about these verses? How do we show that we fear the Lord?

**Proverbs 3:5–7.** To help family members visualize what these verses teach, you could invite them to lean against something sturdy and stable, like a wall. Then they could try leaning against something that is not sturdy, like a broom. Why should we "lean not unto [our] own understanding"? How can we show that we trust Jesus Christ with all our hearts?

**Proverbs 15:1–2, 18; 16:24, 32.** How do our words affect the spirit in our home? Perhaps family members could practice giving "a soft answer" to "grievous words" and try to use what they learn in their interactions with each other. A song like "Kindness Begins with Me" (*Children's Songbook,* 145) could help reinforce this principle.

For more ideas for teaching children, see this week's outline in *Come, Follow Me—For Primary.*

Suggested song: "Where Love Is," *Children's Songbook,* 138–39.

---

### Improving Personal Study

**Words of the scriptures apply to all.** Some scripture passages refer only to men or only to women (such as Proverbs 3:13; 31:10). In most cases, however, the principles in these passages apply to everyone.

"In all thy ways acknowledge him, and he shall direct thy paths" (Proverbs 3:6). *He Leadeth Me,* by Yongsung Kim, havenlight.com

# Prophets and Prophecy

In the traditional Christian division of the Old Testament, the last section (Isaiah through Malachi) is called "the Prophets."[1] This section, about one-fourth of the Old Testament, contains the words of God's authorized servants, who spoke with the Lord and then spoke *for* Him, sharing His message with the people between about 900 and 500 BC.[2]

Prophets and prophecy play a major role throughout the Old Testament. The patriarchs Abraham, Isaac, and Jacob saw visions and spoke with heavenly messengers. Moses talked to God face to face and communicated His will to the children of Israel. The books of First and Second Kings recount the memorable works and messages of the prophets Elijah and Elisha. The Old Testament also speaks of prophetesses like Miriam (see Exodus 15:20) and Deborah (see Judges 4), along with other women blessed with the spirit of prophecy, such as Rebekah (see Genesis 25:21–23) and Hannah (see 1 Samuel 1:20–2:10). And even though the Psalms weren't written by formal prophets, they too are filled with the spirit of prophecy, especially as they look forward to the coming of the Messiah.

None of this comes as a surprise to Latter-day Saints. In fact, the restored gospel of Jesus Christ teaches us that prophets are not just an interesting piece of history but an essential part of God's plan. While some might see prophets as unique to Old Testament times, we see them as something we have in *common* with Old Testament times.

Still, reading a chapter from Isaiah or Ezekiel might feel different from reading a general conference message from the current President of the Church. Sometimes it can be hard to see that ancient prophets had something to say to us. After all, the world we live in today is much different from the one where they preached and prophesied. And the fact that we *do* have a living prophet could raise a question: why is it worth the effort—and it does take effort—to read the words of ancient prophets?

## They Do Have Something to Say to Us

For the most part, people today aren't the primary audience of the Old Testament prophets. Those prophets had immediate concerns they were addressing in their time and place—just as our latter-day prophets address our immediate concerns today.

At the same time, prophets can also look beyond immediate concerns. For one thing, they teach eternal truths, relevant to any age. And, blessed with revelation, they see the bigger picture, the wider perspective of God's work. For example, Isaiah could not only warn people of his day about their sins—he could also write about deliverance for Israelites living 200 years in the future and simultaneously teach of the deliverance that all God's people seek. In addition, he could write prophecies that, even today, are still awaiting their complete fulfillment—like promises of "a new earth" (Isaiah 65:17) that is "full of the knowledge of the Lord" (Isaiah 11:9), where the lost tribes of Israel have been gathered and where "the nations" do not "learn war any more" (Isaiah 2:4). Part of the joy and inspiration that comes from reading the words of Old Testament prophets like Isaiah is realizing that *we* play a role in the glorious day they envisioned.[3]

So when you read ancient prophecies, it's helpful to learn about the context in which they were written. But you should also see yourself in them, or "liken them unto [yourself],'" as Nephi put it (see 1 Nephi 19:23–24). Sometimes that means recognizing Babylon as a symbol of worldliness and pride, not just as an ancient city. It could mean understanding Israel as God's people in any era and understanding Zion as the latter-day cause God's people embrace, instead of as just another word for Jerusalem.

We can liken the scriptures because we understand that a prophecy can be fulfilled in multiple ways.[4] A good example of this is the prophecy in Isaiah 40:3: "The voice of him that crieth in the wilderness, Prepare ye the way of the Lord." To the captive Jews in Babylon, this statement might have referred to the Lord providing a way out of captivity and back into Jerusalem. To Matthew, Mark, and Luke, this prophecy was fulfilled in John the Baptist, who prepared the way for the Savior's mortal ministry.[5] And Joseph Smith received revelation that this prophecy is still being fulfilled in the latter days in preparation for Christ's millennial ministry.[6] In ways we're still coming to understand, ancient prophets *did* speak to us. And they taught many precious, eternal truths that are just as relevant to us as they were to ancient Israel.

*Fulness of Times*, by Greg K. Olsen

## They Testified of Jesus Christ

Perhaps even more important than seeing yourself in Old Testament prophecies is seeing Jesus Christ in

them. If you look for Him, you will find Him, even if He's not mentioned by name. It might help to keep in mind that the God of the Old Testament, the Lord Jehovah, *is* Jesus Christ. Anytime the prophets describe what the Lord is doing or what He will do, they are speaking of the Savior.

You will also find references to an Anointed One (see Isaiah 61:1), a Redeemer (see Hosea 13:14), and a future King from David's line (see Isaiah 9:6–7; Zechariah 9:9). These are all prophecies about Jesus Christ. More generally, you will read about deliverance, forgiveness, redemption, and restoration. With the Savior in your mind and heart, these prophecies will naturally point you to the Son of God. After all, the best way to understand prophecy is to have "the spirit of prophecy," which John tells us is "the testimony of Jesus" (Revelation 19:10).

**Notes**

1. Isaiah, Jeremiah, Ezekiel, and Daniel are often referred to as the Major Prophets because of the length of their books. The other prophets (Hosea, Joel, Amos, Obadiah, Jonah, Micah, Nahum, Habakkuk, Zephaniah, Haggai, Zechariah, and Malachi) are called the Minor Prophets because their books are much shorter. The book of Lamentations is considered part of the Writings, not the Prophets.

2. We don't know how the prophetic books were compiled. In some cases, a prophet may have overseen the collection of his writings and prophecies. In other cases, they may have been recorded and compiled after his death.

3. "Just think of the excitement and urgency of it all: every prophet commencing with Adam has seen our day. And every prophet has talked about *our* day, when Israel would be gathered and the world would be prepared for the Second Coming of the Savior. Think of it! Of all the people who have ever lived on planet earth, *we* are the ones who get to participate in this final, great gathering event. How exciting is that!" (Russell M. Nelson, "Hope of Israel" [worldwide youth devotional, June 3, 2018], supplement to the *New Era* and *Ensign*, 8, ChurchofJesusChrist.org). See also Ronald A. Rasband, "Fulfillment of Prophecy," *Ensign* or *Liahona*, May 2020, 75–78.

4. The Savior, speaking of Isaiah, said, "All things that he spake *have been* and *shall be*, even according to the words which he spake" (3 Nephi 23:3; italics added).

5. See Matthew 3:1–3; Mark 1:2–4; Luke 3:2–6.

6. See Doctrine and Covenants 33:10; 65:3; 88:66.

# Isaiah 1–12

"GOD IS MY SALVATION"

Seek spiritual guidance as you study. The words of Isaiah are best understood when we are "filled with the spirit of prophecy," as Nephi taught (2 Nephi 25:4).

RECORD YOUR IMPRESSIONS

Even if this is your first time reading the book of Isaiah, you might find passages that sound familiar. That's because, of all Old Testament prophets, Isaiah is the one most often quoted in other books of scripture, including by the Savior Himself. Isaiah's words also appear often in hymns and other sacred music. Why is Isaiah quoted so often?

Surely part of the reason is that Isaiah had a gift for expressing the word of God in vivid, memorable language. But it's more than that. Isaiah has inspired prophets for generations because the truths he taught transcended his own generation—the Israelites living between 740 and 701 BC. His role was to open our eyes to God's great work of

redemption, which is much bigger than one nation or one time period. From Isaiah, Nephi learned that he and his people, though separated from the rest of Israel, were still part of God's covenant people. In Isaiah, New Testament writers found prophecies about the Messiah that were being fulfilled right before their eyes. And in Isaiah, Joseph Smith found inspiration for the latter-day work of gathering Israel and building Zion. When you read Isaiah, what will you find?

For more about Isaiah and his writings, see "Isaiah" in the Bible Dictionary. For information about the time when Isaiah lived, see 2 Kings 15–20 and 2 Chronicles 26–32.

# Ideas for Personal Scripture Study

### ISAIAH 1–12

## How can I better understand the teachings of Isaiah?

Speaking of Isaiah's writings, the Savior said, "Search these things diligently; for great are the words of Isaiah" (see 3 Nephi 23:1–3). Yet to many, Isaiah can be difficult to understand. Here are some tips to help you find greater meaning in the words of Isaiah:

- Ponder the symbols and metaphors Isaiah used. For example, ponder what you think Isaiah wanted to communicate when he wrote about a vineyard (see Isaiah 5:1–7), the waters of Shiloh (see Isaiah 8:5–10), an ensign (see Isaiah 5:26), and a flag (see Isaiah 11:10, 12).

- For every chapter you read, ask yourself, "What am I learning about Jesus Christ?" (see 1 Nephi 19:23).

- Look for topics that feel relevant to our day, such as the life and mission of Jesus Christ, the scattering and gathering of Israel, the last days, and the Millennium. You could also keep lists of references from Isaiah that teach about these topics.

- Use study helps where available, such as a dictionary, the Bible footnotes, the chapter headings, and the Guide to the Scriptures.

See also 2 Nephi 25:1–8.

### ISAIAH 1; 3; 5

## "Cease to do evil."

Isaiah continually warned the Kingdom of Judah about their spiritual condition. After reading Isaiah 1, 3, and 5, how would you describe the spiritual condition of the people? What warnings do you find that feel applicable to our day?

In addition to the warnings, you might also make note of messages of hope for sinful Israel (see, for example, Isaiah 1:16–20, 25–27; 3:10). What do you learn about the Lord from these messages?

### ISAIAH 2; 4; 11–12

## God will do a great work in the latter days.

Many of Isaiah's writings are prophecies that have specific meaning for our day. Which of Isaiah's descriptions of the latter days in chapters 2; 4; 11–12 are especially inspiring to you? (Doctrine and Covenants 113:1–6 provides helpful insights about Isaiah 11.) What do you learn about the gathering of Israel and redemption of Zion? What do you feel inspired to do after reading these chapters?

See also Isaiah 5:26; 10:20.

### ISAIAH 6

## Prophets are called of God.

In chapter 6, Isaiah recounted his call to be a prophet. As you read this chapter, what impresses you about what Isaiah experienced? How does this chapter influence the way you think about the Lord, His prophets, and the work they are called to do?

"For unto us a child is born, unto us a son is given" (Isaiah 9:6).

ISAIAH 7–9

## Isaiah prophesied of Jesus Christ.

Early in Isaiah's ministry, the Kingdom of Israel (also called Ephraim) formed an alliance with Syria to defend itself against Assyria. Israel and Syria wanted to force Ahaz, the king of Judah, to join their alliance. But Isaiah prophesied that the alliance would fail and counseled Ahaz to trust in the Lord (see Isaiah 7–9, especially Isaiah 7:7–9; 8:12–13).

As Isaiah counseled Ahaz, he made several well-known prophecies, such as those found in Isaiah 7:14; 8:13–14; 9:2, 6–7. While it's not completely clear what these prophecies meant in Ahaz's time, they clearly apply to Jesus Christ (see also Matthew 1:21–23; 4:16; 21:44; Luke 1:31–33). What do you learn about the Savior from these verses?

# Ideas for Family Scripture Study and Home Evening

**Isaiah 1:16–18.** To help family members understand these verses, you could read the section "Some of Us Feel We Can Never Be Good Enough" from Sister Sharon Eubank's message "Christ: The Light That Shines in Darkness" (*Ensign* or *Liahona,* May 2019, 75). Or you could demonstrate how stains can be removed from clothing. How is the Lord's message in these verses different from what Satan wants us to believe?

**Isaiah 2:1–5.** Family members could pick one of these verses and draw what it describes. What does the temple teach us about the Lord's ways? How are we blessed as we "walk in the light of the Lord"? (Isaiah 2:5).

**Isaiah 4:5–6.** What does the Lord promise us in these verses? What might these promises mean? How is He fulfilling them? (See also Exodus 13:21–22.)

**Isaiah 7:14; 9:1–7.** Using drawings or pictures from Church magazines, you could make a poster illustrating some of the things we learn about Jesus Christ from these verses.

For more ideas for teaching children, see this week's outline in *Come, Follow Me—For Primary.*

Suggested song: "High on the Mountain Top," *Hymns,* no. 5.

---

### Improving Personal Study

**Ask the Lord for help.** To understand the scriptures, we need personal revelation. The Lord has promised, "Ask, and it shall be given you; seek, and ye shall find; knock, and it shall be opened unto you" (Matthew 7:7).

Isaiah taught that the tabernacle would be "a place of refuge" and "a covert from storm and from rain" (Isaiah 4:6). Idaho Falls Idaho Temple

SEPTEMBER 12–18

# Isaiah 13–14; 24–30; 35

"A MARVELLOUS WORK AND A WONDER"

President Bonnie H. Cordon taught, "Scriptures enlighten our minds, nourish our spirits, answer our questions, increase our trust in the Lord, and help us center our lives on Him" ("Trust in the Lord and Lean Not," *Ensign* or *Liahona,* May 2017, 7).

RECORD YOUR IMPRESSIONS

One of the things the Lord asks prophets to do is to warn about the consequences of sin. In the case of Old Testament prophets, this often meant telling the powerful rulers of mighty kingdoms that they must repent or be destroyed. It was a dangerous task, but Isaiah was fearless, and his warnings to the kingdoms of his day—including Israel, Judah, and surrounding nations—were bold (see Isaiah 13–23).

However, Isaiah also had a message of hope. Even though the prophesied destructions eventually did come upon these kingdoms, Isaiah foresaw a chance for restoration and renewal. The Lord would invite His people to return to Him. He would make "the parched ground . . . become a pool, and the thirsty land springs of water" (Isaiah 35:7). He would perform "a marvellous work and a wonder" (Isaiah 29:14), restoring to Israel the blessings He had promised them. Neither Isaiah nor anyone else alive at that time lived to see this marvelous work. But we are seeing its ultimate fulfillment today. In fact, we are part of it!

## Ideas for Personal Scripture Study

### ISAIAH 13:1–11, 19–22; 14:1–20

### The wicked kingdoms of the world and their rulers will fall.

Isaiah 13–14 is called "the burden of" (a prophetic message about) Babylon (Isaiah 13:1). Once a mighty kingdom with a powerful ruler, Babylon is now considered ancient history. So why is the message to Babylon important to us today? In the scriptures, Babylon symbolizes pride, worldliness, and sin, and today we are surrounded by all of these. Think about this symbolism as you read Isaiah 13:1–11, 19–22; 14:1–20. You might also consider questions like these:

- How are Isaiah's warnings to Babylon similar to prophecies about the world prior to the Savior's Second Coming? (see Isaiah 13:1–11; Doctrine and Covenants 45:26–42).

- What similarities do you see between the pride of the Babylonian king and the pride of Satan? (see Isaiah 14:4–20; Moses 4:1–4). What warnings do you find for yourself in these verses?

- How does the Savior provide "rest from thy sorrow, and from thy fear"? (Isaiah 14:3).

*He Comes Again to Rule and Reign,* by Mary R. Sauer

### ISAIAH 24:21–23; 25:6–8; 26:19; 28:16

### The writings of Isaiah point me to Jesus Christ.

The teachings of Isaiah often refer to the Savior's mission, including His atoning sacrifice, Resurrection, and Second Coming. What aspects of His mission come to mind as you read the following verses: Isaiah 24:21–23; 25:6–8; 26:19; 28:16? What other passages do you find that remind you of the Savior?

See also Isaiah 22:22–25.

### ISAIAH 24:1–12; 28:7–8; 29:7–10; 30:8–14

### Apostasy means turning away from the Lord and His prophets.

To warn about the consequences of turning away from the Lord and rejecting His prophets, Isaiah used a variety of metaphors. These include an empty earth (Isaiah 24:1–12), drunkenness (Isaiah 28:7–8), hunger and thirst (Isaiah 29:7–10), and a broken wall or vessel (Isaiah 30:8–14). Based on what you read in these verses, why is it important to keep our covenants? Consider what you are doing to stay true to the Lord and His servants.

See also M. Russell Ballard, "Stay in the Boat and Hold On!" *Ensign* or *Liahona,* Nov. 2014, 89–92; Gospel Topics, "Apostasy," topics .ChurchofJesusChrist.org.

### ISAIAH 29; 30:18–26; 35

### The Lord can restore things that are lost or broken.

When people or societies turn away from the Lord, Satan wants us to think that the consequences are irreversible. However, Isaiah described some of the marvelous things the Lord will do when people repent and turn to Him. What do you learn from Isaiah 29:13–24; 30:18–26; 35 about the Lord, His love, and His power?

One way the Lord has manifested His power in our day is through the Restoration of His gospel. Isaiah 29 contains several passages that have parallels to events of that Restoration. For example:

- Compare Isaiah 29:11–12 with 2 Nephi 27:6–26 and Joseph Smith—History 1:63–65.

- Compare Isaiah 29:13–14 with Doctrine and Covenants 4 and Joseph Smith—History 1:17–19.

- Compare Isaiah 29:18–24 with the title page of the Book of Mormon.

What thoughts or impressions do you have about the Restoration of the gospel as you read these passages?

See also "The Restoration of the Fulness of the Gospel of Jesus Christ: A Bicentennial Proclamation to the World" (ChurchofJesusChrist.org).

## Ideas for Family Scripture Study and Home Evening

**Isaiah 25:4–9.** Has your family ever experienced the blessing of a safe shelter during a storm or of shade on a hot summer day? (see verse 4). Talk about this as you read these verses and other descriptions of the Lord found in Isaiah 25:4–9. How is the Lord like these things?

**Isaiah 25:8–9; 26:19.** Showing pictures of the Savior in Gethsemane, on the cross, and after His Resurrection can help your family see connections between these verses and Jesus Christ (see *Gospel Art Book,* nos. 56, 57, 58, 59). Invite your family to share why they "rejoice in his salvation" (Isaiah 25:9).

**Isaiah 29:11–18.** These verses can help your family discuss the "marvellous work and a wonder" (verse 14) of the Restoration of the gospel and coming forth of the Book of Mormon. Why are these things marvelous and wonderful to us? Invite family members to find objects in your home that represent the marvelous blessings of the Restoration.

**Isaiah 35.** Your family might enjoy drawing pictures of the images in this chapter that help us understand how Jesus Christ is building up Zion in our day. What do we learn from these images? What can we do to help build up Zion?

For more ideas for teaching children, see this week's outline in *Come, Follow Me—For Primary.*

Suggested song: "On a Golden Springtime," *Children's Songbook,* 88.

### Improving Our Teaching

**Let children express their creativity.** When children create something related to a gospel principle, it helps them better understand the principle. Allow them to build, draw, color, write, and create. (See *Teaching in the Savior's Way,* 25.)

"Lo, this is our God; we have waited for him, and he will save us" (Isaiah 25:9). James Tissot (French, 1836–1902). *Woman, Behold Thy Son (Stabat Mater),* 1886–1894. Opaque watercolor over graphite on gray wove paper, Image: 11 11/16 x 6 in. (29.7 x 15.2 cm). Brooklyn Museum, Purchased by public subscription, 00.159.300

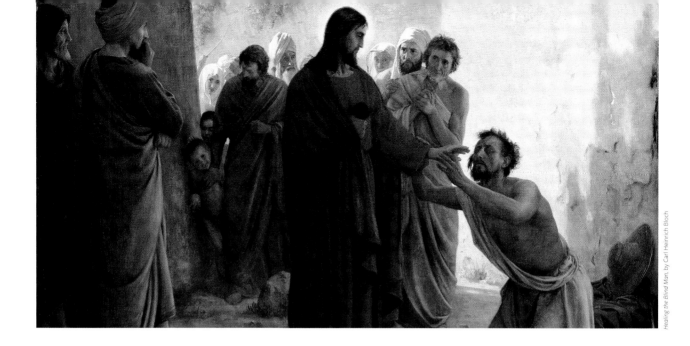

# Isaiah 40–49

"COMFORT YE MY PEOPLE"

Isaiah often used symbolic language. Pay attention to the thoughts and feelings these symbols bring to your mind and heart. This may help you better understand what he taught.

RECORD YOUR IMPRESSIONS

"Comfort" is the first word of Isaiah chapter 40. It marks the beginning of a different tone, a different emphasis in the prophet's message. Where Isaiah's earlier writings warned Israel and Judah about destruction and captivity that would come because of their sins, these later prophecies were meant to comfort the Jews over 150 years in the future—after Jerusalem was destroyed, the temple was desecrated, and the people were taken captive by Babylon. But these prophecies reach even further into the future than to the defeated, disheartened Israelites. They speak to us, who also sometimes feel defeated, disheartened, and even lost.

Isaiah's message to them and to us is simple: "Fear not" (Isaiah 43:1). All is not lost. The Lord has not forgotten you, and He has power over situations that seem out of your control. Isn't the Lord "he that created the heavens, and . . . he that spread forth the earth, and . . . he that giveth breath unto the people upon it"? (Isaiah 42:5). Isn't He more powerful than Babylon, than sin, than whatever is holding you captive? "Return unto me," He pleads, "for I have redeemed thee" (Isaiah 44:22). He can heal, restore, strengthen, forgive, and comfort—whatever is needed for you, in your case, to be redeemed.

To learn how Nephi and Jacob likened Isaiah 48–49 to their people, see 1 Nephi 22 and 2 Nephi 6.

## Ideas for Personal Scripture Study

### ISAIAH 40–49

### Jesus Christ can comfort me and give me hope.

It must have been discouraging, even devastating, for the Israelites to find themselves captive in Babylon. Many may have wondered if they had forever lost their place as God's chosen, covenant people. As you read Isaiah 40–49, look for passages that might have provided comfort and hope. For each passage you find, ponder and record what the Lord might be saying to *you* in these verses. Here are a few verses you might start with:

40:11, 29–31: _____

41:10–13, 17–18: _____

42:6–7: _____

43:1–7, 25: _____

44:1–4, 21–24: _____

46:3–4: _____

49:7–16: _____

How could you share these messages with someone who needs encouragement or hope? (see Isaiah 40:1–2).

See also Jeffrey R. Holland, "A Perfect Brightness of Hope," *Ensign* or *Liahona,* May 2020, 81–84.

### ISAIAH 40:3–8, 15–23; 42:15–16; 47:7–11

### God's power is greater than worldly power.

Isaiah repeatedly reminded his people of God's matchless power, even compared to the oppressive worldly power that surrounded them. Look for this message as you read Isaiah 40:3–8, 15–23; 42:15–16; and 47:7–11 (note that chapter 47 is addressed to Israel's captor, Babylon). What do these passages teach you about worldly things? What do they teach you about God? Ponder why this message might have been valuable to the Jews in captivity. Why is it valuable to you?

See also "Abide with Me!" *Hymns,* no. 166.

### ISAIAH 41:8–13; 42:1–7; 43:9–12; 44:21–28; 45:1–4; 48:10; 49:1–9

### "Thou art my servant."

Throughout Isaiah 40–49 the Lord speaks of His "servant" and His "witnesses." In some passages these words seem to refer to Jesus Christ (see Isaiah 42:1–7), others refer to the house of Israel (see Isaiah 45:4), and yet others refer to King Cyrus, who allowed the Jews to return to Jerusalem and rebuild the temple (see 44:26–45:4). In each case, though, you might also consider how the passages apply to you as a servant and a witness of the Lord. For example, ponder questions like these:

*Isaiah 41:8–13; 42:6; 44:21.* What has the Lord called you to do? Consider formal Church callings as well as other covenant responsibilities to serve Him. How does He support you and "hold [your] hand" (Isaiah 42:6) as you serve? How has He "formed" you to become His servant? (see also Isaiah 48:10).

*Isaiah 43:9–12.* In what sense are you a witness of Jesus Christ? What experiences in your life have shown you that He is the Savior?

*Isaiah 49:1–9.* What messages do you find in these verses that can help when your efforts and service seem to be "for nought, and in vain"? (verse 4).

See also Mosiah 18:9; Henry B. Eyring, "A Child and a Disciple," *Ensign* or *Liahona,* May 2003, 29–32.

## Ideas for Family Scripture Study and Home Evening

**Isaiah 40:3–4.** To explore what it might mean to "prepare . . . the way of the Lord," your family could straighten something that's crooked, clear a cluttered floor, or make a clear path in rocky ground. You could also show pictures of John the Baptist and Joseph Smith (see *Gospel Art Book,* nos. 35, 87). How did they prepare the way for the Lord's coming? (see Luke 3:2–18; Doctrine and Covenants 135:3). How do we help prepare the way for Him? (for example, see Doctrine and Covenants 33:10).

**Isaiah 40:28; 43:14–15; 44:6.** What names or titles of Jesus Christ do we find in these verses? What does each name teach us about Him?

**Isaiah 41:10; 43:2–5; 46:4.** These verses are reflected in the hymn "How Firm a Foundation" (*Hymns,* no. 85). Your family might enjoy singing the hymn together and finding phrases in it that are similar to phrases in these verses. What do these phrases teach us about Jesus Christ?

**Isaiah 44:3–4; 45:8.** After reading these verses, your family could water a plant as you talk about blessings the Lord has poured out on them. What happens to a plant when we water it? What does the Lord expect from us as He blesses us?

**Isaiah 48:17–18.** Consider showing pictures or videos of rivers and ocean waves. How can peace be like a river? How can righteousness be like waves?

By obeying the Lord, we can have "peace . . . as a river" (Isaiah 48:18).

For more ideas for teaching children, see this week's outline in *Come, Follow Me—For Primary.*

Suggested song: "How Firm a Foundation," *Hymns,* no. 85.

### Improving Personal Study

**Define words.** Try looking up definitions of words in the scriptures you don't understand—and even words you think you do understand. Sometimes definitions can help you read a verse differently and gain new spiritual insights.

"The Lord hath comforted his people, and will have mercy upon his afflicted" (Isaiah 49:13). *Balm of Gilead,* by Ann Adele Henrie

*The Mocking of Christ*, by Carl Heinrich Bloch

# Isaiah 50–57

"HE HATH BORNE OUR GRIEFS, AND CARRIED OUR SORROWS"

Ponder the insights from Isaiah 50–57 that help you draw closer to the Savior. Record the impressions you receive.

RECORD YOUR IMPRESSIONS _____

_____

_____

Throughout his ministry, Isaiah spoke of a mighty deliverer (see, for example, Isaiah 9:3–7). These prophecies would have been especially precious to the Israelites centuries later when they were in captivity in Babylon. Someone who could topple the walls of Babylon would be a mighty conqueror indeed. But that isn't the kind of Messiah that Isaiah described in chapters 52–53: "He is despised and rejected of men; a man of sorrows, and acquainted with grief: and we hid as it were our faces from him. . . . We did esteem him stricken, smitten of God, and afflicted" (Isaiah 53:3–4). By sending such an unexpected deliverer,

God taught us about true deliverance. To save us from oppression and affliction, God sent One who Himself "was oppressed, and . . . afflicted." Where some expected a lion, He sent a lamb (see Isaiah 53:7). Surely, God's ways are not our ways (see Isaiah 55:8–9). Jesus Christ frees us not by just opening the prison but by taking our place there. He relieves us from our chains of grief and sorrow by bearing them Himself (see Isaiah 53:4–5, 12). He does not save us from a distance. He suffers with us, in an act of "everlasting kindness" that "shall not depart from thee" (Isaiah 54:8, 10).

# Ideas for Personal Scripture Study

### ISAIAH 50-52

## The future is bright for the Lord's people.

Even though the Israelites spent many years in captivity—and even though that captivity was a result of their own poor choices—the Lord wanted them to look to the future with hope. What hopeful messages do you find in Isaiah 50–52? What does the Lord teach us about Himself in these chapters, and why does this give you hope? (see, for example, Isaiah 50:2, 5–9; 51:3–8, 15–16; 52:3, 9–10).

You might also list everything in chapters 51–52 that the Lord invites Israel to do to make this hopeful future a reality. What do you feel the Lord is inviting you to do through these words? For example, what do you think it means to "awake" and "put on strength"? (Isaiah 51:9; see also Isaiah 52:1; Doctrine and Covenants 113:7–10). Why do you think the invitation to "hearken" (or "listen with the intent to obey") is repeated so often? (Russell M. Nelson, "Hear Him," *Ensign* or *Liahona,* May 2020, 89).

See also Mosiah 12:20–24; 15:13–18; 3 Nephi 20:29–46.

### ISAIAH 53

## Jesus Christ took upon Himself my sins and sorrows.

Few chapters in scripture describe Jesus Christ's redemptive mission more beautifully than Isaiah 53. Take the time to ponder these words. With each verse, pause to contemplate what the Savior suffered—the "griefs," "sorrows," and "transgressions" He bore—for all people and specifically for you. You might replace words like "we" and "our" with "I" and "my" as you read. What feelings or thoughts do these verses inspire in you? Consider writing them down.

You may want to review Mosiah 14; 15:1–13 to see how the prophet Abinadi used Isaiah's words to teach about the Savior.

*Because of Love,* by sculptor Angela Johnson

### ISAIAH 54; 57:15-19

## Jesus Christ wants me to return to Him.

We all have times when we feel distant from the Lord because of our sins or weaknesses. Some have even given up hope that He will ever forgive them. Isaiah 54 and 57 are great chapters to read for reassurance and encouragement during such times. Particularly in Isaiah 54:4–10; 57:15–19, what do you learn about the Savior's mercy and His feelings about you? What difference does it make in your life to know these things about Him?

How do the blessings described in Isaiah 54:11–17 apply to you?

### ISAIAH 55-56

## The Lord invites all to "take hold of my covenant."

For generations, Israel had been identified as God's covenant people. However, God's plan has always included more than just one nation, for "every one that thirsteth" is invited to "come . . . to the waters" (Isaiah 55:1). Keep this in mind as you read Isaiah 55 and 56, and ponder what it means to be God's people. What is God's message to those who feel "utterly separated" from Him? (Isaiah 56:3). Consider marking verses that describe attitudes and actions of those who "take hold of my covenant" (see Isaiah 56:4–7).

## Ideas for Family Scripture Study and Home Evening

**Isaiah 51–52.** As you discuss the Lord's invitations in these chapters, you could invite family members to act them out. For instance, what does it look like to "lift up your eyes to the heavens," "awake, stand up," or "shake thyself from the dust"? (Isaiah 51:6, 17; 52:2). What do these phrases teach us about following Jesus Christ?

**Isaiah 52:9.** After reading this verse, your family could "sing together" a hymn or children's song that brings them joy. What promises in Isaiah 52 cause us to "break forth into joy"?

**Isaiah 52:11; 55:7.** These verses could lead to a discussion about what the phrase "Be ye clean" might mean. As part of this discussion, you could review topics in *For the Strength of Youth* (booklet, 2011) or read scriptures about the blessings of being

spiritually clean (see 3 Nephi 12:8; Doctrine and Covenants 121:45–46).

**Isaiah 53.** To introduce Isaiah's description of the Savior, your family could talk about how stories, movies, and other media often depict heroes who rescue people. You could contrast those depictions with the descriptions of the Savior that you read in Isaiah 53. You could also watch the video "My Kingdom Is Not of This World" (ChurchofJesusChrist.org) and talk about how the prophecies in Isaiah 53 were fulfilled. What are some of the griefs and sorrows the Savior carries for us?

**Isaiah 55:8–9.** How do things look different when you are high above the ground? What does it mean to you that God's ways and thoughts are higher than ours?

For more ideas for teaching children, see this week's outline in *Come, Follow Me—For Primary.*

Suggested song: "I Stand All Amazed," *Hymns,* no. 193.

### Improving Personal Study

**Use music.** Hymns teach gospel principles powerfully. Consider listening to or reading sacrament hymns to help you understand truths about the Atonement of Jesus Christ taught in Isaiah 53. (See *Teaching in the Savior's Way,* 22.)

*His Light,* by Michael T. Malm

*Jesus in the Synagogue at Nazareth*, by Greg K. Olsen

OCTOBER 3–9

# Isaiah 58–66

"THE REDEEMER SHALL COME TO ZION"

As you study Isaiah 58–66, consider how Isaiah's words bring you joy and hope for the future.

RECORD YOUR IMPRESSIONS

Early in His earthly ministry, Jesus Christ visited a synagogue in Nazareth, the village where He was raised. There He stood to read from the scriptures, opened the book of Isaiah, and read what we now know as Isaiah 61:1–2. He then announced, "This day is this scripture fulfilled in your ears." This was one of the Savior's most straightforward declarations that He was the Anointed One, who would "heal the brokenhearted" and "preach deliverance to the captives" (see Luke 4:16–21). This scripture was indeed fulfilled on that day. And, like many other prophecies of Isaiah, it continues to be fulfilled in our day. The Savior continues to heal all the brokenhearted who come unto Him. There are yet many captives to whom deliverance must be preached. And there is a glorious future to prepare for—a time when the Lord will "create new heavens and a new earth" (Isaiah 65:17) and "cause righteousness and praise to spring forth before all the nations" (Isaiah 61:11). Reading Isaiah opens our eyes to what the Lord has already done, what He is doing, and what He will yet do for His people.

# Ideas for Personal Scripture Study

### ISAIAH 58:3–12

## Fasting brings blessings.

These verses suggest that to many ancient Israelites, fasting was more of a burden than a blessing. Many of us can relate to that feeling at times. If you would like to find more meaning and purpose in your fasting, read Isaiah 58:3–12 to find the Lord's answers to the question "Why do we fast?" In your experience, how can fasting "loose the bands of wickedness" and "break every yoke"? (Isaiah 58:6). How has fasting brought you the blessings described in Isaiah 58:8–12? How does Isaiah 58:3–12 affect the way you think about fasting?

In his message "Is Not This the Fast That I Have Chosen?" (*Ensign* or *Liahona,* May 2015, 22–25), President Henry B. Eyring shared several examples of how people have been blessed by fasting and fast offerings. How have you witnessed similar blessings in your life?

See also Gospel Topics, "Fasting and Fast Offerings" (topics.ChurchofJesusChrist.org).

### ISAIAH 59:9–21; 61:1–3; 63:1–9

## Jesus Christ is my Savior and Redeemer.

In Isaiah 58–66 you will find multiple references to the atoning mission of Jesus Christ. Here are a few examples, along with some questions to help you ponder them.

- Isaiah 59:9–21. How would you summarize the spiritual condition of the people described in verses 9–15? What impresses you about the description of the "intercessor" in verses 16–21 and the covenant He makes with those who turn to Him?

- Isaiah 61:1–3. How has Jesus Christ blessed you in the ways described in these verses? What "good tidings" has He brought you? How has He given you beauty in place of ashes?

- Isaiah 63:7–9. What "lovingkindnesses of the Lord" can you mention? What feelings for the Savior do these verses inspire in your heart?

What other references to the Savior do you find in Isaiah 58–66?

See also Mosiah 3:7; Doctrine and Covenants 133:46–53.

"The Lord shall be unto thee an everlasting light" (Isaiah 60:19). *A Gift of Light,* by Eva Timothy

### ISAIAH 60; 62

## "The Lord shall be unto thee an everlasting light."

Isaiah 60 and 62 speak of light and dark, eyes and seeing, to teach about how the gospel of Jesus Christ will bless the world in the last days. Look for these concepts especially in Isaiah 60:1–5, 19–20; 62:1–2. As you read these chapters, ponder how God is gathering His children out of darkness to His light. What is your role in this work?

See also 1 Nephi 22:3–12; 3 Nephi 18:24; Doctrine and Covenants 14:9; Bonnie H. Cordon, "That They May See," *Ensign* or *Liahona,* May 2020, 78–80.

### ISAIAH 64:1–5; 65:17–25; 66
## Christ will reign on earth during the Millennium.

Isaiah spoke of a day when "the former troubles are forgotten" (Isaiah 65:16). While this prophecy has several fulfillments, in its fullest sense, that day is yet to come—when Jesus Christ will return to the earth and establish an era of peace and righteousness called the Millennium. Isaiah described this future day in Isaiah 64:1–5; 65:17–25; 66. Notice how often he used words like "rejoice" and "rejoicing." Ponder why the Savior's return will be a day of rejoicing for you. What can you do to prepare for His coming?

See also Articles of Faith 1:10; Russell M. Nelson, "The Future of the Church: Preparing the World for the Savior's Second Coming," *Ensign,* Apr. 2020, 13–17.

## Ideas for Family Scripture Study and Home Evening

**Isaiah 58:3–11.** Family members might better understand Isaiah's message about fasting if they act out the type of fasting described in Isaiah 58:3–5 and the type of fasting described in Isaiah 58:6–8. How can we make our fasts more like "the fast that [God has] chosen"? What blessings have we seen from fasting?

**Isaiah 58:13–14.** What is the difference between "finding [our] own pleasure" and finding "delight . . . in the Lord" on the Sabbath? How can we make the Sabbath "a delight"?

**Isaiah 60:1–5.** As you read Isaiah 60:1–3, family members could turn on a light when the verses mention light and turn it off when the verses mention darkness. How is the gospel of Jesus Christ like a light to us? What did Isaiah foresee would happen as God's people share the light of the gospel? (see Isaiah 60:3–5).

**Isaiah 61:1–3.** How has the Savior fulfilled Isaiah's prophecies in these verses? You could invite family members to look for pictures of the Savior that they feel illustrate these aspects of His mission (pictures can be found in Church magazines or the *Gospel Art Book*). You might also sing a song about how the Savior blesses us, such as "I Feel My Savior's Love" (*Children's Songbook,* 74–75).

For more ideas for teaching children, see this week's outline in *Come, Follow Me—For Primary.*

Suggested song: "When He Comes Again," *Children's Songbook,* 82–83.

### Improving Personal Study

**Prepare your surroundings.** Our surroundings can affect our ability to learn. Find a place to study the scriptures where you can feel the influence of the Spirit. (See *Teaching in the Savior's Way,* 15.)

"Arise, shine; for thy light is come, and the glory of the Lord is risen upon thee" (Isaiah 60:1). *Light and Life,* by Mark Mabry

OCTOBER 10–16

# Jeremiah 1–3; 7; 16–18; 20

"BEFORE I FORMED THEE IN THE BELLY I KNEW THEE"

Elder David A. Bednar said: "One of the ways I hear [the Lord] is in the scriptures. The scriptures are the prerecorded voice of the Lord" ("'Hear Him' in Your Heart and in Your Mind," ChurchofJesusChrist.org).

RECORD YOUR IMPRESSIONS _____

_____

At first, Jeremiah didn't think he would make a good prophet. "Behold, I cannot speak," he protested when the Lord first called him (Jeremiah 1:6). The Lord reassured him, "I have put my words in thy mouth" (verse 9). Jeremiah felt that he was an inexperienced "child" (verse 6), but the Lord explained that he was actually more prepared than he realized—he had been ordained to this calling even before he was born (see verse 5). So Jeremiah set aside his fears and accepted the call. He warned Jerusalem's kings and priests that their pretended holiness would not save them from destruction. The "child" who thought he could not speak came

to feel God's word "in [his] heart as a burning fire" and could not be silent (Jeremiah 20:9).

Jeremiah's story is also our story. God knew us, too, before we were born and prepared us to do His work on the earth. Among other things, that work includes something Jeremiah foresaw: gathering God's people, one by one, to "bring [them] to Zion" (Jeremiah 3:14). And even if we don't know exactly what to do or say, we should "be not afraid . . . ; for I am with thee, saith the Lord" (Jeremiah 1:8, 19).

For an overview of the book of Jeremiah, see "Jeremiah" in the Bible Dictionary.

# Ideas for Personal Scripture Study

## JEREMIAH 1:4–19; 7:1–7; 20:8–10

### Prophets are called to speak the Lord's word.

As you read in Jeremiah 1:4–19 about Jeremiah's call to be a prophet, ponder the role of prophets in your life. What do you learn about prophets from the Lord's words to Jeremiah? (see also Jeremiah 7:1–7). Jeremiah's preaching was often rejected (see Jeremiah 20:8, 10). What do you learn from Jeremiah's words in Jeremiah 20:9? Keep these thoughts in mind throughout your study of Jeremiah's teachings. What do you find in these teachings that inspires you to follow our latter-day prophets?

## JEREMIAH 1:5

### God knew me before I was born.

Before Jeremiah was born, God knew him and chose him, or foreordained him, to fulfill a specific mission on earth (see Jeremiah 1:5). Why do you think it was valuable for Jeremiah to know this?

God also knew you before you were born and foreordained you to specific responsibilities (see Alma 13:1–4; Doctrine and Covenants 138:53–56; Abraham 3:22–23). What difference can this knowledge make in your life? If you have received your patriarchal blessing, you might prayerfully review it and ask God how to accomplish what He foreordained you to do.

See also Gospel Topics, "Foreordination," "Premortality," topics.ChurchofJesusChrist.org.

People in ancient Israel used cisterns to store precious water.

## JEREMIAH 2; 7

### "They have forsaken me the fountain of living waters."

In the arid region where the Israelites lived, people stored precious water in underground reservoirs called cisterns. Why would receiving water from a fountain be better than relying on a cistern? What does it mean to forsake "the fountain of living waters"? What do you think the "broken cisterns" mentioned in Jeremiah 2:13 might symbolize? As you read Jeremiah 2 and 7, notice how the people were forsaking the Lord's living waters, and think about how you are receiving living water in your life.

Jeremiah 7 is addressed to those who were entering "the gate of the Lord's house . . . to worship the Lord" (Jeremiah 7:2). Yet despite this outward appearance of devotion, they were guilty of great wickedness (see verses 2–11). What messages do you feel the Lord might have for you in verses 21–23?

## JEREMIAH 3:14–18; 16:14–21

### The Lord will gather His people.

When Jeremiah prophesied of the gathering of scattered Israel, he said it would be even more monumental than the Exodus from Egypt (see Jeremiah 16:14–15). In a similar spirit, President Russell M. Nelson said: "You were sent to earth at this precise time . . . to help gather Israel. There is *nothing* happening on this earth right now that is more important than that [gathering]. . . . This gathering should mean *everything* to you" (Russell M. Nelson and Wendy W. Nelson, "Hope of Israel" [worldwide youth devotional, June 3, 2018], supplement to the *New Era* and *Ensign,* Aug. 2018, 12, ChurchofJesusChrist.org).

As you study Jeremiah 3:14–18; 16:14–21, what inspires you about the latter-day gathering of Israel? What do these verses suggest about how that gathering happens? What additional insights do you find in the rest of President Nelson's message cited above?

## Ideas for Family Scripture Study and Home Evening

**Jeremiah 1:5.** You could use this verse to talk about our life with Heavenly Father before we were born. Resources like "I Lived in Heaven" (*Children's Songbook,* 4) and "Introduction: Our Heavenly Father's Plan" (in *New Testament Stories,* 1–5) could help. How can knowing about our premortal life affect the way we live our mortal life?

**Jeremiah 2:13; 17:13–14.** To help family members visualize these verses, you could demonstrate what

happens when you put water in a cracked or broken container. What might the "fountain of living waters" and "broken cisterns" represent? (Jeremiah 2:13). How do we drink from the Lord's living water?

**Jeremiah 16:16.** President Russell M. Nelson has compared the fishers and hunters in this verse to latter-day missionaries (see "The Gathering of Scattered Israel," *Ensign* or *Liahona,* Nov. 2006, 81). Family members could "hunt" for objects around your home and talk about how you can help "fish" and "hunt" for scattered Israel.

**Jeremiah 18:1–6.** To explore these verses, you might discuss or show how pottery is made. What message does the Lord have for Israel in Jeremiah 18:1–6? What does it mean to be clay in the Lord's hands? (see also Isaiah 64:8). For another story that compares us to potter's clay, see Elder Richard J. Maynes's message "The Joy of Living a Christ-Centered Life" (*Ensign* or *Liahona,* Nov. 2015, 27–30).

For more ideas for teaching children, see this week's outline in *Come, Follow Me—For Primary.*

Suggested song: "Israel, Israel, God Is Calling," *Hymns,* no. 7.

### Improving Our Teaching

**Use stories.** The Savior often taught using stories. Think of stories from your own life that can make a gospel principle come alive. (See *Teaching in the Savior's Way,* 22.)

"Behold, as the clay is in the potter's hand, so are ye in mine hand, O house of Israel" (Jeremiah 18:6).

*The Cry of Jeremiah the Prophet*, from an engraving by the Nazarene School

# Jeremiah 30–33; 36; Lamentations 1; 3

"I WILL TURN THEIR MOURNING INTO JOY"

As you record your impressions, think about how the principles in Jeremiah and Lamentations relate to other things you have learned in the Old Testament.

RECORD YOUR IMPRESSIONS

When the Lord first called Jeremiah to be a prophet, He told him that his mission would be "to root out, and to pull down" (Jeremiah 1:10)—and in Jerusalem, there was plenty of wickedness to root out and pull down. But this was only part of Jeremiah's mission—he was also called "to build, and to plant" (Jeremiah 1:10). What could be built or planted in the desolate ruins left by Israel's rebellion? Similarly, when sin or adversity have left our lives in ruins, how can we rebuild and plant again? The answer lies in "the Branch of righteousness" (Jeremiah 33:15), the promised Messiah. The Messiah brings "a new covenant" (Jeremiah 31:31)—one that requires more than a superficial commitment or the outward appearance of devotion. His law must be "in [our] inward parts," written "in [our] hearts." That is what it really means for the Lord to "be [our] God" and for us to "be [His] people" (Jeremiah 31:33). It's a lifelong process, and we will still make mistakes and have cause to mourn from time to time. But when we do, we have this promise from the Lord: "I will turn their mourning into joy" (Jeremiah 31:13).

For an overview of Lamentations, see "Lamentations, Book of" in the Guide to the Scriptures (scriptures.ChurchofJesusChrist.org).

# Ideas for Personal Scripture Study

### JEREMIAH 30–31; 33

## The Lord will bring Israel out of captivity and gather them.

In Jeremiah 30–31; 33 the Lord acknowledged the "lamentation, and bitter weeping" (Jeremiah 31:15) that the Israelites would experience as they went into captivity. However, He also offered words of comfort and hope. What phrases in these chapters do you think would have given the Israelites consolation and hope? What promises do you find from the Lord to His people? How might these promises apply to you today?

### JEREMIAH 31:31–34; 32:37–42

## "They shall be my people, and I will be their God."

Although the Israelites had broken their covenant with the Lord, Jeremiah prophesied that the Lord would again establish a "new" and "everlasting covenant" with His people (Jeremiah 31:31; 32:40). The new and everlasting covenant is "the fulness of the gospel of Jesus Christ [see Doctrine and Covenants 66:2]. It is *new* every time it is revealed anew following a period of apostasy. It is *everlasting* in the sense that it is God's covenant and has been enjoyed in every gospel dispensation where people have been willing to receive it" (Guide to the Scriptures, "New and Everlasting Covenant," scriptures.ChurchofJesusChrist.org; italics added).

As you read Jeremiah 31:31–34; 32:37–42, ponder what it means to you to be part of God's covenant people. How do these verses affect the way you view your covenant relationship with God? What does it mean to have His law written in your heart? (see Jeremiah 31:33).

See also Jeremiah 24:7; Hebrews 8:6–12.

The scriptures can inspire us to repent and turn to the Lord.

### JEREMIAH 36

## The scriptures have power to turn me away from evil.

The Lord commanded Jeremiah to record his prophecies in "a roll of a book," or a scroll, explaining that if the people were to hear these prophecies, "it may be that . . . they may return every man from his evil way; that I may forgive their iniquity" (Jeremiah 36:2–3). As you read Jeremiah 36, consider noting how the following people felt about these prophecies:

The Lord:

_____

_____

_____

Jeremiah:

_____

_____

_____

Baruch:

_____

_____

_____

Jehudi and King Jehoiakim:

_____

_____

_____

Elnathan, Delaiah, and Gemariah:

_____

_____

_____

Ponder how you feel about the scriptures and their role in your life. How have they helped you turn away from evil?

See also Julie B. Beck, "My Soul Delighteth in the Scriptures," *Ensign* or *Liahona,* May 2004, 107–9.

### LAMENTATIONS 1; 3

## The Lord can relieve the sorrow we experience because of sin.

The book of Lamentations is a collection of poems written after the destruction of Jerusalem and its temple. Why do you think it is important that these lamentations were preserved and included in the Old Testament? Consider what the metaphors in Lamentations 1 and 3 help you understand about the great sorrow Israel felt. What messages of hope in Christ do you find? (see especially Lamentations 3:20–33; see also Matthew 5:4; James 4:8–10; Alma 36:17–20).

# Ideas for Family Scripture Study and Home Evening

**Jeremiah 31:3.** How have Heavenly Father and Jesus Christ shown Their "everlasting love" for us? Showing pictures of things Christ created for us or did during His mortal ministry could help your family feel His "lovingkindness."

**Jeremiah 31:31–34; 32:38–41.** Consider making a list of things in these verses the Lord promises when we make covenants with Him. What do these verses teach us about the importance of our covenants?

Family members could also write (or draw) on paper hearts something that shows how they feel about the Savior. What does it mean to have His law written in our hearts? (see Jeremiah 31:33). How do we show the Lord that we want to be His people?

**Jeremiah 36.** How might you use Jeremiah 36 to help your family learn about the importance of the scriptures? (see, for example, verses 1–6, 10, 23–24, 27–28, 32). You might ask one family member to read a verse from this chapter while another family member writes it down, like Baruch did for Jeremiah. Why are we grateful for the efforts of people like Baruch, who preserved the words of the prophets? What can we do to show the Lord we value His words in the scriptures?

**Lamentations 3:1–17, 21–25, 31–32.** As a family, you might talk about how the feelings expressed in Lamentations 3:1–17 can relate to the feelings we have when we sin. How can the messages in verses 21–25, 31–32 influence our lives?

For more ideas for teaching children, see this week's outline in *Come, Follow Me—For Primary.*

Suggested song: "I Feel My Savior's Love," *Children's Songbook,* 74–75.

### Improving Personal Study

**Seek revelation.** As you ponder throughout the day, you may receive additional ideas and impressions about scriptures you studied. Don't think of gospel study as something you make time for but as something you are always doing. (See *Teaching in the Savior's Way,* 12.)

*Jeremiah Lamenting the Destruction of Jerusalem,* by Rembrandt van Rijn

Come, Follow Me, by Scott Sumner

# Ezekiel 1–3; 33–34; 36–37; 47

"A NEW SPIRIT WILL I PUT WITHIN YOU"

Ezekiel was invited to symbolically "eat" God's word—to fill himself with it (see Ezekiel 2:9–3:3, 10). How will you fill yourself with God's word this week?

RECORD YOUR IMPRESSIONS

Ezekiel was a prophet in exile. Along with other Israelites, he had been captured and sent to Babylon several years before Jerusalem was finally destroyed. In Jerusalem, Ezekiel would have been a priest serving in the temple. In Babylon, he was among "them of the captivity," and he "sat where they sat" (Ezekiel 3:15), hundreds of miles from the temple and with little hope of returning to the beloved house of God. Then one day Ezekiel had a vision. He saw "the glory of the Lord" (Ezekiel 1:28)—not back in the temple at Jerusalem but there in Babylon among the exiles. The wickedness in Jerusalem, he learned, had become so severe that God's presence was no longer there (see Ezekiel 8–11; 33:21).

One of Ezekiel's tasks was to warn the Israelites about the consequences of their rebellion—a warning that largely went unheeded. But there was more to Ezekiel's message: he prophesied that, despite how bad things became, there was a way back. If God's people would accept the invitation to "hear the word of the Lord" (Ezekiel 37:4), what was once dead could be revived. A "stony heart" could be replaced with "a new heart" (Ezekiel 36:26). "[I] shall put my spirit in you," the Lord told them, "and ye shall live" (Ezekiel 37:14). And in the last days, the Lord would establish a new temple and a new Jerusalem, "and the name of the city from that day shall be, The Lord is there" (Ezekiel 48:35).

# Ideas for Personal Scripture Study

## EZEKIEL 1–3

### "Thou shalt speak my words."

Reading about Ezekiel's call to the ministry in Ezekiel 1–3 might prompt you to think about opportunities God has given you to "speak with [His] words" to others (Ezekiel 3:4). In Ezekiel 2–3, notice His words of encouragement and instruction to Ezekiel. Although the people you serve probably aren't as rebellious as Ezekiel's people, consider how God's words to Ezekiel affect the way you view your service in the Church, at home, and elsewhere.

See also Ezekiel 33:1–9; D. Todd Christofferson, "The Voice of Warning," *Ensign* or *Liahona,* May 2017, 108–11.

## EZEKIEL 33:10–19

### The Lord wants to forgive.

"If our . . . sins be upon us," the captive Israelites wondered, "how should we then live?" (Ezekiel 33:10). In response, the Lord taught them important truths about repentance and forgiveness. These questions might help you ponder those truths:

- What do you think it means to "trust to [your] own righteousness"? (see Ezekiel 33:12–13).

- What would you say to someone who feels that the righteous person and the wicked person described in Ezekiel 33:12–19 are not being treated fairly? (see also Matthew 21:28–31; Luke 18:9–14).

- What phrases do you find in these verses that help you understand what it means to repent? What additional insights do you find in Ezekiel 36:26–27 and Alma 7:14–16?

## EZEKIEL 34

### The Lord invites me to feed His sheep.

In Ezekiel 34, the Lord refers to leaders of His people as "shepherds." As you read, consider what this title suggests to you about what it means to be a leader. Who are the "sheep" the Lord wants you to feed? How can you follow the example the Savior sets as our shepherd? (see verses 11–31).

See also John 21:15–17.

Ezekiel saw in vision a river flow from the temple and heal the Dead Sea.

## EZEKIEL 37

### The Lord is gathering His people and giving them new life.

The gathering of Israel is portrayed in Ezekiel 37 through two symbols. As you read about the first one—dead bones being restored to life (see verses 1–14)—ponder what you learn about gathering Israel on both sides of the veil (see also Ezekiel 36:24–30).

The second symbol (see verses 15–28) involves two sticks, which many scholars interpret as wooden writing boards joined by a hinge. The stick of Judah can represent the Bible (since much of the Bible was written by Judah's descendants), and the stick of Joseph can represent the Book of Mormon (since Lehi's family were descendants of Joseph of Egypt). With that in mind, what do these verses teach you about the role of the scriptures in the gathering of Israel? What does 2 Nephi 3:11–13 (a prophecy about Joseph Smith and the Book of Mormon) add to your understanding?

See also 2 Nephi 29:14; "The Book of Mormon Gathers Scattered Israel" (video, ChurchofJesusChrist.org).

## Ideas for Family Scripture Study and Home Evening

**Ezekiel 33:1–5.** To illustrate these verses, one family member could pretend to be a "watchman" by looking out a window and telling the rest of the family what is happening outside. How is our living prophet like a watchman for us?

**Ezekiel 33:15–16.** What do these verses teach us about the forgiveness we can receive through Jesus Christ?

**Ezekiel 36:26–27.** Show your family some stones as you discuss what it means to have a "stony heart." Let them suggest words that describe the "new heart" and "new spirit" the Savior gives us (see Mosiah 3:19; 5:2).

**Ezekiel 37:15–28.** Family members could find two sticks and write on one *For Judah (Bible)* and on the other *For Joseph (Book of Mormon)* (see verses 16–19). They could then share stories or scriptures from the Bible and Book of Mormon that help them feel closer to the Savior and become "[His] people" (verse 23).

**Ezekiel 47:1–12.** These verses describe Ezekiel's vision of water flowing from the temple and healing the Dead Sea—a sea so salty that fish and plants cannot live in it. Children might enjoy drawing a picture of this vision. What could the water flowing from the temple symbolize? (see the video "And the River Will Grow," ChurchofJesusChrist.org). How does the temple help heal us? (see Ezekiel 47:8–9, 11).

For more ideas for teaching children, see this week's outline in *Come, Follow Me—For Primary.*

Suggested song: "Dear to the Heart of the Shepherd," *Hymns,* no. 221.

### Improving Our Teaching

**Don't try to cover everything.** You may not be able to explore every truth in Ezekiel with your family. Seek spiritual guidance to determine what to focus on. (See *Teaching in the Savior's Way,* 7.)

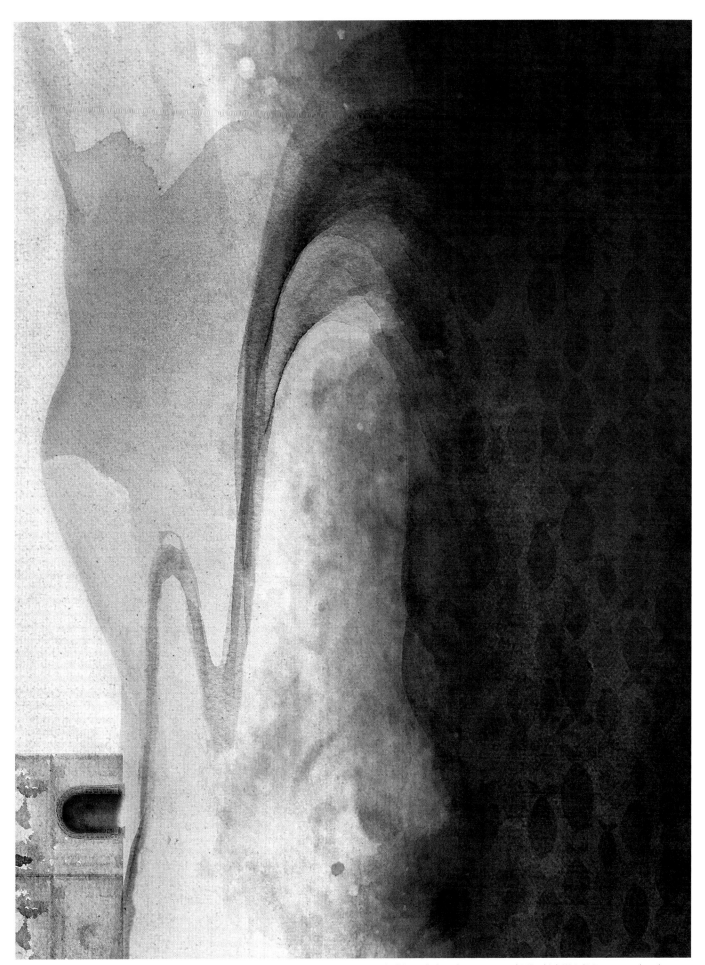

"Behold, waters issued out from under the threshold of the house. . . . And every thing shall live whither the river cometh" (Ezekiel 47:1, 9). Image used under license from shutterstock.com.

OCTOBER 31–NOVEMBER 6

# Daniel 1–6

"THERE IS NO OTHER GOD THAT CAN DELIVER"

Elder Richard G. Scott explained that recording inspiration "shows God that His communications are sacred to us. Recording will also enhance our ability to recall revelation" ("How to Obtain Revelation and Inspiration for Your Personal Life," *Ensign* or *Liahona,* May 2012, 46).

RECORD YOUR IMPRESSIONS

Most likely no one will ever threaten to throw you into a fiery furnace or a den of lions because of your faith in Jesus Christ. But none of us get through this life without a trial of faith. We can all benefit from the example of people like Daniel, Shadrach, Meshach, and Abed-nego, who were taken captive as young men by the mighty Babylonian Empire (see 2 Kings 24:10–16). These young people were surrounded by an unfamiliar culture with different values, and they faced great temptations to abandon their beliefs and righteous traditions. Yet they remained true to their covenants. Like Joseph in Egypt and Esther in Persia, Daniel and his friends

in Babylon kept their faith in God, and God worked miracles that still inspire believers to this day.

How did they find the strength to remain so faithful? They did those small and simple things that God has asked all of us to do—praying, fasting, choosing good friends, trusting in God, and being a light to others. As we are strengthened by doing these same small and simple things, we can face the lions and fiery furnaces in our own lives with faith.

For an overview of the book of Daniel, see "Daniel, book of" in the Bible Dictionary.

# Ideas for Personal Scripture Study

### DANIEL 1; 3; 6

## I can trust in the Lord when my faith is tried.

In a sense, we all live in Babylon. The world around us is filled with many temptations to compromise our standards and question our faith in Jesus Christ. As you read Daniel 1, 3, and 6, note the ways in which Daniel, Shadrach, Meshach, and Abed-nego were pressured to do things they knew were wrong. Have you ever felt pressure to compromise your beliefs? What do you learn from these men that can help you trust in the Lord when you face opposition?

The book of Daniel and many other scriptures record experiences where great faith led to great miracles. But what if our faith doesn't lead to the miracles we seek? (see, for example, Alma 14:8–13). Based on what you read in Daniel 3:13–18, how do you think Shadrach, Meshach, and Abed-nego would have answered this question? How can their example affect how you approach your trials of faith? For more about these verses, see Elder Dennis E. Simmons's message "But If Not . . ." (*Ensign* or *Liahona,* May 2004, 73–75).

The book of Daniel also shows how an individual's righteous choices can lead others to greater faith in the Lord. What examples of this do you find in chapters 1, 3, and 6? Ponder the effects that your choices may be having on others (see Matthew 5:16).

See also Dieter F. Uchtdorf, "Be Not Afraid, Only Believe," *Ensign* or *Liahona,* Nov. 2015, 76–79; David R. Stone, "Zion in the Midst of Babylon," *Ensign* or *Liahona,* May 2006, 90–93.

Illustration of Daniel and his friends refusing the king's food, by Brian Call

### DANIEL 2

## The Church of Jesus Christ of Latter-day Saints is the kingdom of God on earth.

Through revelation, Daniel saw that Nebuchadnezzar's dream foretold future worldly kingdoms, as well as the future kingdom of God, which "shall never be destroyed" (Daniel 2:44). "The Church is that prophesied latter-day kingdom," Elder D. Todd Christofferson taught, "not created by man but set up by the God of heaven and rolling forth as a stone 'cut out of the mountain without hands' to fill the earth" ("Why the Church," *Ensign* or *Liahona,* Nov. 2015, 111). Think about God's latter-day kingdom as you read the descriptions of the stone in Daniel 2:34–35, 44–45. What similarities do you see between the stone and the kingdom? How do you see God's kingdom filling the earth today?

See also Gordon B. Hinckley, "The Stone Cut Out of the Mountain," *Ensign* or *Liahona,* Nov. 2007, 83–86; L. Whitney Clayton, "The Time Shall Come," *Ensign* or *Liahona,* Nov. 2011, 11–13.

### DANIEL 3:19–28

## The Savior will support me in my trials.

What insights come to you as you read about the fourth figure appearing in the fiery furnace with Shadrach, Meshach, and Abed-nego? How can this account help you in the trials you face? You might find additional insights in Mosiah 3:5–7; Alma 7:11–13; Doctrine and Covenants 61:36–37; 121:5–8.

## Ideas for Family Scripture Study and Home Evening

**Daniel 1–2.** As you read Daniel 1 and 2 together, you could look for the blessings that Daniel and his friends received by abstaining from eating the king's meat and wine. (See the video "God Gave Them Knowledge," ChurchofJesusChrist.org.) You could compare those blessings to the Lord's promises to us as we keep His commandments, such as the Word of Wisdom (see Doctrine and Covenants 89:18–21). How has the Lord blessed us for living the Word of Wisdom?

**Daniel 3.** How could you help your family learn about the story in Daniel 3? "Shadrach, Meshach, and Abed-nego" in *Old Testament Stories* could help. What impresses us about Shadrach, Meshach, and Abed-nego? What situations do we face that challenge our faith and require us to show that we trust God?

**Daniel 6:1–23.** Your family may enjoy acting out parts of the story in Daniel 6:1–23 (for example, verses 10–12 or 16–23). What do we learn from Daniel's example? What can we do to be more like him?

**Daniel 6:25–27.** According to these verses, how was King Darius affected when the Lord delivered Daniel from the lions? You could also read in Daniel 2:47; 3:28–29 about how King Nebuchadnezzar was affected in a similar way. What opportunities do we have to influence others? Discuss examples you have seen of how the faith of other people, including family members, has influenced others for good.

For more ideas for teaching children, see this week's outline in *Come, Follow Me—For Primary.*

Suggested song: "I Want to Live the Gospel," *Children's Songbook,* 148.

### Improving Our Teaching

**Teach the doctrine.** The Lord's gospel is beautiful in its simplicity (see Doctrine and Covenants 133:57). Simple activities and discussions focused on doctrine can invite the Holy Ghost to carry the gospel message into the hearts of your family.

*Daniel in the Lion's Den,* 1872. Rivière, Briton (1840–1920). Credit: Walker Art Gallery, National Museums Liverpool/Bridgeman Images

# Hosea 1–6; 10–14; Joel

"I WILL LOVE THEM FREELY"

Invite the Spirit to be part of your study of Hosea and Joel. Make note of the messages the Spirit impresses on your heart and mind.

RECORD YOUR IMPRESSIONS

Israel's covenant with the Lord was meant to be so deep and meaningful that the Lord compared it to a marriage. The covenant, like a marriage, included eternal commitment, shared experiences, building a life together, exclusive loyalty, and most of all, wholehearted love. This kind of devotion came with high expectations—and tragic consequences for infidelity. Through the prophet Hosea, God described some of the consequences the Israelites faced for breaking their covenant. And yet His message was not "I will reject you forever for being unfaithful." Instead it was "I will invite you back" (see Hosea 2:14–15). "I will betroth thee unto me in righteousness," the Lord declared (Hosea 2:19). "I will heal their backsliding, I will love them freely" (Hosea 14:4). This is the same message He gives us today as we seek to live our covenants with love and devotion.

Joel shared a similar message: "Turn unto the Lord your God: for he is gracious and merciful, slow to anger, and of great kindness" (Joel 2:13). "The Lord will be the hope of his people, and the strength of the children of Israel" (Joel 3:16). As you read Hosea and Joel, ponder your own relationship with the Lord. Think about how His faithfulness inspires you to be faithful to Him.

For an overview of the books of Hosea and Joel, see "Hosea, or Hoshea" and "Joel" in the Bible Dictionary.

# Ideas for Personal Scripture Study

## HOSEA 1–3; 14

### The Lord always invites me to return to Him.

Hosea's wife, Gomer, was unfaithful to him, and God pointed to this sad event to teach the Israelites how He felt about them and their covenants with Him. As you read Hosea 1–3, ponder how the Lord views His relationship with His covenant people. You might ponder ways that you, like the Israelites, may have been unfaithful to the Lord and how He has reached out to you. For example, what do Hosea 2:14–23 and Hosea 14 teach you about the Lord's love and mercy? How do you show Him your love and loyalty?

See also Dieter F. Uchtdorf, "Point of Safe Return," *Ensign* or *Liahona,* May 2007, 99–101.

Sinful Gomer, who represents Israel, was offered redemption by the Lord. Illustration by Deb Minnard, licensed from goodsalt.com

## HOSEA 6:4–7; JOEL 2:12–13

### Devotion to God must be felt inwardly, not just expressed outwardly.

The Lord had commanded His people to offer animal sacrifices. But even though the people in Hosea's day were obeying that law, they were breaking commandments of greater importance

(see Hosea 6:4–7). What do you think it means that the Lord "desired mercy, and not sacrifice; and the knowledge of God more than burnt offerings"? (Hosea 6:6). What do you think it means for righteousness to be like a cloud or like dew? What should our righteousness be like? (see Isaiah 48:18; 1 Nephi 2:9–10).

You could also read Matthew 9:10–13; 12:1–8 to see how the Savior used Hosea 6:6 during His ministry. How do these passages help you understand Hosea's words?

When reading Joel 2:12–13, it might help to know that rending or tearing one's clothing was traditionally an outward sign of mourning or remorse (for example, see 2 Chronicles 34:14–21, 27). How is rending our hearts different from rending our garments?

See also Isaiah 1:11–17; Matthew 23:23; 1 John 3:17–18.

## JOEL 2

### "I will pour out my spirit upon all flesh."

When Joel prophesied of "the day of the Lord," he described it as "a day of darkness and of gloominess," "great and very terrible" (Joel 2:1–2, 11). Israel has faced many great and terrible days throughout its history, and God's covenant people will face more in the future. What impresses you about the counsel the Lord gave in Joel 2:12–17? Also notice the blessings He promised in Joel 2:18–32. Why might the blessings promised in verses 27–32 be especially valuable in days like those described in Joel 2, including our day?

What do you think it means that the Lord would "pour out [His] spirit upon all flesh"? (Joel 2:28). How are the prophecies in Joel 2:28–29 being fulfilled? (See Acts 2:1–21; Joseph Smith—History 1:41.)

You might ponder these words from President Russell M. Nelson: "In coming days, it will not be possible to survive spiritually without the guiding, directing, comforting, and constant influence of the Holy Ghost" ("Revelation for the Church, Revelation for Our Lives," *Ensign* or *Liahona,* May 2018, 96). Why is revelation essential to our spiritual survival? How can you increase your capacity to receive personal revelation?

## Ideas for Family Scripture Study and Home Evening

**Hosea 2:19–20.** The Lord used the metaphor of marriage to describe His covenant relationship with Israel (see also Guide to the Scriptures, "Bridegroom," scriptures.ChurchofJesusChrist.org). Your family could discuss why marriage can be a good metaphor for our covenants with God. How does Hosea 2:19–20 help us understand how God feels about us? How can we be faithful to our covenants with Him?

**Hosea 10:12.** Children might enjoy drawing a clock and planning ways they can seek the Lord at different times throughout the day.

**Joel 2:12–13.** To help your family talk about Joel 2:12–13, you could place a picture of the Savior on one side of a room and the word *sin* on the opposite side. Invite family members to take turns facing the sign and then turning toward the Savior as they share things that can help us turn to Him "with all [our] heart." Encourage family members to think about all aspects of their lives, including activities, work, school, and relationships.

**Joel 2:28–29.** What could it mean for the Spirit to be "poured out" upon us? Maybe you could demonstrate this by pouring a liquid and then contrasting it with a drip or a trickle.

For more ideas for teaching children, see this week's outline in *Come, Follow Me—For Primary.*

Suggested song: "Come unto Jesus," *Hymns,* no. 117.

### Improving Our Teaching

**Teach the doctrine.** "Never miss a chance to gather children together to learn of the doctrine of Jesus Christ. Such moments are so rare in comparison with the efforts of the enemy" (Henry B. Eyring, "The Power of Teaching Doctrine," *Ensign,* May 1999, 74).

*Come unto Me,* by Kelly Pugh

NOVEMBER 14–20

# Amos; Obadiah

"SEEK THE LORD, AND YE SHALL LIVE"

The Holy Ghost can open your mind and heart to messages in the word of God that are meant just for you. What do you feel the Lord wants you to learn this week?

RECORD YOUR IMPRESSIONS

God chose Abraham's seed to be His covenant people so that they would "be a blessing" to all people (see Genesis 12:2–3). But instead, by the time of Amos's ministry, many of the covenant people were oppressing the poor and ignoring the prophets, making their acts of worship empty and meaningless (see Amos 2:6–16). True, the nations surrounding them were also guilty of great sins (see Amos 1; 2:1–5), but that has never been an excuse for God's people (see Amos 3:2). So God sent a herdsman from Judah named Amos to preach repentance to the Kingdom of Israel. Later, God also declared through the prophet

Obadiah that although the Kingdom of Judah had been destroyed, the Lord would gather and bless His people again. The covenant people had strayed from the Lord, both prophets testified, but they would not be cast off forever. When God reveals His secrets to His servants the prophets (see Amos 3:7), we can take it as a sign that He still wants to help us live up to the covenants we made with Him.

For more about the books of Amos and Obadiah, see "Amos" and "Obadiah" in the Bible Dictionary.

## Ideas for Personal Scripture Study

### AMOS 3:1–8; 7:10–15

### The Lord reveals truth through His prophets.

In Amos 3:3–6, the prophet Amos presented several examples of causes and effects: because a lion finds prey, the lion roars; because a baited trap is set for a bird, the bird is ensnared. (Note that in the Joseph Smith Translation of verse 6, the word "done" was changed to "known" [in Amos 3:6, footnote *b*].) In verses 7–8, Amos applied this logic to prophets. What causes a prophet to prophesy? What else do you learn about prophets as you read Amos 7:10–15? Ponder why you are grateful that the Lord still "revealeth his secret unto his servants the prophets" (Amos 3:7). What does this truth suggest to you about God?

See also Doctrine and Covenants 1:38; 21:4–8; 35:13–14.

### AMOS 4–5

### "Seek the Lord, and ye shall live."

As you read Amos 4:6–13, note the judgments the Lord had sent upon the people of Israel. What do these verses suggest about what the Lord hoped would happen after each of these experiences? (see also Helaman 12:3). Think about a recent trial you have experienced. While your trial may not have been sent by God, ponder how it might give you opportunities to seek Him.

Read Amos 5:4, 14–15, and ponder how the Lord has been "gracious" (verse 15) to you as you have sought Him, even during your times of trial.

See also Donald L. Hallstrom, "Turn to the Lord," *Ensign* or *Liahona,* May 2010, 78–80.

### AMOS 8:11–12

### The word of the Lord can satisfy spiritual hunger and thirst.

We all experience periods of spiritual hunger and thirst, but there is no need for us to "wander from sea to sea" (Amos 8:12) looking for something to satisfy us. We know what will satisfy that spiritual hunger, and we have been blessed with the word of the Lord in abundance. As you read Amos 8:11–12, think about why a famine is a good comparison for living without the word of God. What additional insights do you find in Matthew 5:6; John 6:26–35; 2 Nephi 9:50–51; 32:3; Enos 1:4–8?

See also Jeffrey R. Holland, "He Hath Filled the Hungry with Good Things," *Ensign,* Nov. 1997, 64–66; Gospel Topics, "Apostasy," topics .ChurchofJesusChrist.org.

We can become saviors on Mount Zion by doing temple and family history work.

### OBADIAH 1:21

### Who are the "saviours . . . on mount Zion"?

President Gordon B. Hinckley gave one possible interpretation of the phrase "saviours on mount Zion," connecting the phrase to temple and family history work: "[In the temple] we literally become saviors on Mount Zion. What does this mean? Just as our Redeemer gave His life as a vicarious sacrifice for all men, and in so doing became our Savior, even so we, in a small measure, when we engage in proxy work in the temple, become as saviors to those on the other side who have no means of advancing unless something is done in their behalf by those on earth" ("Closing Remarks," *Ensign* or *Liahona,* Nov. 2004, 105).

## Ideas for Family Scripture Study and Home Evening

**Amos 3:7.** You might review several recent messages from the President of the Church and discuss what the Lord is revealing to your family through him. Why is it important to have a prophet leading the Church? How have we come to know he is a true prophet? What are we doing to follow his counsel?

**Amos 5:4.** Your family might create a poster to hang in your home with this verse on it. What does it mean to seek the Lord? How do we seek Him? What blessings do we receive when we do? You could invite family members to share and discuss other passages that teach about seeking the Lord, such as Matthew 7:7–8; Ether 12:41; and Doctrine and Covenants 88:63.

**Amos 8:11–12.** Children might enjoy making up actions that go with phrases in these verses. When our bodies are hungry or thirsty, what do we do?

When our spirits are hungry or thirsty, what do we do? You might also watch the video "The Great Apostasy" (ChurchofJesusChrist.org) and talk about how the Restoration of the gospel satisfies our spiritual hunger.

**Obadiah 1:21.** What could it mean to be "saviours . . . on mount Zion"? (For one possible explanation, see the statement by President Gordon B. Hinckley in "Ideas for Personal Scripture Study.") Which of our ancestors need saving ordinances? What will we do to help them?

For more ideas for teaching children, see this week's outline in *Come, Follow Me—For Primary.*

Suggested song: "We Thank Thee, O God, for a Prophet," *Hymns,* no. 19.

### Improving Personal Study

**Use music to invite the Spirit and learn doctrine.** Listening to or reading a hymn can help you learn gospel principles. For example, you could listen to or read "We Thank Thee, O God, for a Prophet" (*Hymns,* no. 19) to inspire greater faith in living prophets. (See *Teaching in the Savior's Way,* 22.)

Santo Domingo Dominican Republic Temple

# Jonah; Micah

"HE DELIGHTETH IN MERCY"

As you record your impressions, think about how the principles in Jonah and Micah relate to what you have been learning in the scriptures.

RECORD YOUR IMPRESSIONS

---

Jonah was on a ship headed for Tarshish. There's nothing wrong with sailing to Tarshish, except that it is far away from Nineveh, where Jonah was supposed to go to deliver God's message. So when the ship encountered a great storm, Jonah knew it was because of his disobedience. At Jonah's insistence, his fellow mariners cast him into the depths of the sea to stop the storm. It looked like the end of Jonah and his ministry. But the Lord hadn't given up on Jonah—just as He hadn't given up on the people of

Nineveh and just as He doesn't give up on any of us. As Micah taught, the Lord does not delight in condemning us, but "he delighteth in mercy." When we turn to Him, "he will turn again, he will have compassion upon us; he will subdue our iniquities; and [He will] cast all [our] sins into the depths of the sea" (Micah 7:18–19).

For an overview of the books of Jonah and Micah, see "Jonah" and "Micah" in the Bible Dictionary.

# Ideas for Personal Scripture Study

### JONAH 1–4; MICAH 7:18–19

## The Lord is merciful to all who turn to Him.

The book of Jonah shows, among other things, how merciful the Lord is when we repent. As you read Jonah, look for examples of His mercy. Ponder how you have experienced that mercy in your life. What do you learn that can help you be more merciful to others?

Witnessing the Lord's mercy often inspires feelings of love and gratitude. However, Jonah was "displeased" and "very angry" (Jonah 4:1) when the Lord extended mercy to the people of Nineveh, who were Israel's enemies. Why might Jonah have felt this way? Have you ever had similar feelings? What do you feel the Lord was trying to help Jonah understand in chapter 4?

Ponder the teachings in Micah 7:18–19. How could these truths have helped Jonah change his attitude about the Lord and the people of Nineveh?

See also Luke 15:11–32; Jeffrey R. Holland, "The Justice and Mercy of God," *Ensign,* Sept. 2013, 16–21.

### JONAH 1; 3–4

## All of God's children need to hear the gospel.

Nineveh was part of the Assyrian empire, an enemy of Israel known for its violence and cruelty. To Jonah, it probably seemed unrealistic that the people of Nineveh were ready to accept the word of God and repent. Yet, as President Dallin H. Oaks taught: "We should never set ourselves up as judges of who is ready and who is not. The Lord knows the hearts of all of His children, and if we pray for inspiration, He will help us find persons He knows to be 'in a preparation to hear the word' (Alma 32:6)"

("Sharing the Restored Gospel," *Ensign* or *Liahona,* Nov. 2016, 58–59). What do you learn from Jonah 3 that inspires you to share the gospel even with those who may not seem ready to change?

It might be helpful to compare Jonah's attitude (see Jonah 1; 3–4) to the feelings of Alma and the sons of Mosiah (see Mosiah 28:1–5; Alma 17:23–25).

See also 3 Nephi 18:32.

We can share the gospel with God's children.

### MICAH 4:11–13; 5:8–15; 7:5–7

## Jesus Christ quoted the writings of Micah.

It is well known that the Savior quoted Isaiah and the Psalms. Did you know that He also quoted Micah several times? Consider the following examples, and ponder why these passages might have been important to the Savior. Why are they important to you?

*Micah 4:11–13 (see 3 Nephi 20:18–20).* The Lord compared the latter-day gathering to a wheat harvest (see also Alma 26:5–7; Doctrine and Covenants 11:3–4). What does this comparison suggest to you about the gathering of Israel?

*Micah 5:8–15 (see 3 Nephi 21:12–21).* What do these verses suggest to you about God's people ("the remnant of Jacob") in the last days?

*Micah 7:5–7 (see Matthew 10:35–36).* According to these verses, why is it important to "look unto the Lord" first? Why is this counsel important today?

MICAH 6:1–8

## "What doth the Lord require of thee?"

Micah invites us to imagine what it might be like to "come before the Lord, and bow . . . before the high God" (Micah 6:6). What do verses 6–8 suggest to you about what is important to the Lord as He evaluates your life?

See also Matthew 7:21–23; 25:31–40; Dale G. Renlund, "Do Justly, Love Mercy, and Walk Humbly with God," *Ensign* or *Liahona,* Nov. 2020, 109–12.

# Ideas for Family Scripture Study and Home Evening

**Jonah 1–4.** Your children might enjoy doing actions that tell the story of Jonah, like pretending to run away, making sounds like a stormy sea, or pretending to get swallowed by a big fish (see "Jonah the Prophet" in *Old Testament Stories*). Ask family members what they learn from Jonah's experience. For one example of a lesson from Jonah, see verse 7 of "Follow the Prophet" (*Children's Songbook,* 110–11).

**Jonah 3.** What did Jonah learn about sharing the gospel? Who do we know that would be blessed by hearing the message of the restored gospel of Jesus Christ?

**Micah 4:1–5.** According to these verses, what will bring peace and prosperity to the Lord's people? What can we do to help fulfill this prophecy in our home?

**Micah 5:2.** You could display a picture of Jesus as a child with His mother (see *Gospel Art Book,* no. 33) on one side of the room and a picture of the Wise Men on another. Read together Micah 5:2 and Matthew 2:1–6. How did Micah's prophecy help the Wise Men find Jesus? Family members could move the picture of the Wise Men next to the picture of Jesus. Your family might also enjoy watching the video "The Christ Child: A Nativity Story" (ChurchofJesusChrist.org).

For more ideas for teaching children, see this week's outline in *Come, Follow Me—For Primary.*

Suggested song: "I'll Go Where You Want Me to Go," *Hymns,* no. 270.

## Improving Personal Study

**Find God's love.** As you read the scriptures, consider noting evidences of God's love that stand out to you. For instance, look for how God showed His love for His children in the story of Jonah.

Illustration by Kevin Carden

"His ways are everlasting" (Habakkuk 3:6). *In the Beginning Was the Word,* by Eva Timothy

# Nahum; Habakkuk; Zephaniah

"HIS WAYS ARE EVERLASTING"

You can study the scriptures for a lifetime and still find new insights. Don't feel that you have to comprehend everything right now. Pray for help to recognize the messages you need today.

RECORD YOUR IMPRESSIONS

Reading the Old Testament often means reading prophecies about destruction. The Lord frequently called prophets to warn the wicked that His judgments were upon them. The ministries of Nahum, Habakkuk, and Zephaniah are good examples. In dreadful detail, these prophets foretold the downfall of cities that, at the time, seemed strong and powerful—Nineveh, Babylon, and even Jerusalem. But that was thousands of years ago. Why is it valuable to read these prophecies today?

Even though those prideful, wicked cities were destroyed, pride and wickedness persist. In today's world, we can sometimes feel surrounded by the evils that were condemned by the ancient prophets. We may even detect traces of them in our own hearts.

These Old Testament prophecies reveal how the Lord feels about pride and wickedness, and they teach that we can turn away from these evils. Perhaps that's one reason we still read these ancient prophecies today. Nahum, Habakkuk, Zephaniah, and the others weren't just prophets of doom—they were prophets of deliverance. The descriptions of destruction are tempered by invitations to come unto Christ and receive His mercy: "Seek ye the Lord . . . ; seek righteousness, seek meekness" (Zephaniah 2:3). This was the Lord's way anciently, and it is His way today. "His ways are everlasting" (Habakkuk 3:6).

For overviews of these books, see "Nahum," "Habakkuk," and "Zephaniah" in the Bible Dictionary.

## Ideas for Personal Scripture Study

### NAHUM 1

### The Lord is both powerful and merciful.

Nahum's mission was to foretell the destruction of Nineveh—the capital of the violent empire Assyria, which had scattered Israel and brutalized Judah. Nahum began by describing God's wrath and matchless power, but He also spoke about God's mercy and goodness. You might consider identifying verses in chapter 1 that help you understand each of these attributes—and other attributes of God that you notice. Why do you think it is important to know each of these things about the Lord?

Some might find it difficult to reconcile the scriptural teaching that "the Lord is good" (Nahum 1:7) with the teaching that He "will take vengeance on his adversaries" (Nahum 1:2). In the Book of Mormon, Alma's son Corianton had similar questions "concerning the justice of God in the punishment of the sinner" (Alma 42:1). To learn more about God's mercy and how it relates to His justice, read Alma's answer to Corianton in Alma 42.

### HABAKKUK

### I can trust the Lord's will and His timing.

Even prophets sometimes have questions about the Lord's ways. Habakkuk, who lived at a time of widespread wickedness in Judah, began his record with questions to the Lord (see Habakkuk 1:1–4). How would you summarize Habakkuk's concerns? Have you ever had similar feelings?

The Lord responded to Habakkuk's questions by saying that He would send the Chaldeans (the Babylonians) to punish Judah (see Habakkuk 1:5–11). But Habakkuk was still troubled, for it seemed unjust for the Lord to stand by "when the wicked [Babylon] devoureth the man that is more righteous [Judah]" (see verses 12–17). What do you find in Habakkuk 2:1–4 that inspires you to trust the Lord when you have unanswered questions?

Chapter 3 of Habakkuk is a prayer of praise to God and an expression of faith in Him. What impresses you about Habakkuk's words in verses 17–19? How is the tone of these verses different from Habakkuk 1:1–4? Ponder how you can develop greater faith in God, even when life seems unfair.

See also Hebrews 10:32–39; 11; Doctrine and Covenants 121:1–6; Robert D. Hales, "Waiting upon the Lord: Thy Will Be Done," *Ensign* or *Liahona*, Nov. 2011, 71–74.

### ZEPHANIAH

### "Seek ye the Lord, all ye meek of the earth."

Zephaniah prophesied that the people of Judah would be completely destroyed by the Babylonians because of their wickedness. "I will utterly consume all things from off the land, saith the Lord" (Zephaniah 1:2). And yet Zephaniah also said that a "remnant" would be preserved (Zephaniah 3:13). As you read these prophecies, notice the kinds of attitudes and behaviors that led Judah and other groups to destruction—see especially Zephaniah 1:4–6, 12; 2:8, 10, 15; 3:1–4. Then look for the characteristics of the people God would preserve—see Zephaniah 2:1–3; 3:12–13, 18–19. What message do you feel the Lord has for you in these verses?

Zephaniah 3:14–20 describes the joy of the righteous after the Lord "hath cast out thine enemy" (verse 15). What blessings promised in these verses stand out to you? Why is it important to you to know about these blessings? You might compare these verses to the experiences described in 3 Nephi 17 and ponder how Jesus Christ feels about His people—including you.

# Ideas for Family Scripture Study and Home Evening

**Nahum 1:7.** How is the Lord like "a strong hold"? Perhaps your family could build a simple stronghold or fortress in your home and discuss Nahum 1:7 while inside it. What makes our day a "day of trouble"? How do Jesus Christ and His gospel fortify us? How do we show that we "trust in him"?

"The Lord is good, a strong hold in the day of trouble" (Nahum 1:7).

**Habakkuk 2:14.** How can we help fulfill the prophecy in this verse?

**Habakkuk 3:17–19.** What do we learn from Habakkuk's example in these verses?

**Zephaniah 2:3.** You could play a game in which family members have to find the words "righteousness" and "meekness" on a page with many other words. They could then talk about examples of righteousness and meekness they have seen in each other. What does it mean to seek righteousness and meekness?

**Zephaniah 3:14–20.** What do we find in Zephaniah 3:14–20 that makes us want to "sing, . . . be glad and rejoice with all the heart"? Perhaps your family could sing hymns or songs that come to mind as they read these verses.

For more ideas for teaching children, see this week's outline in *Come, Follow Me—For Primary.*

Suggested song: "Seek the Lord Early," *Children's Songbook,* 108.

## Improving Personal Study

**Be patient.** Sometimes we want answers to our questions right away, but spiritual insights take time and cannot be forced. As the Lord told Habakkuk, "Wait for it; because it will surely come" (Habakkuk 2:3).

"The Lord thy God in the midst of thee is mighty" (Zephaniah 3:17). *He Comes Again to Rule and Reign,* by Mary R. Sauer

DECEMBER 5–11

# Haggai; Zechariah 1–3; 7–14

"HOLINESS UNTO THE LORD"

Reading the scriptures invites revelation. Be open to messages that the Holy Ghost reveals to you as you read Haggai and Zechariah.

RECORD YOUR IMPRESSIONS

After decades of captivity, a group of Israelites, probably including the prophets Haggai and Zechariah, were allowed to return to Jerusalem. Some in this group remembered what Jerusalem looked like before it was destroyed. Imagine their feelings as they saw the rubble that had once been their homes, their places of worship, and their temple. To those who wondered whether the temple would ever again resemble the Lord's "house in her first glory" (Haggai 2:3), the prophet Haggai spoke the Lord's words of encouragement: "Be strong, all ye people of the land, saith the Lord, and work: for I am with you, . . . fear ye not." "I will fill this house with glory, . . . and in this place will I give peace." (Haggai 2:4–5, 7, 9.)

But it wasn't just the holy temple that needed rebuilding. In many ways, God's people were spiritually in ruins. And rebuilding a holy people takes more than hewing stones and aligning them to build a temple wall. Today, temples bear the inscription "Holiness to the Lord," and those words apply not just to a building but to a way of life. Engraving these words on "the bells of the horses" and "every pot in Jerusalem" (Zechariah 14:20–21) is helpful only if they are also engraved on every heart. True holiness requires that the Lord's words and laws "take hold" (Zechariah 1:6) in us, allowing His power to change our natures so that we become holy like Him (see Leviticus 19:2).

For an overview of the books of Haggai and Zechariah, see "Haggai" and "Zechariah" in the Bible Dictionary.

# Ideas for Personal Scripture Study

### HAGGAI 1; 2:1–9

## "Consider your ways."

There were many important things to do to rebuild Jerusalem. But after roughly 15 years had passed since the Israelites' return, the Lord was displeased that the rebuilding of the temple had not been given higher priority (see Haggai 1:2–5; see also Ezra 4:24). As you read Haggai 1; 2:1–9, consider questions like these: What consequences did the Israelites face because they had not finished the temple? What blessings did the Lord promise them if they finished building His house? You might take this opportunity to "consider your ways"—to think about your priorities and how you could align them with the Lord's.

See also Doctrine and Covenants 95; Terence M. Vinson, "True Disciples of the Savior," *Ensign* or *Liahona,* Nov. 2019, 9–11.

### ZECHARIAH 1–3; 7–8; 14

## The Lord can make me holy.

Sister Carol F. McConkie taught: "Holiness is making the choices that will keep the Holy Ghost as our guide. Holiness is setting aside our natural tendencies and becoming 'a saint through the atonement of Christ the Lord' [Mosiah 3:19]. . . . Our hope for holiness is centered in Christ, in His mercy and His grace" ("The Beauty of Holiness," *Ensign* or *Liahona,* May 2017, 9–10). Keep these teachings in mind as you read the Lord's words, given through the prophet Zechariah, urging Israel to become

more holy: Zechariah 1:1–6; 3:1–7; 7:8–10; 8:16–17. Note the things the Lord asked Israel to do so He could make them holy. How is He helping you become more holy?

Zechariah 2:10–11; 8:1–8; 14:9–11, 20–21 describe what life will be like in a future day when we all dwell with the Lord in a state of holiness. What might these descriptions have meant to those rebuilding Jerusalem in Zechariah's time? What do they mean to you?

"Behold, thy King cometh unto thee: he is just, and having salvation; lowly, and riding upon an ass" (Zechariah 9:9). *Triumphal Entry,* by Harry Anderson

### ZECHARIAH 9:9–11; 11:12–13; 12:10; 13:6–7; 14:1–9

## Jesus Christ is the promised Messiah.

Several of Zechariah's writings point to the earthly ministry of Jesus Christ and also His eventual Second Coming. Compare the following prophecies from Zechariah with related passages from other books of scripture:

- Zechariah 9:9–11 (see Matthew 21:1–11; 1 Peter 3:18–19)

- Zechariah 11:12–13 (see Matthew 26:14–16; 27:1–7)

- Zechariah 12:10 (see John 19:37; Revelation 1:7)

- Zechariah 13:6–7; 14:1–9 (see Matthew 26:31; Doctrine and Covenants 45:47–53)

What did you learn about the Savior as you studied these passages? Why is it important to you to understand these passages?

See also Guide to the Scriptures, "Messiah" (scriptures.ChurchofJesusChrist.org).

## Ideas for Family Scripture Study and Home Evening

**Haggai 1:2–7.** These verses may prompt your family to "consider your ways." Maybe family members could act out the phrases in verse 6. What does this verse teach about valuing the things of the world over the things of God? You might counsel together about your family's priorities. Singing a song like "I'm Trying to Be like Jesus" (*Children's Songbook,* 78–79) could help your family evaluate what you are doing well and areas in which you can improve.

**Haggai 2:1–9.** To introduce these verses, you could share the story of the Provo City Center Temple, which was rebuilt from a beloved tabernacle that had burned down (see the video "Provo City Center Temple Completed," ChurchofJesusChrist.org). As your family reads Haggai 2:1–9, you might ask family members to think of something in our lives that might be like the work of rebuilding the temple

that had been destroyed. How does the Lord rebuild us after tragedy or adversity?

**Zechariah 3:1–7.** As you read these verses, you could show your family some dirty clothes. How might Joshua have felt when he stood before the angel in dirty clothes? How is sin like dirty clothes? What does Zechariah 3:1–7 teach us about forgiveness? You could then clean the clothes together and talk about the cleansing power of the Savior's Atonement.

**Zechariah 8:1–8.** What impresses us about Zechariah's vision of the future of Jerusalem? What do we find there that we would like to see in our community? How can we invite the Savior to "dwell in [our] midst"? (see Gary E. Stevenson, "Sacred Homes, Sacred Temples," *Ensign* or *Liahona,* May 2009, 101–3).

For more ideas for teaching children, see this week's outline in *Come, Follow Me—For Primary.*

Suggested song: "I'm Trying to Be like Jesus," *Children's Songbook,* 78–79.

### Improving Personal Study

**Take opportunities for self-evaluation.** As you study the scriptures, you will often be inspired to ponder your own commitment to Heavenly Father and Jesus Christ. Act on the impressions you receive.

# From Tabernacle to Temple

## Rebuilding a House of God

**1882**
Ground broken for tabernacle in Provo, Utah, USA

**2010**
Tabernacle largely destroyed by fire

**2012**
Reconstruction begins for Provo City Center Temple

**2016**
Provo City Center Temple dedicated

# Malachi

"I HAVE LOVED YOU, SAITH THE LORD"

The name Malachi means "my messenger" (Bible Dictionary, "Malachi"). As you study Malachi's message to Israel, what messages do you find for your life? How do Malachi's words relate to our day?

RECORD YOUR IMPRESSIONS _____

_____

_____

"I have loved you," the Lord told His people through the prophet Malachi. But the Israelites, who had suffered generations of affliction and captivity, asked the Lord, "Wherein hast thou loved us?" (Malachi 1:2). After all Israel had been through, they may have wondered whether the history of ancient Israel is really a story of God's love for His covenant people.

As you reflect on what you have read in the Old Testament this year, what evidence do you find of God's love? It's easy to see many examples of human weakness and rebellion. Yet throughout all of that, God never stopped reaching out in love. When the sons of Jacob mistreated their brother Joseph, the

Lord still prepared a way to save them from famine (see Genesis 45:4–8). When Israel murmured in the wilderness, God fed them with manna (see Exodus 16:1–4). Even when Israel abandoned Him, turned to other gods, and were scattered, God never fully abandoned them but promised that if they repented, He would gather and redeem them "with great mercies" (see Isaiah 54:7).

Viewed this way, the Old Testament is a story of God's patient, enduring love. And this story continues today. "The Sun of Righteousness [will] arise with healing in his wings," Malachi prophesied (Malachi 4:2). Jesus Christ did come, bringing physical and spiritual healing to all who come unto Him. He is the greatest evidence of God's love for ancient Israel and for all of us.

For more information about the book of Malachi, see "Malachi" in the Bible Dictionary.

## Ideas for Personal Scripture Study

### MALACHI 1–4

### "Return unto me, and I will return unto you."

In Malachi's day, the Israelites had already rebuilt the temple in Jerusalem, but as a people they still needed to rebuild their relationship with the Lord. As you study Malachi, look for questions that the Lord asked the Israelites or that they asked Him. Consider asking yourself similar questions (some examples are suggested below) to help you evaluate your relationship with the Lord and draw closer to Him.

How have I felt the Lord's love for me? (see Malachi 1:2).

Do my offerings to the Lord truly honor Him? (see Malachi 1:6–11).

In what ways do I need to "return" to the Lord? (see Malachi 3:7).

Am I robbing God in any way? (see Malachi 3:8–11).

How does my attitude during difficult times reflect my feelings toward the Lord? (see Malachi 3:13–15; see also 2:17).

See also D. Todd Christofferson, "As Many as I Love, I Rebuke and Chasten," *Ensign* or *Liahona,* May 2011, 97–100.

### MALACHI 1:6–14

### The Lord asks for "a pure offering."

The Lord's words in Malachi 1 indicate that the Israelite priests were offering blemished and sickly animals as sacrifices in the temple, which the Lord had forbidden (see Leviticus 22:17–25). What do these sacrifices suggest about the priests' feelings toward the Lord? (see Malachi 1:13). Why does the Lord ask us to give Him our best offerings? Think about the sacrifices the Lord has asked you to make. What can you do to give Him "a pure offering"? (Malachi 1:11; see also 3:3).

See also Moroni 7:5–14.

### MALACHI 3–4

### Malachi's prophecies are being fulfilled in the latter days.

When the Savior visited the Americas, he quoted Malachi 3–4 to the Nephites (see 3 Nephi 24–25). In 1823, the angel Moroni shared portions of these same chapters with Joseph Smith (see Joseph Smith—History 1:36–39; see also Doctrine and Covenants 2). Why do you think Malachi's words are repeated so often in the scriptures? (see also Doctrine and Covenants 27:9; 110:13–16; 128:17–18). In your opinion, what messages from Malachi 3–4 seem especially important for our day?

When Moroni quoted Malachi 4:5–6 to Joseph Smith, he did so "with a little variation from the way it reads" in the Bible (Joseph Smith—History 1:36). What does Moroni's variation add to our understanding of this prophecy? To learn more about the coming of Elijah and how this prophecy is being fulfilled today, see Doctrine and Covenants 110:13–16 and Elder David A. Bednar's message "The Hearts of the Children Shall Turn" (*Ensign* or *Liahona,* Nov. 2011, 24–27). Why are you grateful that Elijah has come?

MALACHI 3:8–12

## Paying tithing opens the windows of heaven.

As you read Malachi 3:8–12, think about your own experiences with paying tithing. What does the phrase "open you the windows of heaven" (verse 10) mean to you?

# Ideas for Family Scripture Study and Home Evening

**Malachi 1:2.** How would your family answer the question found in Malachi 1:2—"Wherein hast [the Lord] loved us?" What are some evidences of the Lord's love for us?

**Malachi 3:8–12.** As you read Malachi 3:8–12, invite family members to share their thoughts or feelings about tithing. What temporal and spiritual blessings have we seen from paying tithing? (see David A. Bednar, "The Windows of Heaven," *Ensign* or *Liahona,* Nov. 2013, 17–20). Family members might enjoy drawing pictures to represent these blessings and hanging the pictures on a window.

**Malachi 3:13–18.** What does it mean to us to belong to the Lord and to be one of His "jewels"?

**Malachi 4:5–6.** After reading these verses, your family could identify the answers to the following questions about Malachi's prophecy: Who? What? When? Where? Why? (see also Doctrine and Covenants 2).

Illustration of Elijah appearing to Joseph Smith and Oliver Cowdery in the Kirtland Temple, by Robert T. Barrett

How do we turn our hearts to our fathers? How are we blessed when we do? You might ponder these questions while watching the video "The Promised Blessings of Family History" (ChurchofJesusChrist .org). What will we do as a family to receive these blessings?

For more ideas for teaching children, see this week's outline in *Come, Follow Me—For Primary.*

Suggested song: "Family History—I Am Doing It," *Children's Songbook,* 94.

## Improving Personal Study

**Ask questions as you study.** As you study the scriptures, questions may come to your mind. Ponder these questions, and look for answers.

*Mourning's Hosanna,* by Rose Datoc Dall. A woman named Mourning stands in the spirit world, surrounded by her ancestors. She celebrates their deliverance from spiritual captivity.

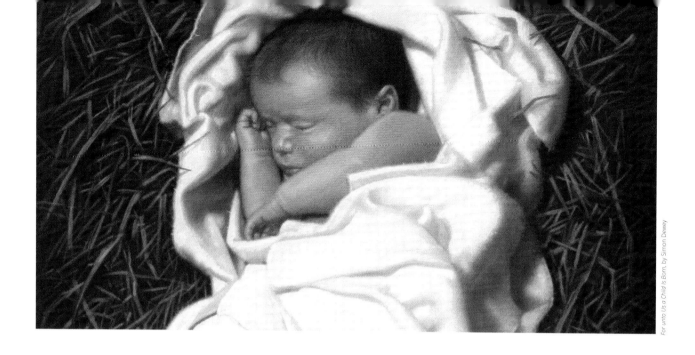

# Christmas

"WE HAVE WAITED FOR HIM, AND HE WILL SAVE US"

During this Christmas season, consider how the Old Testament has strengthened your testimony of Jesus Christ throughout the year.

RECORD YOUR IMPRESSIONS _____

_____

_____

The Old Testament carries a spirit of eager anticipation. In that way, it's a little bit like the Christmas season. Beginning with Adam and Eve, Old Testament patriarchs, prophets, poets, and people looked forward to better days, filled with hope for renewal and deliverance by the Messiah. And the Israelites were frequently in need of that hope—whether they were in captivity in Egypt or Babylon or held captive by their own sin or rebellion. Through it all, prophets reminded them that a Messiah, a Deliverer, would come "to proclaim liberty to the captives" (Isaiah 61:1).

That hope began to be realized when Jesus Christ was born in Bethlehem. The mighty Deliverer of Israel was born in a stable and laid in a manger (see Luke 2:7). But He wasn't just the Deliverer of the ancient Israelites. He came to deliver you—to bear your grief, to carry your sorrows, to be bruised for your iniquities, so that with His stripes you can be healed (see Isaiah 53:4–5). This is why Christmas is so full of joyful anticipation even today. The Messiah came over 2,000 years ago, and He continues to come into our lives whenever we seek Him.

# Ideas for Personal Scripture Study

## I rejoice in my Redeemer.

Christmas is known as a joyful season because of the joy that Jesus Christ brings to the world. Even people who don't worship Jesus as the Son of God can often feel the happiness of Christmas. Ponder the joy you feel because Heavenly Father sent His Son.

Centuries before the Savior was born, Old Testament prophets also felt joy as they spoke of the coming Messiah. Read some of the following passages, and think about why they would have been precious to those who looked forward to the Savior's mission: Psalm 35:9; Isaiah 25:8–9; 44:21–24; 51:11; Zephaniah 3:14–20; Moses 5:5–11. Why are these passages precious to you?

See also Russell M. Nelson, "Joy and Spiritual Survival," *Ensign* or *Liahona,* Nov. 2016, 81–84.

## Symbols can help me remember Jesus Christ.

Many of the traditions associated with Christmas can have symbolic meanings that point us to Christ. Star-shaped decorations represent the bright star that shone the night of Jesus's birth (see Matthew 2:2). Carolers can remind us of the angels who appeared to the shepherds (see Luke 2:13–14). As you studied the Old Testament this year, you may have noticed many symbols of the Savior. A few are listed below. Consider studying these and recording what they teach you about Him.

*Lamb* (Genesis 22:8; Exodus 12:5; 1 Peter 1:18–20).

_____

*Manna* (Exodus 16:4, 12–21, 31; Deuteronomy 8:3; John 6:30–40).

_____

*Water* (Exodus 17:1–6; Jeremiah 2:13; Ezekiel 47:1–12; John 4:7–14).

_____

*Brass serpent* (Numbers 21:4–9; John 3:14–15).

_____

*Rock* (1 Samuel 2:2; 2 Samuel 22:2–3; Psalm 118:22–23; Isaiah 28:16; Ephesians 2:20).

_____

*Branch* (Isaiah 11:1–2; Jeremiah 23:5; 33:15).

_____

*Light* (Psalm 27:1; Isaiah 9:2; 60:19; Micah 7:8; John 8:12).

_____

What other symbols, passages, and accounts have you found in the scriptures that testify of Jesus Christ?

See also 2 Nephi 11:4; Mosiah 3:14–15; Moses 6:63; "Types or Symbols of Christ," in Guide to the Scriptures, "Jesus Christ," scriptures.ChurchofJesusChrist.org.

## "His name shall be called Wonderful."

Jesus Christ is referred to by many different names and titles. What titles do you find in the following verses? Psalms 23:1; 83:18; Isaiah 7:14; 9:6; 12:2; 63:16; Amos 4:13; Zechariah 14:16; Moses 7:53. What other titles can you think of? You might even enjoy listing titles of Jesus Christ that you find in Christmas hymns. How does each title influence the way you think about Him?

# Ideas for Family Scripture Study and Home Evening

**Christmas traditions can point to Jesus Christ.** Israelite families had traditions, such as the Passover and other feasts, that were meant to point their hearts and minds to the Lord (see Exodus 12). What traditions does your family have at Christmastime that help you focus on Jesus Christ? What traditions do you know about from your family history? You might consider discussing as a family some traditions you want to start. Some ideas might include serving someone in need (for ideas, see ComeuntoChrist.org/light-the-world), inviting a friend to watch the First Presidency Christmas Devotional with you (broadcasts.ChurchofJesusChrist.org), writing your own Christmas song, or finding a creative way to share the message of Christ's birth.

**"The Christ Child: A Nativity Story."** How can you help family members feel the reverence and joy of Christ's birth? You might watch the video "The Christ Child: A Nativity Story" (ChurchofJesusChrist.org) or read together Matthew 1:18–25; 2:1–12; Luke 1:26–38; 2:1–20. Each family member could choose a person from the video or scripture account and share how that person felt about the Savior. Family members could also share their own feelings about Him.

**Finding the Savior in the Old Testament.** As you prepare to study the life of Jesus Christ in the New Testament next year, consider reviewing with your family what they have learned about Him this year in the Old Testament. You might review the outlines in this resource and any personal study notes to help you remember what you've learned. Younger children might benefit from looking through *Old Testament Stories* or the pictures in this resource. What prophecies or stories stood out to us? What have we learned about the Savior?

For more ideas for teaching children, see this week's outline in *Come, Follow Me—For Primary.*

Suggested song: "O Little Town of Bethlehem," *Hymns,* no. 208.

## Improving Our Teaching

**Listen to your family members.** "Listening is an act of love. It requires that we care more about what is in another person's heart than what is next on our agenda or outline. . . . As you pay careful attention to [family members'] spoken and unspoken messages, you will come to better understand their needs, their concerns, and their desires. The Spirit will help you know how to teach them" (*Teaching in the Savior's Way,* 34).

*The Nativity,* by N. C. Wyeth